THE LAST ENFORCER

THE LAST ENFORCER

OUTRAGEOUS STORIES FROM THE LIFE AND TIMES OF ONE OF THE NBA'S FIERCEST COMPETITORS

CHARLES OAKLEY

WITH FRANK ISOLA

GALLERY BOOKS

NEW YORK   LONDON   TORONTO   SYDNEY   NEW DELHI

G

Gallery Books
An Imprint of Simon & Schuster, Inc.
1230 Avenue of the Americas
New York, NY 10020

First Gallery Books hardcover edition February 2022

GALLERY BOOKS and colophon are registered
trademarks of Simon & Schuster, Inc.

For information about special discounts for bulk purchases,
please contact Simon & Schuster Special Sales at 1-866-506-1949
or business@simonandschuster.com.

The Simon & Schuster Speakers Bureau can bring authors
to your live event. For more information or to book an event,
contact the Simon & Schuster Speakers Bureau at 1-866-248-3049
or visit our website at www.simonspeakers.com.

Interior design by Michelle Marchese

Manufactured in the United States of America

10 9 8 7 6 5 4 3 2 1

Library of Congress Cataloging-in-Publication Data

Names: Oakley, Charles, 1963– author. | Isola, Frank, author.
Title: The last enforcer : outrageous stories from the life and times of
    one of the NBA's fiercest competitors / Charles Oakley with Frank Isola.
Identifiers: LCCN 2021035847 (print) | LCCN 2021035848 (ebook) |
    ISBN 9781982175641 (hardcover) | ISBN 9781982175665 (ebook)
Subjects: LCSH: Oakley, Charles, 1963–. | African American basketball
    Players—Biography. | Basketball players—United States—Biography. |
    Basketball—Social aspects—United States.
Classification: LCC GV884.O22 A3 2022 (print) | LCC GV884.O22
    (ebook) | DDC 796.323092 [B]—dc23
LC record available at https://lccn.loc.gov/2021035847
LC ebook record available at https://lccn.loc.gov/2021035848

ISBN 978-1-9821-7564-1
ISBN 978-1-9821-7566-5 (ebook)

To my grandfather Julius Moss,
who believed in hard work, and being a man of your word

CONTENTS

FOREWORD BY MICHAEL JORDAN

It doesn't matter who you are or how confident a person you are: when you're going into a tough situation, it always helps to have some protection, to have someone you can count on by your side, to have your back. For me, in the game of basketball, that was Charles Oakley. He truly was my enforcer.

Oak came to the Chicago Bulls as a rookie in 1985 and almost immediately announced his presence. In training camp, you could tell right away that he had what it took to make it in the NBA. I broke my foot three games into the season and didn't get to play with Charles much at first. But as I sat on the bench in street clothes, I watched. And I liked what I saw. The league was a lot more physical back then, and Oak was perfectly suited for it. He was a hard worker, smart, competitive, and no matter the situation or who he was up against, he was not going to back down. Simply put—you did not mess with Oak.

I knew that when I returned to the court, I'd have a bodyguard. I had become a target for other teams, and Oak wasn't afraid to mix it up with players who came after me who might have been bigger than him, but definitely weren't tougher. I truly appreciated his willingness to take on that protective role, and we quickly became close friends.

For all his grit and physicality, though, Oak was also a great player—far from one-dimensional. He could score, rebound, and pass, in addition to throwing that well-timed elbow or punch when he felt it was necessary.

It's no secret that I was not happy when Charles was traded to the Knicks in 1988. Because when someone you trust has your back, you don't want that someone playing for your opponent. But I wasn't just going to miss Oak on the court, I was also going to miss seeing and being around my friend every day.

The Bulls met the Knicks in the NBA playoffs five times between 1989 and 1996, and our rivalry was among the fiercest in league history. Getting past Oak, Patrick Ewing, and the rest of the Knicks was never easy. In 1992, they took us to Game 7 for one of only two times during our two championship runs. The stakes could not have been higher, and the intensity was off the charts. I knew what we were up against and knew that Oak, in particular, wasn't going to just lie down for us, friends or not. This was old-school basketball, with each team pushing the other to its limits.

Oak and I briefly reunited as teammates on the Washington Wizards during my last season. And I hired Oak as an assistant coach for my then–Charlotte Bobcats team in 2010 because I knew our players would benefit from his experience, his competitive nature, and his legendary toughness.

Has Oak changed over the years? Well, I'm not sure I would have predicted he'd ever compete on a show like *Dancing with the Stars* or become such a great cook. The man is a master behind the grill, but believe me, he definitely makes a mess. But Oak is still Oak. He still doesn't back down, and you can't intimidate him. He's uniquely himself. It's been a long time since we shared a basketball court, but if I should find myself in a tough situation, there is no doubt who I would want by my side as my enforcer.

1 | KNOCKING OUT A JACKASS

I did not punch Charles Barkley.

Do you need me to repeat that? I will if it means people will stop spreading lies about me. Enough is enough. I'm going to set the record straight because for more than twenty years, that rumor—the one of me allegedly punching Barkley before an important NBA Players Association meeting in 1999—has been told over and over, to the point that it's become something of an urban legend. But the story is false. So for the last time, I did not punch Charles Barkley.

I did, however, slap the shit out of him.

Barkley had it coming to him. He was talking a lot of shit about me. That's what he does. He talks too much. So I did what I do. Mention my name to Barkley today and he'll still go the other way.

You get hit with a lot of words in the league. You get hit with a lot of elbows, forearms, shoulders, and occasionally fists, too. You don't have to hit first, you just have to make sure you get in the best shot. And I got Barkley pretty good.

I was a power forward in the NBA for nearly two decades with the Chicago Bulls, New York Knicks, Toronto Raptors, Washington Wizards, and Houston Rockets, and I had plenty of run-ins over those years. I played in the golden era of physical play, the 1980s and '90s, and combat was part of my job description. According to the record books, I had almost as many rebounds (12,205) as points (12,417), which tells you what my role was on every team. That's a lot of work in the paint, and that's where things tend to get nasty. There's one more telling statistic: I rank fourth all time for personal fouls (4,421), just behind Robert Parish, Karl Malone, and Kareem Abdul-Jabbar. I'd like to think that most of the fouls were worth it. A lot were used to prevent a dunk or a layup. In New York, Pat Riley got credit for saying we had a "no layup rule."

I played by that rule my whole life.

In addition to Barkley, I mixed it up with Xavier McDaniel, Rick Mahorn, Bill Laimbeer, Alonzo Mourning, and even Larry Johnson, who later became my teammate with the New York Knicks. When you really think about it, that's not so many fights over the course of nineteen seasons. Most of the violence in the eighties and nineties NBA was controlled, and contrary to popular belief, I didn't fight all the time. I fought when I needed to. I fought when it mattered. Was I a physical player? Absolutely. Dirty? No. But if you fucked with me or one of my teammates, I wasn't going to back down. Never. I've been that way my entire life, and I'll be that way until the day I die.

I wasn't the first guy in the NBA who was wired like that, but I might have been the last. Before me, there were bruisers like Maurice Lucas, Lonnie Shelton, and Kermit Washington. A few months after the Portland Trail Blazers won their one and only title, Lucas was featured on the cover of *Sports Illustrated*. It was the magazine's NBA season preview issue, and the photo was of Lucas positioning himself for a rebound by sticking his elbow in the throat of the Seattle SuperSonics' Dennis Johnson. The headline was "The Enforcers."

I liked that, "Enforcer." That nickname stuck with Lucas and it made an impression on me. I was the guy who would do all the little things to help my team win: rebound, defend, and be physical. That was my mentality in every game.

In one of my final seasons with the Knicks, we played in Portland, and Mo Lucas came into our locker room to talk to me after the game. We had a nice conversation. He said he admired the way that I went about my business. The guy was a legend. He died of bladder cancer in 2010 at the age of fifty-eight, one year older than I am as I write this. I think about that a lot.

I think about a lot of things that happened during my career. I think about getting traded by the Bulls before they won the first of their six NBA Championships over eight seasons. Or losing to the Houston Rockets in the 1994 NBA Finals after taking a 3–2 series lead with the Knicks. The Knicks traded me prior to the 1998–99 season, and they went back to the NBA Finals that year, though they were beaten by the San Antonio Spurs, who were led by David Robinson and a young Tim Duncan.

That Knicks trade wasn't the last time the organization threw me aside. All those years of taking a charge and landing on my back or jumping into the front row for a loose ball didn't mean anything twenty years later to the guy then running the franchise. They dragged my ass out of Madison Square Garden.

They started that fight, not me. But that's true of all the fights I've had. Someone starts it, I end it.

Because I fight like a man.

That's the way I was raised.

Cleveland, Ohio, is my hometown. It's a tough and proud city. I grew up on East 123rd Street and Superior. It was a nice house with a front porch. The neighborhood was mostly Black; probably

95 percent Black and we all looked out for one another. That's just how it was.

Right down the street, there was a barbershop where the older guys would shoot dice and play cards. When I was about ten or eleven years old, I'd clean up the place and they'd give me money. They'd send me to the store to buy them food. They'd throw me a $20 bill and I'd keep the change. When I was a few years older, they'd let me roll dice and play cards with them. It was a good hustle—when I won.

In the neighborhood you had the barbershop, Laundromat, record store, seafood place, food market, and a corner store with a barbecue counter where they made the famous Polish Boys. That's a sausage sandwich with kielbasa on a bun. You cover it with French fries, coleslaw, and barbecue sauce. The Polish Boy is big in Cleveland. We invented the thing, and this place in my neighborhood had the best barbecue sauce going.

I used the money from the barbershop and the dice games to buy food. I never told my mother, Corine, that I got the money from gambling, because I didn't want to get in trouble. I wasn't sneaky, I was smart. My mother wouldn't have been happy about me playing cards with the old guys, but she was okay with me playing cards with her. That was fine. We'd play poker or Tonk, a card game that was popular among blues and jazz musicians from the South going all the way back to the 1930s. You can play with either two or four players, so me and my mom would play a lot. My mom was good. She'd talk a lot of smack when she played, but she kept it together. She never drank or smoked. That wasn't her thing. She worked in a bar for fifteen years and never drank. My mom still lives in Cleveland, and we're still very close. I'm there all the time.

I didn't know my dad much. My father, Charles Oakley II, came from a big family; he was one of ten kids, and when I was growing up, they owned five gas stations in Cleveland. He was always working. He lived with his brothers, while my siblings and I lived with our mother. I seen him, but I didn't see him a lot, you know what I mean? Then he died of a heart attack in 1971. He was only thirty-five and I was nine. It's just one of those things.

I grew up the youngest of six children, with one brother, Curtis (eleven years older than me), and four sisters: Saralene (seven years older), Carolyn (five years older), Diane (three years older), and Yvonne, who is twelve years older than me, but Yvonne lived in York, Alabama, with our grandparents on our mom's side. I'm sure you've never heard of York. It's in Sumter County, close to Mississippi. It's about a two-hour drive northwest to Birmingham and about a five-hour drive to Atlanta. I can make it in four.

According to the local records, the town was established in the early 1830s. It was a farming and cotton town, and during the Civil War, the railroad passed through York on its way to a military hospital in Meridian, Mississippi. After World War II, the train traffic slowed down and people started to move out. It's a mostly Black town, and yet the first African-American mayor wasn't elected until 1996. Progress, like life in general, moves slowly in York. But I still love it there.

When I was seven years old and in the second grade, my sister Diane and I moved to York to live with our maternal grandparents, Julius and Florence Moss, and join Yvonne. Curtis, Saralene, and Carolyn stayed behind in Cleveland with my mother. My mom was trying to get established. She was living in an apartment and needed more money to buy a house, so it was easier for her to send the two youngest kids to Alabama for a few years.

It wasn't bad in York. My mother would visit three times a year, and in the summer she would stay for a few weeks. I was fine with it because I had a lot of cousins in Alabama and I was spending a lot of time with them—my dad's side of the family was from there, too. Out of maybe one thousand people in York alone, I was probably related to three hundred of them. It was like being away at camp year-round. We all protected each other.

That doesn't mean it was all fun and games. I did go to school. Education was important to my family. A lot of the people in my family worked in the school system, either as teachers or administrators, and a few of my aunts attended the University of Western Alabama. We didn't mess around when it came to school. Or church.

My grandfather Julius was a deacon, so every Sunday we were in church. He'd make a few trips in his car on Sunday morning for those of us who needed a ride. You didn't have a choice. My grandfather baptized me in the pond down the street. He walked into the pond with his boots on, tilted my head back, and that was it.

I learned at an early age that my parents and grandparents would not tolerate any bullshit. If I talked back or, God forbid, used profanity, I was in trouble. My grandparents would lay me across their laps and give me the beating of my life. The only voices you heard in that house were my grandparents and the television. And the TV went off every night at nine o'clock, so it got quiet early there. There wasn't a lot of nonsense going on.

Julius Moss was a special man. He was born in Alabama in 1906, so you can imagine how life was for him. Growing up in the Jim Crow South, my grandfather saw it all. Shit, by the time he was twenty-five, he had probably seen more than he wanted to see. But he was a proud man, with an incredible work ethic that was second to none. On top of being a deacon in the church, he was a blacksmith, a farmer, and a coal miner. He hunted deer. He built his own house, starting with three rooms and eventually adding on four more. He slept four or five hours every night and never complained.

My grandfather was tough. His hands were so rough and covered with calluses that he could pick up a piece of hot coal. He was six-foot-three and strong. When I was a kid, my uncles would tell a story about the time my grandfather knocked a mule out. One day he was in the field and the mule didn't want to work. He was pushing and prodding, and I guess the mule got real aggressive. It was either my grandfather or the mule, so he knocked the mule out. Is the story true? I don't know. Like I said, my grandfather was tough. I'd pick him over the mule. I've knocked out a few jackasses in my life as well.

We'd all help my grandfather with his farming—he'd have us out in the field picking cucumbers and tomatoes to feed the family. In the summer, we'd help him with a side job that he had, going to a big farm up the road to feed their many horses and cows. It was farm owned by white people, and it had a big white fence around it. Ain't no Black people with a farm that big with a white fence around it. My grandfather had some horses of his own, about six or seven cows, and one bull. He wasn't big-time. He just did what he could.

He passed away when I was in my second year in the NBA. Julius Moss wasn't big into sports, so the fact that I made the league didn't mean a lot to him. But I know he was proud. He was happy I had a job and was earning an honest living.

My father passed away while I was living with my grandparents. When I think about it now, he died so young. The funeral was in Alabama, and it was big; there were a lot of people there, family and friends, and they were all crying. I was only nine, so I didn't really process everything that was happening.

I spent four years in Alabama before my mom came to take me and Diane back to Cleveland. When she said I had to leave, I hid under the bed. I didn't want to go back. I was having a good time with my cousins. We were playing football and basketball all the time. Why would I want to leave? But my mom had gotten herself established in Cleveland, as she'd been working to do, and had bought a house. So it was time to move on.

Those years in Alabama helped me become the man and player I turned into. Because of my grandfather's example, I never bitched about basketball practice or playing back-to-backs. I never made excuses. I practiced and played hard every day, and even when I wasn't at my best I didn't quit. I treated basketball as my job. It could be difficult, but I'd seen what real work looked like.

I was developing that attitude already when I moved back to Cleveland and started playing basketball at a local YMCA every Sunday. By the time I was thirteen, I was playing against guys who were sometimes four and five years older than me. There were a lot of old-school guys who would try to take your head off when you went to the basket. I decided that my attitude would be to stand tall and tough. If they're going to give it to you, you got to give it to them. I wouldn't fight for no reason, but if somebody crossed me, insulted me, or attacked me, then we'd have a problem.

The first time I really had to put that theory into practice on a basketball court was with this one guy at the games who knew karate, and made sure that everybody was aware of that. For a long while, he gave me a hard time. Everyone else at the games knew he was testing me. They were wondering if and when I was going to respond. Well, one day he tried to get me and I went after him. All that karate didn't help him, because once I threw my hands up, there was nothing he could do.

I played a lot of football in the street as a kid. When you grow up playing on concrete and in a lot of cold weather, you either get tough quickly or you do something else, like watch a lot of television. I was big and strong even as a kid, so football seemed like the natural sport for me. A lot of kids in Ohio dream of playing for Ohio State, but I didn't really focus on that. I figured if I'm good enough, someone will find me. Learning to play football helped me with basketball because you learn how to take a hit and give a hit.

When you're playing football in that setting and you got guys talking shit, there's going to be some minor fights. Nothing big. The next day you get over it and you go back to playing. But there was one time when I was playing organized peewee football and that rule didn't hold. It was ugly. There were these twin brothers from the neighborhood who were getting mad at me because I was whoopin' their asses in practice. I was probably twelve or thirteen. One day after practice, the twins and their uncle, who was probably nineteen, jumped me. They got me pretty good. In fact, they broke my arm. When I got home, I told my mother I got hurt in practice. I didn't tell her anything about getting jumped because I decided that wasn't going to change anything. I had to fight for myself. My mother shouldn't have to do that. I wasn't mad. I wasn't scared. My thing was I needed to do a better job of protecting myself.

Years later, when I was in the NBA, I returned to Cleveland during the off-season, and I saw the twins' uncle sitting at a bus stop. I was with some friends who knew the story and wanted to scare the guy. I told them, "Leave him alone," and I walked into the restaurant we were going to. Did my friends listen? It doesn't seem that way—all I know is, he didn't catch that bus that day. I see the twins every now and then, and they both keep their distance. That's a smart move.

If my toughness and work ethic came from my grandfather, then my love of cooking came from my mother. My mom is a great cook. She makes incredible ham hocks, chitlins and collard greens, string beans, and pound cake and sweet potato pie for dessert. All my aunts can cook, too. When I was growing up, they would cook and I would ask questions about the meal. I never cooked when I was a kid, but I watched and learned from them, and once I got into the league I started cooking. When we were on the road, you'd eat either room service or go to a restaurant. I always thought the food was bland. So when I got home, I wanted to eat healthy and make things the way I liked to make them. And whenever we played games in Cleveland, my mom would cook for the whole team. She would make smoked turkey for Patrick Ewing because Pat didn't like pork. One downside of all that good food is that I ended up being picky and demanding about the quality of what I eat. People hate to go out to eat with me because they know there's a good chance I'm going to send the meal back.

My high school in Cleveland was called John Hay. Not John Jay (a mistake a lot of people make). It's John Hay High School. A few years ago the city honored me with a street sign—Charles Oakley Way—in front of my alma mater. But back when I was a student, I was just another kid trying to figure things out. Shit, just getting to school was a job: I had to take two buses to get there. Not school buses—public transportation. I would either take the No. 6 to the No. 3 or the No. 10 to the No. 40. The other option was to walk two and a half miles. If we had lived a few houses down, I would have been in another school district that had actual school buses. The crazy thing is, when people see you on a school bus, they look at you as a student. When they see you on a public bus, they start wondering if you're skipping school and if you're up to no good, especially if you're a Black kid.

There was one day, I was probably fifteen years old, and after waiting a long time for the second bus, I decided to start walking home. I walked past the Green Door, which was a bar where guys sold a lot of weed. All of a sudden a car pulled up; two undercover cops got out and threw me against the wall. In the neighborhood we called these two cops "Starsky and Hutch." They drove around in unmarked cars and harassed people in the hood. They accused me of selling drugs. I didn't have anything on me, so they threw me in the car and drove me around for three hours. What the fuck did I do?

They told me, "We're going let everyone see you, and we're gonna tell them you've been snitching." That's fucked up.

So walking home wasn't the best option. Taking two buses was the safer bet.

At John Hay, I was considered to be better at football than basketball. I was being recruited as a defensive end by Ohio State and Bowling Green. But I cared about basketball more, and I also wanted to get out of Ohio. There was a lot of stuff going on, a lot of bullshit like drugs and crime. I wanted a change of scenery. So I worked my ass off, and accomplished my goals when I got a scholarship offer to play basketball at Virginia Union, a historically Black university in Richmond.

The importance of leaving Ohio and getting a fresh start in Richmond was made even more obvious to me the summer before I left for college. I was seventeen and saw a man get shot four times. It took place in the basement of a house in Cleveland, where a guy was running a game of craps on a pool table. I had won some money gambling the week before, so I decided to take $1,500 and test my luck, seeing if I could make some more before I headed off to college. It seemed like most of the people in the basement knew each other and like they were all having a good time as they were shooting dice. I was standing off to the side near the staircase, watching and waiting for my turn. I had been there for about fifteen minutes when one guy pulled out a gun and said: "This is a stickup. Give me all the money."

I was thinking this must be a joke. How was he going to rob everyone and get away with it when most of the people there knew exactly who he was? But he wasn't playing around. He took some of the money off the table and started making his way to the staircase.

All of a sudden, there was a series of loud "bap, bap, bap, bap" sounds. It was either four or five shots. The guy who had taken the money started falling back down the stairs. Someone had shot him as he was trying to get away. This was all happening right next to me. I got the fuck out of there as quickly as I could and never looked back. I never asked anyone about it, and no one ever questioned me about what I saw. All I knew was that I didn't want that life.

Having spent most of my life in Cleveland and Alabama, I didn't know what to expect when I got to Richmond. Little did I know that in the early eighties the murder rate in Richmond was worse than Chicago and Compton. It was safer in Cleveland.

I saw the effects of being in that environment quickly. Two weeks after arriving on campus, there was a student gathering at the Henderson Center on the Friday night before the Saturday football game. A few local guys, guys from the hood, snuck in and were causing problems.

I was talking to some girls, these guys were trying to talk to them, too, and one thing led to another. You know that story. It wasn't a fight. The thing was broken up before it started. But they sent word that I shouldn't show up at the football game. That was a threat. And they weren't talking about fighting anymore. If they saw me, they were going to start shooting.

It turns out that our point guard, Kenny Thompson, was from Richmond and knew a few of the guys who were threatening me. He talked to them. I think he said I was cool, but I didn't really care. I was going to be here for four years. I wasn't about to spend my time looking over my shoulder. I was here to go to school and play ball. I wasn't going to be a punk. I went to the game, and it was all fine, nothing happened.

My attitude even at that young age was to defend not only myself but my teammates and my friends. Sometimes, that circle could extend further than you might think. There was one time my college roommate and I traveled to North Carolina to watch our Virginia Union football team play Fayetteville State University. A brawl broke out during the game between the players of the two teams. My roommate and I were just there as fans, but we ran out onto the field and joined our fellow VUU student athletes to take on the Fayetteville players. It seemed like the right thing to do.

Thankfully, this kind of thing didn't happen often, and I settled into campus life and my role on the basketball team pretty quickly. I looked at college as a chance to make a name for myself, even at a small school. My dream was to make it to the NBA. Virginia Union is not UCLA, North Carolina, Duke, Kentucky, or Indiana. But HBCU schools have sent some great players to the NBA. Earl Monroe (Winston-Salem State), Willis Reed (Grambling), and Sam Jones (North Carolina Central) are all enshrined at the Naismith Hall of Fame in Springfield, Massachusetts. Bobby Dandridge, who is from Richmond and attended Norfolk State, should be in the Hall of Fame. He scored more points in the NBA Finals during the 1970s than any other player—and that includes Lew Alcindor, who later became Kareem Abdul-Jabbar.

Virginia Union itself has a few players who made it to the NBA besides me: Terry Davis, A. J. English, and Ben Wallace. I met Ben when he came to a summer basketball camp I was running at Sumter High School in South Carolina when I was in the league and Ben was about twelve years old. My sister Yvonne worked in the school system there and asked me to do the camp. We were charging $25 a week at the time, but a lot of kids didn't have the money, Ben included, and we didn't turn anyone away. I later helped Ben get recruited to Cuyahoga Community College in Cleveland, and then he transferred to VUU. Ben wound up having a great NBA career, especially for a guy who went undrafted. He won a championship with the Detroit Pistons, made the All-Star team four times, and was the Defensive Player of the Year four times. The Pistons even retired his number.

So Virginia Union had pedigree and talent, but because it was a Division II school, our games weren't televised nationally. That made it harder to get noticed by NBA scouts, especially for my first two college seasons. But in my junior year, that started to change when we made it to the quarterfinals of the NCAA Division II tournament, which got us some recognition. (We lost by one point to Kentucky Wesleyan, coached by Wayne Chapman, whose son, Rex Chapman, was a star at Kentucky and went on to play in the NBA. That's how it works in basketball; it's all like one big family tree.)

Then, my senior year, both the team and I had an incredible season. We went 31-0, and I averaged 24 points and 17.3 rebounds. And I put up 43 points in a game against Elizabeth City State. NBA scouts were suddenly showing up to our games, including the Bulls' general manager Jerry Krause. He came to see me play more than once. We came into the NCAA tournament as the team to beat, and were matched up in the first round against Winston-Salem State, which was coached by Clarence "Big House" Gaines, who won 828 games and is now in the Hall of Fame. It turned out to be a disaster. We lost 44–42. I went from scoring 43 points in a single game to losing in the tournament in a game where our whole team scored 42.

It wasn't the way I wanted it to end. I had been named Division II Player of the Year, and finished my college career with 2,379 points and 1,642 rebounds, but I worried it might not be enough. (Just for comparison, Patrick Ewing, who also graduated in 1985, had 2,184 points and 1,316 rebounds in four years at Georgetown. No question, the competition was better in the Big East and in Division I.) The great Moses Malone, one of the top five centers of all time, who led Philadelphia to the title in 1983 and outplayed

Kareem Abdul-Jabbar, apparently knew who I was. He lived close
by, loved to be around women, and every once in a while he'd show
up on campus, riding around in his Rolls-Royce. He'd go to the
club near campus, stand in the corner drinking a Coke, and talk
to college girls. One night, he showed up at the club and started
yelling: "Where is Oakley? Where's Oakley?" I guess he had heard
about me. That was pretty cool—but did it mean I was getting
enough attention from the people who mattered to give me a shot
at getting to the NBA?

I didn't know.

In late March 1985, I got invited to play in a college All-Star
Game. This was right around the time when Patrick Ewing and
Georgetown lost to Villanova in the NCAA Finals. The All-Star
roster was all Division I players and me. Dean Smith, the legendary coach at North Carolina, was my coach for the All-Star Game.
Coach Smith and my college coach, Dave Robbins, knew each
other, which is probably one reason I got invited to the game. They
were good guys and good coaches. Coach Robbins went 713-194
and won three Division II championships over thirty years at Virginia Union. Dean Smith coached at North Carolina for thirty-six
years and finished with an 879-254 record and two national titles.
He's one of the best of all time.

I still remember Coach Smith telling the guys they had to pass
at least two times before shooting. That sounded like a reasonable
request. But the game started, guys weren't passing, and so Smith
pointed at a guy on the court and told me to take his spot. Dean
Smith wasn't having it, even at an All-Star Game.

I played a lot of minutes that day. I don't know if that exposure
helped me in the NBA Draft, but it didn't hurt. It also helped that
Dean Smith was saying good things about me to NBA teams.

With the NBA Draft set for June 18, I stayed around Virginia
and waited for the day to come. (I was focused on the draft, so I

didn't graduate that year, but a few years later I completed one final course at summer school and graduated from Virginia Union with a degree in business administration.) People were telling me I would get drafted, maybe in the second or third round, but I really wasn't sure. I stared at the calendar for those couple of weeks, eager to find out what my future would hold.

2 | WELCOME TO THE LEAGUE

The 1985 NBA Draft was the league's first-ever lottery-style draft. Before that, the draft order was determined solely by the records of the teams in the previous season. But teams had started tanking intentionally to up their place in the draft. So, in 1985, the NBA decided to do things differently. On May 12, in Manhattan, about a month before the actual draft, envelopes were made up for each of the seven teams that hadn't made the playoffs. Each team's logo was put into an envelope, and the envelopes were put into a plastic drum, which was cranked by hand to mix them all up. Then, NBA commissioner David Stern picked the envelopes out on by one, counting down from the seventh pick to the first, all while CBS televised the drama nationally. This meant each team had the same chance to win the number one overall pick—at least theoretically.

Today, the NBA still does a lottery-style draft but uses Ping-Pong balls, and the draft order is determined by the combination of the numbers on the balls that are drawn. It's a lot more complicated, and a lot more random. In 1985, because of the way it was done, there was talk of a conspiracy. Patrick Ewing, the three-time all-American center from Georgetown, was the big player coming out who everyone wanted and knew would be the number one pick. Less than a week before the lottery, Sam Goldaper, the *New York Times* basketball writer, wrote that "there is a strong feeling among league officials and television advertising executives that the NBA will benefit most if he winds up in a Knick uniform." The league had Magic Johnson in Los Angeles, Larry Bird in Boston, and Michael Jordan finishing his rookie season in Chicago. New York needed a star.

There was a lot of suspense as David Stern drew the envelopes one by one from the drum, and then a lot of excitement when the Knicks won. But then, of course, everyone was saying it was fixed. The conspiracy theories abounded.

One of them was that the corner of the Knicks envelope was creased. Another was that the Knicks envelope was put in dry ice before going into the plastic drum, so that it would be cool to the touch. Another said X-ray glasses were involved. Combined, these are often considered the most popular conspiracy theories in NBA history.

I don't know what happened that day, but I know that when I watched the lottery on TV, I wasn't thinking about Patrick or the Knicks or any damn conspiracy. Like most of the other players who were eligible that year, I was just focused on where I could be going during the actual draft, which was coming up on June 18, also in Manhattan.

When the day arrived, I didn't go to New York because I didn't know where or when I would be selected. I stayed in Virginia, and since I didn't have cable in my place, my draft day was spent at the house of my college coach, Dave Robbins. His wife and kids were my big entourage that day. We watched and waited as Patrick was

THE LAST ENFORCER | 19

selected by the Knicks first overall, as everyone knew he would be. Wayman Tisdale, a good low post scorer out of Oklahoma, went second, to Indiana. Benoit Benjamin, another big man, went to the Clippers. The league was different back then. Everyone was looking for big men. Xavier McDaniel went to Seattle, and then two big white guys were taken: Jon Koncak went to Atlanta and Joe Kleine was drafted by Sacramento. Chris Mullin, who had a great college career at St. John's, was picked by the Warriors seventh overall, followed by the German, Detlef Schrempf, who had played college ball at Washington, at the eighth spot. Not many people had heard of Schrempf. Just about no one had heard of me.

That's why I couldn't believe it when the Cleveland Cavaliers— my hometown team—called me to say they were going to draft me ninth overall but trade me right away. They didn't tell me what team they were making a deal with, so I was a little confused, but to be honest I was glad I wouldn't be playing in Cleveland. I'm not sure it would have been the best thing for me. I had a lot of friends there who were getting in trouble. I didn't need to get caught up in that.

When I hung up the phone and the commissioner said my name as the ninth draft pick, my coach said, "You did it, Big Fella. That's a great honor to get drafted, especially when you're from a historical Black college." That's when being drafted really hit me.

The next thing that happened sent my head spinning. The general manager of the Chicago Bulls, Jerry Krause, called to say that it was him who was trading with Cleveland for me. Under league rules, the Bulls couldn't announce the deal until after the first round, but the pieces soon fell into place. Krause drafted center Keith Lee with the Bulls' first-round pick, at eleventh overall. Lee had led Memphis to the Final Four before losing to Villanova. Then Cleveland selected guard Calvin Duncan out of Virginia Commonwealth with their other first-round pick, at thirtieth overall. Chicago then traded Keith Lee and their point guard Ennis Whatley, who had been drafted in the first round in 1983, to Cleveland in exchange for me and Calvin Duncan. I was a Bull.

Chicago fans, who had gathered at the team's draft headquarters at the Hyatt Regency in downtown Chicago, booed the news of the deal. Krause had just been named general manager a few months earlier, after spending years bouncing around as a scout for both basketball and baseball teams. But he believed in me. He had seen me play in the Portsmouth Invitational Tournament, an annual pre-draft camp for college seniors, a few months earlier. He was also close with coach Clarence "Big House" Gaines at Winston-Salem State, whose teams had played against me for four years, and who told Krause what kind of player I was. Nothing against Keith Lee, but he didn't make the trade—Krause had engineered the whole thing, and it was bringing me to Chicago that drove it. I remember telling the *Chicago Tribune* after the draft that I wasn't worried about the first reaction from fans: "Talk is cheap and actions speak louder than words. I'm the real deal," I said.

Jerry Krause gave me my start. I'll never forget that. And he brought me to a team where I'd meet a guy who would not only become one of the greatest athletes of all time, but one of my best friends: Michael Jordan.

A year earlier, with a little luck, the Bulls had managed to draft Michael Jordan when he fell into their lap with the third pick. Jerry Krause might be considered the luckiest beneficiary of inheriting a team with Michael on it, even though Michael and Krause would end up butting heads. In fact, Michael would come to really hate Krause. He gave him the nickname "Crumbs," because Krause was a fat little guy who usually had crumbs on his shirt. I'll admit that I laughed at that joke from time to time. But most of that would come later—when I arrived in 1985, Michael would say shit here and there about Krause but not a lot. Their conflict really didn't come to a boiling point until they started winning championships. As I saw it, Krause was a scout at heart who knew talent. Later, when the documentary series *The Last Dance* came out and people were blaming Krause for all sorts of things, I saw him as the fall guy. Jerry Reinsdorf was and still is the owner of the Chicago Bulls. His name is on the checks, and the buck stops with him. Jerry Krause knew basketball and put the team together. He did his job. He would prove that again and again in the coming years, drafting Scottie Pippen, Horace Grant, and building a dynasty.

When Michael came into the league, he had the whole package— he was talented, good-looking, professional, and had a great work ethic—and of course I knew all about him already as I prepared to join the team. Basketball fans everywhere, not only in Chicago, had fallen in love with Michael right away. By December 1984, in his rookie year, he had been on the cover of *Sports Illustrated*, and the headline was "A Star Is Born." He averaged 28.2 points that season, started in the All-Star Game, and was named Rookie of the Year. Most of all, he was competitive and motivated. That's a lethal combination. Mike was always looking for something to fuel him. Sometimes it was Krause. Sometimes it was a story in the newspaper or something a player had said. It's one of the things that made him great.

As a team, the 1984–85 Bulls, coached by Kevin Loughery, had won thirty-eight games and reached the playoffs for the first time in four years. They got knocked out by the Milwaukee Bucks in the first round, but the organization knew it had a budding superstar. Now they needed to build around him. And that's where I came in.

In early July, a few weeks after the draft, I arrived in Chicago and got right to work. I was excited to prove that I belonged. They have one of the best summer leagues, and I started playing ball as soon as I arrived. That's when Michael and I first got to know each other. By the time training camp started, he had seen that I was a hard worker and that I wasn't taking anything for granted.

I had a good first training camp and preseason. There were a lot of veterans on the team, including Sidney Green, David Greenwood, and Orlando Woolridge. Green, Greenwood, and Woolridge weren't comfortable with me out there. When the coaches blew the whistle, I didn't stop. They had to blow it twice. I wanted to play. I thought of it as a wrestling match with these guys who were ahead of me, to get the chance to play. I came in with the attitude that I'd make my name by outworking and outlasting everyone else on the court.

Mike saw the work I was putting in and recognized I had the same type of drive and work ethic as him. That first year in Chicago I was all business. They said to be at work at 10 a.m.; I was there at 8:30. I was about doing whatever it took to win. I knew that Michael was watching me. I didn't take shortcuts. I put the work in. He wanted to see how I carried myself on the court. He wanted to see how I carried myself off the court, too.

He was twenty-two, and I was twenty-one, but he cared about what it meant to be a gentleman. We'd go out to eat and he would make sure my manners were good. He wanted me to be respectful. That's just how Michael was. That's how he began to trust me. Michael grew up in the South. He was a country kid, and his mom and pops raised him the right way. My mom raised me the right way as well. We could see that in each other.

Back then, Mike didn't talk a lot of shit. There were vets out there. They weren't going to put up with a lot of talking from a young player. That's the way the league was. It was like having a driver's license—you had to pass a test. And if you talked, you had to back it up. Michael knew his place. Everyone talks about how he was constantly getting on Steve Kerr and Scott Burrell in the nineties. But in Mike's early seasons, he waited his turn to become a leader. Everyone knew it was coming. It's like he was the FBI, gathering evidence, studying what it took to lead. It took him a while to get there, but he certainly did.

So that first training camp, I just played hard and didn't say much either, even if I was pissing off some of the older veterans with my tenacity on the court. I think the coaches and the front office knew I could help right away. I also think that's one of the reasons Krause made a big move by trading David Greenwood to the San Antonio Spurs on October 24, 1985, the day before our season opener against Cleveland.

At the time I didn't think much of the trade, but Michael was pissed. He didn't like it for a number of reasons. On top of trading a veteran player who Michael liked, the Bulls released Rod Higgins on the day of the Greenwood trade. Rod was and still is one of Mike's best friends. So that pissed him off.

But the biggest problem of all may have been the person who Krause had traded Greenwood to San Antonio for: the one and only Iceman, George Gervin. There was some bad blood there. Eight months earlier, at the 1985 All-Star Game in Indianapolis, Michael felt that George had tried to fuck him over.

I know I'm going on a tangent to say all this, but I think the story gives an interesting picture of what life was like in the NBA when I came into the league—and just how rich and dramatic the friendships and feuds could be. I'm referring to the infamous "Freeze Out" All-Star Game, when a small group of veterans, including Gervin, had a plan to keep the ball away from Michael as much as possible and not help the rookie out on defense. Gervin was involved, but it was principally Isiah Thomas's idea.

Why? In my opinion, it's because Isiah Thomas was jealous of Michael. He was from the West Side of Chicago, and he loved to talk about how Chicago was his town. He felt Chicago belonged to him, even though he was playing in Detroit. Michael becoming the king of the town as a rookie pissed Isiah off. (For the record, as I see it, nobody fucking cares that Isiah is from Chicago. Even to this day when I see Isiah he tells me, "We need to sit down with Michael." Man, he's not sitting down with you. Kick rocks. You and Magic Johnson sat down and talked about your problems, but Michael is not going to do that.)

The plan was that Isiah, with the help of some veteran teammates on the Eastern Conference roster, would keep the ball out of Michael's hands. Isiah also planned for two of his friends on the Western Conference roster, Magic Johnson and George Gervin, to attack Michael on defense and wear him out.

Why would Magic and George and Isiah's Eastern Conference teammates get involved in this plan?

There were a bunch of crazy rumors about what happened before the game that could explain it, though I really think that most of it is stupid shit. There was one report that Michael refused to acknowledge Isiah in a hotel elevator the night before the All-Star Game.

Another version is that, on the Saturday before the game, during workouts, Michael wore his Nike warm-ups in violation of the NBA protocol. He was promoting Nike. So the veteran guys got upset, saying, "Who the heck is this rookie? He's not acting the way he should."

Whatever the reason, Michael ended up playing twenty-two minutes, the fewest among all ten starters on the Eastern Conference team. He scored seven points on 2-for-9 shooting. Six players on the East roster took more shots, including the Bucks' Terry Cummings, who managed to shoot seventeen times in sixteen minutes. Gervin did, in fact, attack Michael on both defense and offense, and scored 23 points.

Mike tried to keep the feud from going public. After the game he simply said: "This being my first All-Star Game, I was very tentative. I didn't want to be perceived as a rookie going out to steal the show. I was just happy to be there."

Isiah wasn't quite so professional, though in his own way he tried to laugh it off, and he's always claimed that the whole freeze out thing never happened. In response to the rumor that Michael snubbed him in an elevator, he said that if "Michael Jordan ever walked by me without saying hello, I'd probably turn around and punch him in the face." Isiah was laughing when he said it.

A lot of the bad blood that had started at the 1985 All-Star Game continued for a long time. Isiah thinks that Mike kept him off the 1992 Dream Team. My opinion: Isiah can't be mad at Mike when his own coach, Chuck Daly, didn't want him on the team. Isiah had too much baggage. USA Basketball didn't want that luggage going to the Olympics in Barcelona. Even Magic says that Mike had nothing to do with keeping Isiah off the Olympic team. Magic also claims he wasn't involved in the All-Star "Freeze Out." All I can say is, birds of a feather flock together. Magic is a very controlling guy. Isiah is the same way.

Two days after the All-Star Game, the Bulls beat the Pistons 139–126 in overtime. Michael scored 49 points, at the time his career high. He played forty-five minutes and took thirty-one shots. That's how motivated Michael was by the incident in Indiana. As I joined him on the Bulls, and we became players and teammates, I came to see that quality up close and learn from it.

All of this is to say that Jerry Krause wasn't being completely honest when he said of the trade for George Gervin just before my first real NBA game: "I don't think we'll have any problems with him." George being in Chicago did cause a problem with Michael.

Personally, I didn't have any problem with George. In fact, Iceman became one of my mentors during my rookie year. Michael wasn't the biggest fan of that, but it didn't matter to me: I was of the opinion that rookies should listen to vets. When you enter the league, you always have one or two veteran players who look out for you as a rookie. It's a tradition that still exists—I became the vet for a lot of first-year players during my career. And I was George's "rook." George was originally from Detroit. He could score, and he had one of the best Nike posters ever. You know the one: in the photo George is wearing a gray track suit and is sitting on blocks of ice while holding two basketballs.

Iceman would always call me "young fella." That was his thing. He and I lived close to each other in Chicago, so we saw each other a lot, and we talked on the phone a lot, too. He didn't mind trying to talk to young players and help them. He was thirty-three when he got traded to Chicago. I'd hung around with my uncles when I was growing up, so I was used to being around guys more than ten years older than me. (Years later, Iceman and I coached against each other in the Big3—that's the three-on-three league run by another Ice: Ice Cube.)

George was a star in both in the ABA and the NBA with the San Antonio Spurs. He averaged 33 points per game one season for the Spurs. He was the team's all-time leading scorer and held the record for most points scored in a quarter with 33 against New Orleans in 1978. Carmelo Anthony tied that record, and then in 2015 Klay Thompson scored 37 against the Sacramento Kings.

Iceman was scoring points in an era when you were really allowed to play physical defense. Before David Robinson and Tim Duncan came along, George was the best player in Spurs history. The year before we traded for him Ice averaged 21 points, but he was unhappy with the Spurs. A few days before George was traded, he was a no-show at two practices. George didn't like that he was going to be on the bench behind Alvin Robertson and Wes Matthews. San Antonio's owner at the time, Angelo Drossos, fined George and asked him if he wanted to retire. George wasn't ready to call it a career, so the Spurs instead traded him to the Bulls.

When the reporters asked Michael about the Bulls trading for Gervin, Mike didn't hide his feelings.

"I have no comment on the trade," he said. "Just say I am unhappy."

Maybe this was a case of Krause trying to motivate Michael by making him angry. Or maybe the trade, which was a big one to make the day before the season started, was meant to be a distraction from some bigger issues that had been swirling around the team. On the eve of my rookie season, the Chicago Bulls had more to worry about than whether their budding superstar could peacefully coexist with a legendary veteran.

3 | BASKETBALL JUNKIE

When the Bulls traded for George Gervin in October 1985, there was already a player on our team, named Quintin Dailey, who wore the number that Gervin had on his jersey his entire career, 44. So Gervin took number 8 with the Bulls. It turned out that Gervin probably should have been given 44 all along, because just as he was arriving to the team, Dailey was in Pasadena Community Hospital's drug rehabilitation center, being treated for cocaine addiction. He spent thirty-one days there and missed our first thirteen games. Then, in February, he had a relapse and returned to the same facility after failing to show up for a home game against the Detroit Pistons.

This guy was always involved in some type of controversy. When Quintin was a rookie with the Bulls in 1982, there were women's groups picketing outside of Chicago Stadium because he had pled guilty to an assault charge in an incident involving a woman when he played college ball at the University of San Francisco. He was sentenced to three years' probation in that case.

He once gained thirty pounds during a season. I had heard the famous story before coming to the Bulls about him having a ball boy get him a slice of pizza and a soda during a game in 1984 and eating it on the bench. He had attempted suicide, and violated the league's drug policy twice. A third violation would have meant the NBA would kick him out of the league for at least two years. That didn't happen, but when he was sent to rehab in February 1986, he never played for the Bulls again. Dailey died of heart disease in 2010 at the age of forty-nine. It's sad, and I have to think that his drug use had something to do with it.

Dailey's case was extreme, but honestly, not all that extreme.

The NBA had a serious drug problem when I got to the league. In the early 1980s, the *Washington Post* estimated that "40 to 75 percent" of the league was using cocaine, and that maybe 10 percent were freebasing.

"There is not a team in the league you can confidently say does not have a drug problem," Frank Layden, the general manager of the Utah Jazz said in August of 1980. "Every team could benefit from a rehabilitation program. I had two [drug] cases out of eleven players last year. We need a place to send these people [for help]."

In January of 1980, the Jazz forward Bernard King, who made his name with the Knicks, had been arrested on charges of sodomy and possession of cocaine. Later, Terry Furlow, a guard with the Jazz, died in a car accident. The autopsy showed traces of valium and cocaine in Furlow's system.

Larry O'Brien was NBA commissioner in the early eighties. The NBA actually formed a special committee to look into the drug problem. When that report came out, O'Brien said, "The NBA, of course, recognizes that the use of drugs is a problem in our society today. We have no indication that the percentage of players in our league who may have tried drugs exceeds the percentage of the general population which has experimented with drugs."

David Stern took over for O'Brien in 1984 and wanted to do more to actually address the drug problem. He could have easily started with our locker room in Chicago. There were drugs everywhere.

In *The Last Dance*, the documentary about the nineties Bulls, Michael told a crazy story about the drug use he encountered on the team when he was a rookie in 1984. Michael said: "Look, guys were doing things that I didn't see. I had one event, preseason, I think we were in Peoria [Illinois]. I was in the hotel trying to find my teammates. So I start knocking on doors, and I get to this one door and knock on the door and I can hear someone say 'Shhhh. Someone's outside.' And then you hear this deep voice [say] 'Who is it?' I said 'MJ.' And they said 'Ah, fuck, he's just the rookie, don't worry about it.' So they open up the door, I walk in, and practically the whole team was in there, and it was like, things I've never seen in my life as a young kid. You got your lines [of cocaine] over here, you got your weed smokers over here, you got your women over here.

"So the first thing I said was 'Look, man, I'm out.' Because all I could think about was if they come raid this place right about now, I am just as guilty as everybody else that's in this room. From that point on, I was more or less on my own."

The problem didn't seem any better the next season, when I was a rookie. Michael and I became fast friends and did just about everything together. I was spending a lot of time with Michael from the start, and maybe one of the reasons we got along, other than being the same age, is that we didn't do drugs. We went to dinner all the time, worked out together, went on vacation. Mike flew me to the All-Star Game in Dallas my rookie year. I only played with Michael for three seasons in Chicago, but I probably went out to dinner with him eighty times. I played ten years with Patrick Ewing and went out to dinner two or three times with him. Patrick liked to keep to himself.

Mike and I really had a low-key lifestyle. On a typical night on the road I'd go to Mike's room, play spades, and we'd just talk. We didn't hang out at clubs. There would be times we'd go out to dinner and maybe meet up with people, but we weren't going out drinking and clubbing the night before a game. You've got to be focused. At least that was my philosophy. I never smoked weed or did cocaine.

I saw drugs all the time when I was growing up. I had family members and friends who were freebasing. I knew kids in the sixth and seventh grade who were doing that. My thinking always was: Why would I take something and allow it to control my mind?

Like I told you, everyone was hustling in my neighborhood in Cleveland. You had guys dealing and other guys stealing. I grew up with a kid named Forest Gilliam who was robbing stores left and right. They called him Robin Hood because he was stealing from the rich and giving to the poor. Really, he'd give the people in the neighborhood a discount when he resold the luxury items he stole. He'd have diamonds, mink coats, and purses. He stole a $15,000 watch and sold it for $7,000. The drug dealers were paying for merchandise with their drug money.

Forest was a good football player, but he's spent his life in and out of jail. A few years ago he was arrested in Port St. Lucie, Florida, attempting to rob cash registers at Walmart. The police had him connected to nearly thirty similar crimes nationwide.

Shit, when Forest got busted, the cops found $7,000 in cash as well as cash drawer keys and a handwritten list of Walmart stores in the area. Forest used two friends to run the scam. One was a woman from Akron named Amy J. Gallo, who they figured no one would suspect because she's white. The getaway driver, Garland Ware, was from University Heights, Ohio. They were driving around the country like old-time bank robbers.

Forest was a smart guy, but he loved to steal. Believe me, the day they let him out of jail, he's going to do the same thing. I stayed away from people like that. Just like I stayed away from drugs. If I didn't do it as a stupid kid, why would I start once I made it to the NBA?

But I really can't overstate it: the drugs were everywhere. Remember, it was easy to get to the players in the eighties. It's not like today, when players have friends working for them and they're surrounded 24/7 by people they trust. It's hard to get to guys now. But in the eighties there would be guys waiting in the lobby with drugs. All the hot spots were in the big cities: New York, Chicago, Oakland. In fact, Oakland was one of the worst places. The number one hub was and still is the Marriott in Oakland, which is where the Warriors used to practice before moving to San Francisco. There were people doing drugs right in the hallway. And there are still drugs in the league today. I would say 60 to 70 percent of the guys in the league today smoke weed. A lot of them play like they're high, that's for sure.

Even with all the drugs, back in the eighties, most of the guys were serious about their craft. The perception that every night in the NBA was one wild party, with women, weed, and booze, was not really the case when I entered the league. Guys were committed, and they could play. Every position was also deep. It's not like today's NBA, where they fill out the rosters with guys who can't play. It was competitive and you had to keep up. We were committed to the grind. Most of the guys who weren't too deep into drugs waited until the summer to really go out. That's your time to do what you want. That's when you start going out and seeing girls. Hanging out was a summer thing, not a winter thing.

Shit, a lot of this was because if you think the NBA is a grind today, imagine what it was like in the 1980s. We were flying commercial back then, and we were playing a lot of back-to-backs. That means we were taking the first flight out after a game, sometimes at 5:30 or 6 a.m., and flying to another city to play a game that night. We'd be up at four, carrying our own bags, heading to the airport. When we got to the airport, we'd have to eat breakfast on the run. And of course the airport had the worst food in the world.

I always complained to my teammates about that—as I said, I love food, but I'm picky about what I eat—I like it made a certain way. My regular meal before games was steak and broccoli. I thought that was a good, healthy choice. For lunch, especially on the road, I'd go out and get a turkey sandwich and a bag of chips. I didn't like hotel food, so I would go out to look for something better. Michael was picky about food and had his routines, too. I ate steak before most games, but Michael literally had steak before 100 percent of his games. And before 90 percent of our practices, he ate McDonald's breakfast.

Today, the players whine about how hard they got it. It's not that hard, especially when it comes to travel. Every NBA team flies charter. I think that 20 percent of today's guys would be tough enough to play in our era. Maybe not even that many.

Another thing that's different today is that players on big-city teams typically live where the action is, because the practice facilities are built closer to the main stadium. A few years ago, the Bulls built a practice facility across the street from the United Center and the players moved downtown. But when I was with the Bulls, our practice facility was the Deerfield Multiplex in suburban Chicago. I didn't want to be more than ten minutes from where we practiced, since that's where I would be spending most of my time. So most of the Bulls players, myself and Mike included, lived north of the city. I was ten minutes from practice and about twenty minutes from O'Hare Airport. If it was snowing, it would take thirty minutes. Michael's first wife, Juanita Vanoy, would drive us to O'Hare in those early days. They started dating in 1985 and got married in 1989.

I played seventy-seven games and made thirty starts as a rookie. My first career start was on February 14, 1986, against the Indiana

Pacers at Chicago Stadium. I had a decent game: 17 points, 13 rebounds in thirty-five minutes. I made eight of twelve shots I took. But Herb Williams, the Pacers' big man, who eventually became my teammate in New York, had 39 points, and we lost the game. He got us pretty good.

The big man was a dominant force in the NBA when I got into the league. My "Welcome to the NBA" moment had come a few months earlier when we played the Houston Rockets, who started Hakeem Olajuwon and Ralph Sampson. I played nine minutes that night, and it wasn't the best nine minutes of my career. Hakeem had all the great spin moves and had a jumper. Olajuwon finished with 33 points and 15 rebounds and the Rockets blew us out. The story was a little different when we played the Rockets again in February. Hakeem still scored 33 with 11 rebounds. But I had 19 points and 17 rebounds. Sidney Green started but played just nine minutes. I played thirty-eight off the bench.

They weren't running plays for me, so I had to get my points any way I could. I could get offensive rebounds and score on put-backs. I also understood our defensive schemes, so that part came easy to me. My philosophy was just to keep my man off the boards. If he is averaging 30 points, try to hold him to 20.

I didn't care about shots. I wanted to win. It's like a music group. I'm playing bass, so my job is not to jump in front of the lead singer. Mike was our lead singer. In New York, Patrick Ewing wasn't strong enough to be the number one option. A lot of people said we didn't have a number two option with the Knicks and that's why we didn't win. I disagree. Patrick was the number two option. I was number three. We didn't have a number one.

Winning during my rookie season in Chicago was a struggle though, because Michael was out for much of it. He broke his foot in our third game and didn't play again until March. Not being able to play was killing Mike. And it was killing our record.

Krause and the front office didn't want to rush Mike back. The feeling was the management wanted a high draft pick. But Michael didn't care about that. He had every intention of playing and getting us into the playoffs. That's just the way Mike is built. He's a competitive guy who wants to win. That's the way I'm built, too. I agreed with the way he was thinking: let's get into the playoffs and give it our best shot. Who knows, maybe we can make a run. Fuck tanking. We're here to play. We're here to win.

Michael eventually came back, on March 15, and we lost our next five games. He was frustrated with losing, but he was also frustrated with his restricted playing time. The front office wanted to limit Mike's minutes. In those first five games he played thirteen, fourteen, fifteen, sixteen, and sixteen minutes. He wasn't having it. Michael is not the kind of guy who wants to be on a minutes restriction. I know that's a big thing in the NBA now, which is a load of shit, in my opinion. If you can play, play. No one is ever really 100 percent healthy. By the time you get to late March and early April, no one is healthy. That's just how it is.

Even with Michael struggling with his minutes and us struggling to get a win, we did get into a good groove over the final two weeks of the regular season. We managed to win four of our last six games and get into the playoffs with a 30-52 record. That's a bad record, but we were in the playoffs. That's all we cared about. Iceman was big for us. He played all eighty-two games and started seventy-five. Even though Mike didn't like George, and George wisely kept his distance from Michael all season—they never really talked or got much closer—the trade proved to have been a smart move by Krause.

By the end of the regular season I had started to learn the league and play with more confidence. But nothing you do during the regular season can prepare you for the playoffs, especially when you're playing the Boston Celtics. After losing the 1985 NBA Finals to the Los Angeles Lakers, Boston went 67-15 in 1985–86 and won forty home games. That team had five future Hall of Fame players: Larry Bird, Kevin McHale, Robert Parish, Bill Walton, and Dennis Johnson. We didn't stand a chance.

We knew what Boston was. They were going to get the calls. Back then, Los Angeles and Boston got all the calls. Even when we played in Chicago, they were still the home team. Superstars get the calls. I noticed that early on. Then in the last two minutes the refs bite the whistle. I don't like that. That's cheating to me. If it's a foul early in the game, it should be a foul late in the game.

I was still in college when Kevin McHale of the Celtics clotheslined Kurt Rambis of the Los Angeles Lakers in the 1984 NBA Finals. The Celtics thought that shit was the turning point of the series. Danny Ainge called that foul "inspirational." Imagine if that foul happened today? They would call in the National Guard. It was a nasty foul, no question about it. Both benches spilled onto the court. And guess what? Forget being suspended, McHale didn't even get kicked out of the game. It was a different league, and the Celtics were a different kind of team: physical, nasty, and fucking good. They didn't need help from referees, but they got it.

Bird was slow, but he could shoot. The game was played at a different pace back then, and Boston was like a YMCA team. They moved the ball and had good shooters. I loved playing against Parish, McHale, and Bird. McHale was like Karl Malone, both of them cried and flopped all the time, even if they had good moves. But for the most part the Celtics were professional.

Michael scored 49 in Game 1 in Boston, but we lost by 18. Game 2 was Michael's breakout performance. He scored 63 points against the Celtics inside the Boston Garden. Afterward, Bird said it was "God disguised as Michael Jordan." That sounds about right. I watched all 63 because I didn't get one pass from him. I kept waiting for Mike to miss, but he didn't miss many. It was a beautiful thing to see him score like that in back-to-back playoff games.

But at the end of the day Boston was too tough. We lost that game in double overtime. Then they blew us out in Game 3 back in Chicago to complete the sweep, and went on to win the championship. Still, everyone knew that Michael was special, and it seemed like we were headed in the right direction. In a lot of ways we were. The next year, with Doug Collins as our head coach, we improved by ten wins, but all it did was get us another playoff series with Boston. And the Celtics swept us again.

Michael was steaming. In three seasons he'd lost each year in the first round of the playoffs. His postseason record was 1-9. A lot of people forget that when they talk about the greatest of all time. It started slow for Michael. He didn't win his first playoff series until his fourth season, when he was twenty-four years old.

4 | PROTECTING MJ

By my third season with the Chicago Bulls, and Michael's fourth, 1987–88, you could tell that we were a team ready to make a big jump. I was a year older, wiser, and tougher. We had John Paxson, who joined the team from San Antonio my rookie year, at point guard. Midway through the season, we picked up Sam Vincent in a trade with Seattle, and he took over starting at point. Brad Sellers, who was our first-round draft pick in 1986, was coming off a solid rookie season.

Jerry Krause had worked his magic once again in the 1987 NBA Draft by making a trade for an unheralded player from a small college. Sound familiar? The first overall pick was David Robinson, who everyone knew. With the fifth overall pick, the Seattle SuperSonics selected Scottie Pippen out of Central Arkansas, who very few people knew. He was a mystery, but he was about to become our mystery. The Bulls selected Olden Polynice out of Virginia eighth and immediately traded him, plus a future first-round draft pick, for Pippen. No one realized it at the time, but Krause had just made one of the greatest draft-day trades in NBA history.

Krause also had the tenth overall pick, and he used it to select Horace Grant out of Clemson. I wasn't really sure how to take it when the Bulls drafted a power forward. They already had one: me. But I couldn't worry about that stuff. I was the starter and things were looking up for me and the team. I figured we were maybe a year or two away from contending for a championship.

Michael had become a superstar, and as long as he was healthy, we would be a team to reckon with. When you played the Chicago Bulls, the goal was to stop Michael by any means necessary. And the bigger Mike got, the bigger the target got on his back, especially in the late 1980s, when physical play was so commonplace. Luckily, physical play was my strength.

When you have a superstar on your team, that player usually has the ball a lot and gets fouled a lot. That's part of the game. When the fouls became excessive or borderline dirty, that's when I would step in. Michael was the NBA version of Wayne Gretzky, the young NHL star. They were both highly skilled players who could leave their opponents frustrated and with no other choice but to get physical to try to stop them from scoring. Those types of players need protection. In the NHL every team has an enforcer. The same was true of the NBA in the eighties and nineties.

You always remember the "firsts" from your NBA career: first points, first rebound, first dunk, first playoff game, and of course, first fight. I had had my first NBA fight the year before, my second season with the Chicago Bulls. The location was the MECCA. Not the basketball Mecca, which is what basketball players call Madison Square Garden. I'm talking about the MECCA in Milwaukee. There was nothing special about the MECCA Arena, but there was something special about the Milwaukee Bucks.

They were a good, tough team, and I liked going up against them. Milwaukee was an easy ninety-mile road trip for us. The short drive from Chicago to Milwaukee also meant a lot of our fans would make the trip. The Bucks had Terry Cummings, Ricky Pierce, and Sidney Moncrief. Their coach was Don Nelson, a guy who later replaced Pat Riley in New York for the 1995–96 season and coached me for fifty-nine games before the Knicks fired him. The Bucks had won fifty-seven games my rookie year. They'd knocked off the Philadelphia 76ers in the second round of the playoffs that year, beating future Hall of Famers Julius Erving, Maurice Cheeks, Bobby Jones, and Charles Barkley. Then they'd gotten swept in the Eastern Conference Finals by the Celtics.

Unlike today's NBA, where teams like to play small and in some cases will use a lineup with a six-foot-seven center, the NBA in the eighties was a big man's league. The Bucks had two big white seven-footers—Paul Mokeski and Randy Breuer—and they would sometimes play together. Neither guy was a great player, but they could both be physical. I found that out late in the third quarter when I had the ball in the post with both Mokeski and Breuer guarding me. I banged into Mokeski, trying to create space and make a move to the basket, and as he went to slap down at the ball, he got me in the chin with his left elbow. Then he reached out and raked me across the face with his left hand. Even though I was just a second-year player, I wasn't going to let him beat me up on the court. My reaction was to punch him. I popped him pretty good. That was how most NBA fights start. Heat of the moment, a hard foul, an elbow to the head, and then it's on.

Mokeski weighed about 255 pounds and had a few inches on me. He told reporters after the game that "there was a lot of elbowing and pushing and shoving. I was trying to get position and keep him away from the basket. He made a good move and I fouled him hard. I didn't want him to make a basket and get a three-point play. He didn't like it and he threw an elbow. I pushed and he pushed. Then whatever happened, happened."

What happened was, I broke his nose.

We both got ejected. I had 17 points and 10 rebounds, and we were leading 79–76. Mokeski hadn't scored a point, which made it a good trade-off for the Bucks. I won the fight; the Bucks won the game, 120–105. And then the league had their say. Mokeski was fined $1,000 and I was fined $2,500. I thought, OK, so the winner gets the bigger prize money?

"The reason for the difference in fines is Oakley punched Mokeski" is how Rod Thorn, the NBA vice president of operations and former general manager of the Bulls, described it at the time. Thorn's title was a fancy way of saying he was the Dean of Discipline. "Oakley punched him first," Thorn said, "and when Mokeski went after him, Oakley punched him again as he was backpedaling. . . . Anyone who throws a punch gets fined. Anyone who connects gets fined more. Mokeski did foul him hard, but there is no justification for punching a guy in the face."

Justification? Mokeski was holding me and fouling me. Then he came walking at me, and he hit me first when he put his hand on my face.

I realized that my version of events wasn't the same as the NBA's, which only means that my version doesn't matter. But I'd had my first fight, and neither the fine, nor the bogus explanation, was going to be enough to stop me from playing hard and doing what was necessary to protect myself and my teammates.

So by my third year in the league, players knew that I could play, and they knew that I would protect my guys. Dennis Rodman knew it. Charles Barkley knew it. Mention my name to Barkley today and he'll go the other way. Everyone thinks I'm Michael Jordan's bodyguard, but the truth is I provided protection for all my teammates.

Also, just because I looked out for Michael, that doesn't mean he was soft. He was mentally and physically tough. He had to be to survive.

I remember doing a radio interview a few years ago and the host asked me, "What made Michael Jordan so tough?" I looked at the guy, paused, and said, "I did." I'm not taking credit for his skill level or work ethic. I had nothing to do with that. I always tell Michael: "You're God's first child. I don't know who the second is, but you're the first." I just think that I helped him learn that mindset of toughness that he needed to play basketball as his game and superstar status developed, and to be a leader in the way he became.

There were only twenty-three teams in the league in 1987–88 and only two divisions for each conference. The Atlantic Division had five teams, but in our eyes only one of them really mattered: the Celtics. We still thought of them as the clear team to beat in the East. They'd made it to the NBA Finals the past three consecutive years, losing to the Lakers in 1985, then defeating the Rockets in 1986 for the championship, and then losing in 1987 to Magic Johnson, Kareem Abdul-Jabbar, and the Los Angeles Lakers again. The Celtics had experience, talent, tradition, and the best front line in the league with Bird, McHale, and Parish. They were a force.

But they weren't the only strong team in the conference. The Central Division, which we played in, was the toughest division in the league. It had six teams: us, the Detroit Pistons, the Atlanta Hawks, the Bucks, the Cleveland Cavaliers, and the Indiana Pacers. Atlanta had Dominique Wilkins, Kevin Willis, and Doc Rivers, and the Bucks were still a good team with Terry Cummings, Sidney Moncrief, and Paul Pressey. We thought we could handle Atlanta and Milwaukee, and that Boston was who we'd need to contend with to make a run in the playoffs. But the Detroit Pistons were another team on the rise, and we had to worry about them, too.

In today's NBA you play teams in your division four times. When I joined the league, we played each team in our division six times. Six games is a lot. That's how rivalries start. That's good for the league. It also leads to bad blood, which leads to fights, which in theory isn't bad for the league either. When it came to blood, fights, and general contempt, the Pistons stuck out for us above all the rest. There wasn't much we liked about them or they liked about us. Both of our teams wanted to prove that we belonged and were the threat to Boston in the East. The Pistons had made it to the Eastern Conference Finals in '87, where they pushed Boston to seven games, so they had a leg up. Every game between us was going to be a battle.

The Pistons weren't the Bad Boys just yet. They got that nickname when they won back-to-back titles in '89 and '90. But the key players were already in place: Isiah Thomas, Joe Dumars, Adrian Dantley, Vinnie Johnson, Rick Mahorn, John Salley, and Dennis Rodman. That's a lot of talent. They also had Bill Laimbeer, who was an asshole.

We opened the 1987–88 season by winning seven of our first eight games. Michael was having a great start to the season. Two weeks in, we had a home-and-home series with the Washington Bullets. That's when you play each other in home games, one in each team's city, over consecutive days. In the first meeting Michael scored 11 points in the last six minutes to carry us to a victory. The following night he scored eight points in the last two and a half minutes and we won again. Two nights later against the Atlanta Hawks, Michael sank two free throws to give us a 94–92 lead. He then blocked Dominique Wilkins's jumper to preserve the victory. Michael was getting it done on both ends of the court.

Our next game was at home against the Pistons on November 21. We were feeling confident in our chances to compete in the

East. It was a close game, which you would expect. We went up 122–119 after Michael made two free throws with seven seconds left, but Isiah, playing in his hometown, hit a three-pointer with two seconds remaining, and we went to overtime. We blew our chance. The Pistons went ahead on back-to-back baskets from John Salley and Dennis Rodman, and we were done. Adrian Dantley scored 6 of his 45 points in overtime. Isiah had 27. Michael scored 49 before fouling out in overtime.

Even in the loss, we, and Michael, felt we had made a strong statement. Detroit caught a break because we were playing our fourth game in five nights. And we went to overtime. That's a worst-case scenario. Michael played forty-four minutes and would have played forty-six of the fifty-three minutes had he not fouled out. Our thing was if you were healthy you played. It's pretty simple. Shit, some people have to go to work seven days a week and don't even make that much money. In the NBA the money got bigger and the game got weaker.

As I mentioned, in our day there was no such thing as load management. That's something Kawhi Leonard started with the San Antonio Spurs. In Michael's third season, my second, he played all eighty-two games and averaged 37.1 points per game. He also averaged forty minutes per game. That's pretty remarkable when you think about it. Mike had only played eighteen games the previous season due to a foot injury, yet the next season he was at forty minutes a game for all eighty-two.

Today's stars play fewer minutes and the league has fewer back-to-backs. But they need more rest? Guys were hungrier back when I played. We knew what it meant every night to be on the floor. If you weren't playing, you were showing weakness. You didn't want anyone to see that. If you were at 70 percent, you still played.

In that November 21 overtime loss to Detroit, I played thirty-six minutes. I also finished with 21 points, 12 rebounds, and 5 assists.

Those are good numbers, but I didn't give a fuck about that. The goal is to win and we didn't get the job done.

Three weeks later, on December 15, 1987, we went to Pontiac, Michigan, to play the Pistons at the Silverdome. The arena was thirty miles north of downtown Detroit, and it was too big for basketball—a huge stadium where the Detroit Lions once played. The Pistons played there for ten years starting in 1978, before moving into the Palace of Auburn Hills, another suburban arena, for the start of the 1988–89 season. They won three championships in the suburbs before moving back to the city, where they belonged, for the start of 2017–18 season.

On this cold December night, the Silverdome had 23,729 fans come see the Pistons and the Bulls. In those days that was a great crowd for an NBA regular season game. In fact, it still is.

We played another competitive game that night, only to lose again in overtime. Michael scored 38 points, and it was clear that even though the Pistons had already beaten us in the first two meetings, they knew Michael was becoming a big problem. They had to do something about him. Really, it was Isiah Thomas who wanted to do something about Michael.

Isiah was always trying to fuck with Michael's head, but those mind games weren't working. Michael is mentally tough. He was one of the most focused players to ever put on the uniform. Isiah and the Pistons knew that Michael couldn't be messed with.

But they damn sure tried.

On January 16, 1988, we played the Pistons again, at home. Our record was 19-14, while the Pistons were in first place with a 20-10 record. Every game was more intense than the last. Laimbeer had taken a shot at Scottie Pippen in December, so it was pretty obvious where this was headed. Tensions boiled over in the third quarter when Rick Mahorn fouled Michael by grabbing him around the waist and throwing him to the floor. Mahorn was big and strong and wanted to send a message.

We had no choice but to go right back at him. I immediately went after Mahorn, and two of my teammates, Mike Brown and Brad Sellers, were pushing Mahorn as well. The fight drifted toward our bench, where our coach, Doug Collins, went to grab Mahorn around the neck. I give Doug credit for sticking up for Michael, but Mahorn tossed Doug on the scorer's table like a rag doll. Both benches ended up on the court. It was crazy.

Me and Mahorn were immediately ejected from the game. Mahorn wound up being the only player suspended: he got one game plus a $5,000 fine. I got fined $2,000, but I wasn't suspended. Doug Collins was hit with a $1,500 fine, while a few of my teammates—Scottie Pippen, Horace Grant, and Granville Waiters—were fined $500 each for leaving the bench. The Pistons' John Salley and Vinnie Johnson were also fined $500 each for leaving the bench.

That's a bargain by today's NBA standards. If you leave the bench now, you get an automatic one-game suspension. We might not have made a lot of money when I first came into the league, but the league office also didn't take a lot of money when punches were thrown. I'm not saying the league encouraged hard fouls and fighting, but they were treated differently. It's too costly to fight now, and as a result, the league has gotten less physical, and players have gotten softer. When Joel Embiid of the Philadelphia 76ers and Karl-Anthony Towns of the Minnesota Timberwolves got into a fight early in the 2019–20 season—nothing but a "pillow fight," as I call it—they were both suspended for two games, and Embiid lost about $40,000 in wages. It's especially not smart to fight in the playoffs. When I was on the Knicks, we learned that lesson the hard way during our 1997 playoff series against the Miami Heat. Our fight in Game 5 cost us the series, as well as my last legitimate chance at winning an NBA title. The NBA's stance on fighting was getting stricter at that time.

But in the late eighties, the league viewed fighting differently. The fines for our fight with the Pistons were announced by Rod

Thorn. In his statement to reporters, Thorn said: "The Board of Governors adopted a resolution in October making it clear that flagrant fouls in half-court play will not be tolerated and will be subject to the most severe penalties. This was a blatant example of the very type of action the Board of Governors was trying to eliminate."

Rod said I was fined for "escalating the incident" and Doug was fined for "acting as other than a peacemaker during the altercation." I look at it as money well spent. We had to defend ourselves, and these are the types of moments that bring a team together. I always stuck up for my teammates. If I was wearing the same uniform as somebody, I got his back.

I knew Michael appreciated how we responded to the foul in that moment and throughout the game. Two things happened that night: we didn't let the Pistons push us around, and we won the game, 115–99. Of course, the focus afterward in the media was on the melee featuring the two heavyweights, myself and Mahorn.

When the fines were announced, Michael told Chicago reporters: "I think my teammates really cared about the way I was being treated. Charles Oakley is a very caring person. I'm very grateful he came over and tried to take up for me."

Michael wanted to return the favor by offering to pay our fines, but Doug and I declined. Doug wanted to pay his fine to make sure the league knew that he stood against fighting. He said: "I don't incite my players to fight and I don't condone fighting. Fighting isn't a part of basketball."

Well, not exactly. Maybe guys in the NBA didn't go into a game looking for a fight, like they might in hockey. But in basketball you have to be ready to stand up for yourself if someone knocks you or your teammate down. We couldn't let the Pistons intimidate us. I remember telling the reporters after the game, "If it didn't get through to them, it will if they ever do it again. If they do something wrong they're going to get checked. No matter what player they mess with, somebody will retaliate. In Detroit earlier this year, Bill Laimbeer hit Scottie. I ran out and told him the next time it happens, something is going down. I knew something was going to happen. The fine will get paid and then it will be forgotten. But you've got to protect yourself at all times."

Over the years, the Bad Boys took more cheap shots than anything. Isiah was usually the one egging guys on. He knew how to get Mahorn and Rodman going.

Guys know who to pick on and who to avoid. It's part of the game. Your response is to not let anyone punk you. They were going out of their way to get to Michael. Mahorn thought he could go after Michael, but he got me instead. And Mahorn knew what I do. I'm the police. I was never going to start the fight but I would end it.

We lost two of our final three regular-season meetings with the Pistons, although on April 3, 1988, Michael had one of those magical performances. He went off for 59 points. It was similar to the game he'd had thirteen months earlier against the Pistons when he scored 61 points by making twenty-two of thirty-nine shots. Me and Mike combined for 68 points that night. Michael said after that game on March 4, 1987: "Nobody's ever really unstoppable but I felt close to it tonight." You know that drove the Pistons crazy.

We were coming. We finished with a record of 50-32 in 1987–88. It was the Bulls' first 50-win campaign since the 1973–74 season. And things only got better. Our first-round opponent was the Cleveland Cavaliers, and in Game 1 Michael scored 50 points, and we broke our team's seven-game playoff losing streak. In Game 2, Michael went off for 55.

We were on a roll with Michael. Even after we lost Game 3, the headline in the *Chicago Tribune* the next day told the story about where the series was headed. It read: "Cavs bring Bulls back to earth . . . Limit Jordan to 38 points."

Cleveland was tougher at home and forced a Game 5 back in Chicago. But in that fifth and decisive game, on May 8, 1988, Michael had his postseason breakthrough. He scored 39, Pippen scored 24, and I grabbed 20 rebounds for our first playoff series victory. I felt I had won the battle, and the war. The player the Cavs traded me for on draft day almost three years earlier, Keith Lee, missed the regular season and the playoffs with a leg injury.

"Nothing against Keith Lee, but Cleveland had to get up on the wrong side of the bed when they made that trade," my former teammate, Gene Banks, once said.

Lee never played another game for the Cavaliers. The following season he joined the New Jersey Nets, and after one year his career was done. My career was just getting going, and I was excited about having another crack at the Pistons, who we were up against next in the playoffs.

We lost Game 1 in Detroit, then managed to tie the series by winning Game 2 as Michael scored 36 and Sam Vincent 31. That game from Michael was something of a wake-up call for the Pistons. When we went back to Chicago for Games 3 and 4, the Pistons Hall of Fame head coach, Chuck Daly, introduced "The Jordan Rules." The Rules were a defensive strategy to slow down and bruise the best player on the court. According to Daly, the Pistons would try and force Michael left and double-team him. If he was on the right, they would run a double-team late at him. And they would send a big man at him any time he went in the box.

"The other rule was, any time he went by you, you had to nail him," Daly said. "If he was coming off a screen, nail him. We didn't want to be dirty—I know some people thought we were—but we had to make contact and be very physical."

That's exactly what the Pistons did in the first quarter of Game 3. Mike tried to fight through a Bill Laimbeer screen at the foul line, and the next thing you know, Laimbeer slapped at Mike's arm. Michael retaliated by throwing a punch, and I immediately jumped in and shoved Laimbeer away. Isiah Thomas wrapped his arms around me to guide me away from the fray and the thing calmed down pretty quickly.

Since this was the 1980s, the only punishment referee Earl Strom handed out was a technical foul on Michael and an offensive foul on Laimbeer. I didn't get anything. But the Pistons set a tone. Michael scored 24 on eight of twenty shooting with five turnovers and Detroit beat us easily, 101–79. We lost Game 4 and scored only 77 points.

I had a strong Game 5 with 19 points and 15 rebounds, but what did it mean? I even got into a shoving match with Mahorn because that's what he and I did. We both received technical fouls and that was it. We lost, and our season was done. The Pistons had successfully shut Michael down enough over the last three games to do the trick. He averaged 24 points as the Pistons dared the rest of us to beat them. It worked. Ultimately, it turned out that we weren't ready to beat the Pistons in a best-of-seven series.

The season was over, but we definitely felt as if we had accomplished something and that our future was bright. Scottie was the real deal. And Michael was a true superstar. The Pistons went on to beat the Celtics in the next round, which told us that the Celtics were fading. Our main competition was now Detroit, and we were ready for that challenge. If they wanted to get nasty, we were down for that. Next season couldn't come soon enough.

Little did I know, however, that when I walked off the court in Detroit, it would be my last game as Michael's teammate with the Chicago Bulls.

5 | THE BOMB SQUAD

Everybody has a plan until they get punched in the mouth."
I'd like to take credit for that line, but those words belong to Mike Tyson, the former heavyweight champion of the world. It's a great quote because it applies to everybody in all walks of life, not just boxers and professional athletes, and it sums up a valuable lesson: your life and your situation can change at a moment's notice. The key is to be able to react and adjust.

Michael Spinks and I learned that the hard way on June 27, 1988.

That night Spinks was fighting Tyson in Atlantic City for the undisputed heavyweight championship. Both fighters were undefeated, and the fight promoters were calling the bout "Once and for All."

I enjoyed going to the fights. When I was young, there was nothing like a big fight. Muhammad Ali, Joe Frazier, George Foreman, Marvin Hagler, Thomas Hearns, Sugar Ray Leonard, Evander Holyfield, and "Iron Mike" Tyson were the guys you wanted to see. Today, mixed martial arts has taken some of the attention away from boxing, but back in the late eighties and early nineties a Tyson fight was where you wanted to be.

I had met Tyson a couple of times before the Spinks fight. I wouldn't say we were best friends, but I knew his boxing promoter, Don King, who was a Cleveland guy, and I'd run into Tyson and King before. Mike and I stayed in touch, and I even visited him in prison a few years after the Spinks fight. He was convicted of rape in 1992 and was at the Plainfield Correctional Facility, about twenty miles from downtown Indianapolis. I was in Indiana for a game in 1993, had a day off, and rented a car to spend a little time with Tyson. Getting a visitor was like a vacation for him.

He was released after serving three years of a six-year prison term and then moved to Southington Township in Ohio, about an hour from my hometown of Cleveland. That's where Don King had a big mansion. Over the years after that, when we were both in New York, I'd hang out with Tyson in Harlem. He had his pigeons. We'd go out to dinner. Go to a club.

In his prime, Tyson boxed like a lion eating raw meat. He wasted no time pummeling his opponents. His fights were quick, so if you had a ticket the idea was to get to your seat before the first round because Tyson wasn't playing around. In 1988, I wasn't going to miss the Tyson-Spinks fight at the Atlantic City Convention Hall. I was traveling with Michael Jordan and Richard Dent, the former Chicago Bears defensive end who was the Most Valuable Player of Super Bowl XX in 1986. That was the Super Bowl when the Bears gave William "Refrigerator" Perry the chance to run for a late touchdown instead of giving the ball to the great Walter Payton. Richard retired after the 1987 season and eventually ended up in the Hall of Fame. That didn't stop someone from stealing Richard's wallet right before the fight. The Super Bowl MVP got himself pickpocketed. You know how it works for all these marquee boxing matches: these fights attract everyone, including the con artists. You get the celebrities, professional athletes, Donald Trump, call girls, strippers, and the punks who steal wallets.

We made it to the fight on time, which was good since Tyson needed just ninety-one seconds to end Spinks's career. That's it. One round, a few good punches, one knockdown, and fight over. Tyson stays unbeaten. As for Spinks, he got punched in the mouth, and his plans had to change. He never fought again.

I got punched in the mouth that night as well, though in my case, it wasn't literal. On the night of the Tyson-Spinks fight I learned I was being traded from the Chicago Bulls to the New York Knicks. Jerry Krause had brought me to Chicago and he was responsible for trading me away, but I know it was really coach Doug Collins who wanted me gone. Doug didn't like it when I asked him to run some plays for me. He never would do it. Opposing teams put so much pressure on Michael when he had the ball. I thought I could help more with some offense. In the playoffs, all the basketball analysts would say that one of the big weaknesses with our team was that no one could score besides Michael. My thing was "How are we going to score if there are no plays run for the rest of us?"

Instead, Doug Collins would say, "Just rebound and play good defense." Doug was a good coach, but I didn't think he was playing me to my potential. I had three good years under my belt and I wanted to do more. I wasn't afraid to speak up. If I felt something needed to be said, I said it. That bothered Doug.

There was one incident in particular back in 1986 that had seemed small, but I think it stuck with him. We were playing the Knicks on Christmas Day and then had one day off before a game against the Indiana Pacers on the 27th. Before the Knicks game, Doug said we could all go home after to be with our families. I honestly didn't care about that—I was okay being by myself around the holidays, I was used to being on my own. My contract said I played for the Bulls, that was my priority, so my feeling was there was no point wasting my time trying to rush home. But other guys, especially Brad Sellers, were looking forward to going home, even if it was just for a day.

We lost that game to the Knicks 86–85 though, and afterward Doug walked into the locker room crying, "Ya stunk up the place. We played like shit. We're all going back to Chicago."

I thought that was wrong, so I said something. "Doug, that's not right," I said. "You told guys they could go home. They bought plane tickets."

I could tell he was mad that I'd challenged him. I'm sure he thought I was complaining, but I was just being honest with him. If I felt something needed to be said, I said it.

I'm convinced that incident and a few others like it led Doug to go to Jerry Krause and whine about me, pushing him to make a move. In 1988, after my third season, I was hearing rumors about a potential deal to send me to the Seattle SuperSonics. There was also talk about me going to Dallas for Mark Aguirre, a Chicago guy who'd attended DePaul and was one of the league's best scorers. Where there is smoke there is fire. And sure enough, Doug got his way. The night of the Tyson-Spinks fight in June 1988, the Chicago Bulls traded me to the New York Knicks for thirty-one-year-old center Bill Cartwright.

Honestly, I was fine with it. The Bulls didn't want me and clearly the Knicks did. Rick Pitino, the Knicks head coach, told reporters that he was "ecstatic" about me joining the team. Might as well go to a team that wants you, I figured.

"We've acquired one of the top power forwards in the game of basketball," Rick said. "He has strength and youth."

With so many reporters at the fight in Atlantic City, word started to spread that I was getting traded. I don't remember who actually gave me the news that it had happened, but when I heard about it

I asked Michael point-blank, "Did they ask you about trading me? You had to know something about it. You're their best player."

"They brought it up but they didn't say when," Michael told me.

Michael knew something was up, but he wasn't happy about it, and not for one second do I believe he wanted me to leave. That's why I wasn't mad at Michael. He told me that it meant "no more picks, no more outlets." Meaning, he was going to miss all the little things I did on the court, rebounding, setting screens to free him up. Trades were not something he could control. I had no control over it either. If they didn't want me or need me, that's life. It's not like today, when some players can veto a trade. So I let it play out. I didn't lose my job, I was only getting traded. What sense does it make to bitch and moan? Once you sign that contract, a team can do whatever they want. Except for a handful of players, just about everyone gets traded. Kareem Abdul-Jabbar was traded. Dr. J, Julius Erving, was traded. Teams trade Hall of Fame players, so they can certainly trade Charles Oakley.

The Bulls were in the market for a center, but they didn't want to pay close to $3 million for Moses Malone. So they traded for Cartwright. He was an offensive player. I remember saying at the time that with Scottie Pippen, Horace Grant, Cartwright, and Michael, the Bulls now had four offensive guys. At my press conference in New York I questioned whether the Bulls could adjust going from one guy having the ball to four, when they couldn't go from one guy to two last year.

When Chicago reporters contacted Michael, he didn't give the deal a ringing endorsement, which I'm sure bothered Krause.

"We're giving up the best rebounder in the league," he said. "How are we going to replace that?"

Michael also denied rumors that I was a troublemaker on the team. I understood the term troublemaker in this case to mean me not being afraid to speak up. The Bulls certainly couldn't complain about my performance and work ethic. I showed up for work early every day. I played hurt. I was productive. But this is what NBA teams do when they make a trade. They leak shit to the media to create their own narrative. It's clear that the narrative they wanted out there was that I was trouble in the locker room. Yet you ask any of my teammates, and they'll tell you that I was a team-first guy. Always was, always will be.

"A lot of people felt that we had conflict, but we never had conflict," Michael said after the trade became official. "I thought he was part of the nucleus here. I thought we were more or less progressing with youth. I don't understand their reasoning, but I guess there is some reasoning behind it or they wouldn't have done it."

Remember how upset Michael was with the George Gervin trade? Well, this was the second trade orchestrated by Krause that Michael disagreed with. And Michael made that known when reporters asked if he understood why the deal was made.

"I don't know. You're dealing with the Executive of the Year."

That was a little dig at Krause. It wasn't Michael's first, and it was far from being the last. But the Bulls were no longer my concern. I was now with the Knicks and ready to play whatever role they asked me to.

I was leaving Chicago, I was leaving the Bulls, and I was leaving Michael. But something told me I'd be seeing him and the Bulls again come playoff time.

When I arrived in New York in 1988, I was joining an organization that was fifteen years removed from winning its second NBA Championship. They had missed the playoffs eight of the previous thirteen seasons. But things for the team were looking up. Coach Rick Pitino was a young guy with a lot of energy. He was thirty-four years old when the Knicks hired him after he led Providence College to the 1987 Final Four. In the Elite Eight, Providence knocked off Patrick Ewing's college team, Georgetown. The Providence point guard was future NBA head coach Billy Donovan, and two of Rick's assistants were future NBA head coaches Stu Jackson and Jeff Van Gundy.

Pitino had replaced Hubie Brown for the 1987–88 season, and in that first year, he led the Knicks to 38 wins, a 14-win improvement over the previous season. He took the team to the playoffs, but they were eliminated in the first round. That off-season they acquired me from the Bulls and drafted point guard Rod Strickland, who grew up in the Bronx and went to DePaul University, with the nineteenth overall pick, even though the incumbent point guard, Mark Jackson, had just been named Rookie of the Year. Patrick Ewing had averaged at least 20 points in his first three seasons since being drafted with the first overall pick and was our best player. We also had a good young core, which included Kenny Walker, Johnny Newman, Trent Tucker, and Gerald Wilkins. When we acquired Kiki Vandeweghe midway through the season, he was our only player over the age of thirty.

Rick had a system and a style that he felt could work with our young roster. He wanted to run and press, tire teams out, and shoot threes. Rick was trying to do an early version with our team of what the Golden State Warriors would later do with Steph Curry and Klay Thompson in 2015. I liked what he was trying because it was different. He knew the way he wanted to coach and felt he had the players to run that system. We had to adapt to him. Today, coaches adapt to the players.

In addition to winning games, Pitino said his edict was to play an exciting brand of basketball that would draw fans to Madison Square Garden. Even with Ewing on the team, the Knicks were struggling at the box office. Pitino was committed to changing that.

"I had to fill the Garden," Rick said. "And the best way to do that was to play an entertaining style that would produce wins. That's exactly what the three-point shot brought to the game."

We did as Rick asked, and shot a lot of threes. You might remember the great poster featuring Jackson, Strickland, Newman, Wilkins, and Tucker dressed as World War II fighter pilots called "The Bomb Squad." It was a cool picture and it was accurate. During the 1988–89 season we took 1,147 threes—400 more than the next team. We made an NBA-record 386 threes.

To show you how much the league has changed in the last thirty years, the Golden State Warriors made—that's right, made—1,087 threes during the 2018–19 season. That was the team with Curry, Thompson, and Kevin Durant. We weren't quite at that level, but we did lead the league in attempted threes (14) per game and three-point field goals (4.7) per game.

We started off slowly by opening the season with consecutive road losses at Boston and New Jersey. On November 9, 1988, we played the Chicago Bulls in our home opener. The Knicks fans had booed Bill Cartwright during his final season with the team, but they gave me, the guy he was traded for, a nice ovation when I was announced before the game. Only Michael got a louder ovation. I didn't have my best performance—6 points and 6 rebounds in twenty-seven minutes—but Johnny Newman outscored Michael Jordan 35–31, and we won the game. It was good to beat the team that had just traded me. I still had a lot of friends on that team, but now that I was wearing a different uniform, it was all business on the court. Michael knew that. Plus, the Knicks desperately needed a win, and that victory over the Bulls became the start of a five-game winning streak. It turned out to be a great way to kick off the season and bring the team together.

The only bump we hit early on in that season occurred at about thirty thousand feet, on a flight back to New York after a win. Rod,

Mark, and Pete Myers were sitting in the back of the plane playing cards and fucking around. They were throwing grapes toward the front of the plane where the veterans were sitting, including Sidney Green, who had been my teammate during my rookie season with the Chicago Bulls. I was in the back of the plane with those guys, but I wasn't throwing grapes.

You have to understand that Sid could be a little stubborn. When I first got to Chicago, we were cool. He took me to workouts and brought me to his house to eat. We went at it all the time in practice because we were both fighting for playing time, but that's what you're supposed to do.

One night during my rookie season, Sid joined me and Michael Jordan for dinner in Seattle, and when the check came Sid was telling MJ that he should pay for the meal since he was an All-Star. Sid, who was from Brooklyn and attended UNLV, was the fifth pick of the 1983 NBA Draft. He had money and that's exactly what MJ told him.

"I'll pay for what I ordered and you pay for what you ordered," Michael told him.

"No, motherfucker, I'm not paying" was Sid's response.

It got real heated. Sid jumped up, and I told him, "I'm not gonna let you just jump MJ. Come on, why are you complaining? It's not like you don't have money."

The Bulls had traded Sidney Green to Detroit in 1986, and Detroit traded him to the Knicks in 1987, so now we were back together in New York. He didn't like getting hit with grapes, and he told those guys, "The next motherfucker who throws a grape is going to get his ass beat."

Of course, once Sid threatened them, Rod, Mark, and Pete all threw a grape at him at once. But Sid came back and accused me.

I said, "Sidney, you don't have eyes in the back of your head so you have no idea who did it. Just stop."

He told me he was going to "take me down," and as he walked toward me, I hit him. Got him pretty good. I busted his lip open. He was bleeding and getting angry. Then, Sid went after Pete Myers. Suddenly we had some turmoil on the team. Pitino was hot. The next day he wanted to meet with everybody to find out who threw the grapes. Rick was real close with Mark Jackson, but Mark wouldn't rat anyone out, including himself.

As players, you get over that kind of stuff. Our group was already getting pretty tight after a first week of good basketball to start the year, and that set the tone for the rest of our season. We turned out to be a great home team. We tied a franchise record by going 35-6 at MSG, which included a franchise record twenty-six-game home winning streak. It started after we lost to the Los Angeles Lakers on November 22 and ended on March 16, 1989, when Charles Barkley and the Philadelphia 76ers beat us 121–112. We were missing Mark Jackson, who had knee surgery, and Pitino was ejected in the fourth quarter of that loss after picking up two technical fouls. In our previous three games Barkley had scored a total of 104 points and made thirty-five of forty-eight shots. I took that shit personally. But Barkley had a huge night in the game that ended our home winning streak: 43 points, 12 rebounds in forty-six minutes. He made seventeen of eighteen free throws. I had 25 points and 18 rebounds, but it wasn't good enough, because afterward Pitino admitted that his biggest concern was "the way we played Barkley."

Four nights later we were in Philadelphia and things were different. We won 129–109, and although Barkley scored 28 points, he was just 3 for 7 in the first half and 8 for 14 overall.

"Oakley did a great job against Barkley," Pitino told reporters after the win.

I also got involved offensively, making three of four threes. I came into the game with two made three-pointers all season. It was an important moment for us because it looked as if we would draw Philadelphia in the first round of the playoffs, and we needed a statement win after they'd ended our home winning streak. It was the type of win that brings a team close together. Ewing played and scored 31 despite having a cold and knee soreness.

"After the 76ers ended our streak, there was a lot of talk, especially from Barkley, about the playoffs," Patrick said. "We wanted to prove we were the better team."

We were the surprise team in the league in 1988–89. We ended up winning fifty-two games, marking the franchise's first fifty-win season in eight years, dating back to when Hall of Fame coach Red Holzman was on the bench. In fact, it was the most wins since Holzman's second title, in 1973. Pitino accomplished both of his preseason goals as we drew 746,851 to Madison Square Garden, the third-best attendance figure in the NBA.

We earned that record just like we earned the second overall seed in the Eastern Conference and a date with Philadelphia in the best-of-five first-round series. The home court advantage held up as Mark Jackson and Gerald Wilkins hit huge shots late in Games 1 and 2, respectively. In Game 3, we clinched the series in overtime at the Spectrum even on an off night from Patrick, who made just three of twelve shots. Mark had 24 points and 9 assists. Gerald, who came within 2 assists of a triple-double, hit the biggest shot of the game: a twenty-footer with six seconds left in overtime, for the 116–115 victory. I contributed 17 points and 17 rebounds. And we kept Barkley, who missed a potential game-winning shot with two seconds left, in check for the most part.

"We should have been the ones sweeping them," Barkley said. "Three shots changed the outcome of all three games."

It was a close series—we outscored the Sixers by a total of 8 points—and a bunch of us celebrated by pushing a broom across the court. In the first quarter, Barkley had thrown the ball at Mark and I started pushing Barkley. He was doing a lot of talking, and now it was time for us to have some fun. Me, Mark, Sidney Green, Johnny Newman, and Eddie Lee Wilkins all grabbed the broom and swept Barkley away.

Not everyone liked it. Ira Berkow, the basketball writer from the *New York Times*, wrote: "They did it gaily, gloriously and with utter disdain for good taste and the gods of chance."

Honestly, it's not that deep. We just won the game, the broom was there, and I don't really care if it annoyed Barkley and the Sixers. Let them worry about that. We were the team advancing.

While we were doing our thing in Philadelphia, Michael Jordan was producing one of the iconic moments of his career: his famous last-second shot over Cleveland's Craig Ehlo in their pivotal Game 5. The win meant that it would be the Knicks against the Bulls in the Eastern Conference Semifinals.

I know reporters like to ask, "Does it mean more to you playing your former team?" The answer, really, is no. I couldn't get caught up in that. My job was to defend, rebound, and make shots. I was not going to try to score more against the Bulls because they'd traded me. That's not how it works, at least not for me. It's not how I operate. Our best chance of winning was for all of us, myself included, to play our game, not get caught up in the storylines . . . and hope that Jordan had a rough series.

The series opened on May 9, 1989, at the Garden, and it took us fifty-three minutes to lose a 12-point fourth-quarter lead and home court advantage. The Bulls rallied to force overtime and then just rolled, 120–109. Michael recorded his first playoff triple-double—34 points, 12 assists, and 10 rebounds—and he scored 9 of Chicago's 17 points in OT.

It was a bad sign for that series, and ultimately a harbinger of things to come for the Knicks. Michael was a great player who always found a way to win. He got the benefit of the doubt from the officials, which was bullshit. He shouldn't have gotten every call, but he had talent and he knew how to win. And Michael was very good at not allowing one bad performance to carry over into the next game.

For example, we held Michael to 15 points in Game 2 to draw even in the series. Then, because the league and its television partner, CBS, wanted to air Michael's games on Saturday and Sunday, we played back-to-back in Chicago on May 13 and 14. Jordan was at his best in those games, coming off of the loss. He scored 40 points with 15 rebounds, 9 assists and 6 steals in Game 3, and the Bulls crushed us, 111–88. The claim was that he injured his groin in the process though, and he was being listed as questionable for Game 4, which was less than twenty-four hours away.

No one—Rick Pitino, myself, or anyone else on our team—thought that Michael would sit out Game 4. We weren't buying that. The next night, Mother's Day, he was limping, and he still scored 47 points, including 18 in the fourth quarter. CBS named Mike's mom, Deloris Jordan, the MVP of the game. Well, Mrs. Jordan and Michael got some help from the referees as well. Michael attempted twenty-eight free throws and made twenty-three. As a team, we took just twenty-two free throws.

"I never saw the officials call a game tighter than they did today," Gerald Wilkins said after the game. "Every time we went near him, they sent him to the free-throw line. He doesn't need that kind of help."

Michael and the refs were a problem, but so was Patrick's overall play. He was awful in Game 4: our All-Star did not shine bright. He made just five of fifteen shots and finished with 15 points, while Cartwright, the Bulls' center, scored 15 of his 21 points in the first quarter. It was the worst possible time for Patrick to have one of his worst games. We were down 3–1 in the series after that loss, and Michael, like a Great White Shark, was smelling blood in the water.

"According to Coach Pitino, I've been faking the injury all the time," Michael said. This is the kind of stuff Michael doesn't forget. Rick didn't back down. He reminded the media that a year earlier, on April 19, 1988, Michael had reported to work for a game against the Knicks with an upset stomach "and scored 47 against us." I never thought that Michael was faking an injury or an illness, but Rick wasn't buying the groin injury.

Ewing answered the bell in Game 5 with 32 points. I added 18 points and 13 rebounds, and we forced the series for Game 6 back to Chicago, where we hadn't won all season. We caught a break in the third quarter when Scottie Pippen and Kenny Walker were ejected for fighting. And our luck continued when Trent Tucker tied the game with six seconds left by converting a three as he was fouled by Craig Hodges. We had a chance. They had Michael. He drew a questionable foul with four seconds left, sank both free throws, and that was it. Jordan finished Game 6 with 40 points. His series average was 35 points, 9 rebounds, and 8 assists.

Pitino called Jordan the "best player to ever put on a uniform," which was saying something real at that point, considering Michael and the Bulls were headed to their first Eastern Conference Finals. He hadn't won anything yet. And the Bulls went on to lose to the Pistons in the next round. But Michael's time would come, of course. I, on the other hand, was heading home for the second straight year with a loss in the conference semifinals, and more change on the way.

There had been reports that Pitino and Knicks general manager Al Bianchi were feuding. I never picked up on that. Nor did I care. I thought Rick was doing a great job, and the system he'd implemented was working. We just ran into Jordan in the second round, and he was great.

But Rick, who was from New York, was being romanced by the University of Kentucky. It was one of the best college jobs in the country, even though the Wildcats were on three-year probation for violating recruiting rules. Pitino took the job anyway.

"I wasn't looking to get into professional basketball," Pitino said on the day he was introduced as Kentucky's coach. "I wanted to be a part of the turnaround here with the New York Knickerbockers. I wish it could have lasted longer, but you have to know who you are and I'm a college basketball coach and I think that's where my heart is."

With Rick, I thought we had a chance to be a really good team. He was young and we were young. It was a good fit. But management was getting in his way. I couldn't blame him for doing what was best for him. I just didn't think it was the best thing for the Knicks.

6 | THE PRICE OF BEING LATE

The Knicks didn't look very far to find Rick Pitino's replacement. They simply promoted Stu Jackson, who had been Pitino's assistant in New York after working for him at Providence College. At thirty-three, Jackson was the second youngest head coach in league history, and one of his first moves was to make the coaching staff even younger by hiring twenty-seven-year-old Jeff Van Gundy, whom Stu had lured away from McQuaid Jesuit High School in Rochester, New York, to work on Pitino's staff at Providence. Jeff had spent the previous season at Rutgers University before being reunited with Stu. Like I said, this is how things work in the NBA. It's all a big family tree.

Stu inherited a good roster from Pitino; eight players were returning from a team that had won fifty-two games the year before. But Stu was also inheriting some of Pitino's problems. Rod Strickland was unhappy being Mark Jackson's backup and asked to be traded midway through the season.

"Looking back, I screwed that up," Stu said. "Rod deserved to play more. I should have made that work. Rod could be hard to coach. He was late for practice. He'd forget his sneakers. But for years it bothered me the way things went down. Our relationship was strained. I told Rod years later that I should have handled things better."

With age comes experience. Stu wasn't much older than his players when he became head coach. He was learning on the job and he had a player who wanted out. It's not an easy situation. The front office tried to make a deal with the Denver Nuggets for Lafayette (Fat) Lever, but the Nuggets rejected two offers. The longer it went on, the worse it got for management.

One day, after Rod arrived late for practice, he got called into a meeting with GM Al Bianchi and Stu. He showed up fifteen minutes late to that. I'm not even sure if Rod was doing it intentionally. He was always late. After Mark Jackson retired, his friends organized a roast and a charity auction. Rod bought an expensive watch, and when it was time for Pitino to address the crowd, he cracked a joke about Rod being late his entire career and deciding now to buy a watch. The audience enjoyed that.

But in 1990, Bianchi and Stu didn't find it funny that Rod arrived fifteen minutes late for an important meeting. It was only a matter of time before a trade would happen, and on February 21, 1990, Strickland was dealt to the San Antonio Spurs for Maurice Cheeks. It was a swap of point guards; the twenty-three-year-old Strickland for the thirty-three-year old Cheeks, who had won an NBA Championship with Philadelphia in 1983. Mo was happy to join our team, and he fit right in with the guys in the locker room. Cheeks is a veteran and a leader.

When the trade was made, Charles Barkley and his big mouth had to chime in. Barkley said: "Are they [the Knicks] crazy? I love Maurice Cheeks, but I just don't know how much he has left. But I do know that all Rod needs is the opportunity to play and he'd be a star."

The Knicks should have figured out a way to make it work with Rod and Mark. The NBA was different in the early nineties. It wasn't as guard-dominant as it is today. When you have talent like that, you don't get rid of it. But management wanted to end a controversy that was becoming a bigger and bigger story in the New York media.

I liked Rod and didn't want to see him go. But I was ready to play with Cheeks, who knew how to run an offense. Unfortunately, my season took a dramatic turn when I suffered a hand injury one month after we acquired Cheeks. The injury knocked me out for the remainder of the regular season. I'm not exactly sure when it happened initially, but my left hand was hurting so much before our March 20 game against the Orlando Magic that I told our team physician, Dr. Norman Scott, that I thought I'd broken it. Dr. Scott looked at it for a second, touched it, and said, "I think you're right. Let's get an X-ray."

I told him it would have to wait until after the game.

"You're not playing tonight," he said.

Well, I didn't listen to him. I played the game. In fact, I played forty minutes, scored 14 points, and grabbed 19 rebounds. Then I went for an X-ray, and sure enough, it showed that I had broken the fourth metacarpal bone in my non-shooting hand, which put me in a cast and ended the regular season for me.

The cast was removed on April 16, ten days before our playoff opener and just seventeen days after doctors had treated me. It was a lot faster than the recommended time for full recovery. Our medical staff wasn't certain I would be ready to play. My thinking was, if the cast is off and I'm wearing this splint, that tells me I'm ready.

"There is very good healing," Dr. Scott told the media. "There is no tenderness. I can't say he will be ready for the playoffs. Since there is risk of re-fracture, the ultimate decision will be made by Charles after he sees how the hand feels. Any fracture like the one Charles sustained normally takes three months to heal."

I heard that as: I could fully recover over the summer. Even though I hadn't played for a couple of weeks, I was keeping myself in shape. The playoffs were coming and there was no way I wasn't playing.

I wasn't available for our last three regular season games, which we lost to the Bucks, the Hawks, and the Cavaliers. We finished 45-37 and drew the Boston Celtics in the first round. The Celtics were getting older, but they were still formidable. We started the series on the road and quickly fell behind 0–2 in the best-of-three, including a 157–128 loss in Game 2. Ewing bailed us out in Game 3 at Madison Square Garden by producing 33 points and 18 rebounds. I had 14 points and 13 rebounds in thirty-eight minutes before fouling out. At least we were making things interesting.

"The biggest thing we did in the series is switching Charles on Robert Parish and Patrick on Kevin McHale," Stu Jackson said. "For whatever reason, we did a better job defensively with those matchups."

In Games 3 and 4 McHale and Parish combined for 28 and 34 points respectively, but Patrick had another monster game, with 44 points, and we blew the Celtics out 135–108 to force a Game 5 in Boston. We had life, but the Celtics had history on their side. The Knicks franchise hadn't won at Boston Garden in twenty-six games, including eight playoff games. That streak of futility dated back to February 29, 1984. Trent Tucker was the only player left on the roster who had won in Boston with the Knicks.

Patrick called it our "destiny" to snap the losing streak, and on May 6, 1990, we did just that. We hung tough throughout the game, and early in the fourth I scored a putback off of a Johnny Newman miss; then I converted a pass from Ewing into a layup and we went up by 6 with 8:15 to play. But two plays really changed the game and ultimately the series. Up 101–99, Patrick hit a short hook in the lane over Parish. On the next possession Larry Bird drove to the basket for an uncontested reverse dunk, and the most incredible thing happened: Bird blew the dunk with 4:30 left.

"I remember saying, 'We got them, we got them,'" Stu said. "The Celtics were a little older and in Game 5 they were tired. We were younger and fresher."

Larry Legend didn't miss shots like that. We buried the Celtics for good when I threw a pass to Patrick that missed its mark and bounced toward the corner. Patrick chased it down in front of our bench, and with the shot clock running down and our medical trainer Mike Saunders screaming "Shoot it! Shoot it!" Patrick turned and fired. The shot was perfect. Patrick had made just one three-pointer all season, back in March against the Washington Wizards. And yet here he was back in his hometown of Boston plunging the dagger into the Celtics' hearts. That basket made it 113–101 with 2:03 left, and we eventually won 121–114.

"This is about as low as it gets since I've been here," Bird said.

Bird's missed dunk changed the series. Boston was like Chicago; they got all the calls. But Bird was the only guy who could put the ball on the floor against us and do something. We just tried to stop him. We weren't worried about the rest of the guys. Patrick finished with 31 points and came within 2 rebounds of a triple-double. I had one of the best games of my career; 26 points on just eleven shots with 17 rebounds in forty-four minutes. I couldn't beat Bird and the Celtics when I was in Chicago, but I got my revenge with the Knicks.

We were flying high, and we didn't have to face Michael Jordan in the second round. Instead, it was the Detroit Pistons, the defending NBA champions. We didn't put up much of a fight. Two nights after our big win in Boston, the Pistons brought us back to reality with a 35-point beatdown. With Isiah Thomas, Joe Dumars, Bill Laimbeer, and Mark Aguirre, the Pistons had too much talent and experience. They were physical like Boston, but more dynamic, and had the best record in the Eastern Conference. We took just one game in the series—Game 3 at home—and failed to score more than 97 points in the four losses.

We ended up with a new coach just fifteen games into the 1990–91 season, when Stu Jackson was fired after a 7-8 start. He was replaced by John MacLeod, who was fifty-three years old and had coached fourteen seasons with the Phoenix Suns and three seasons with the Dallas Mavericks. Al Bianchi had been MacLeod's assistant coach for eleven seasons at Phoenix and had tried to hire him in 1987 before he hired Rick Pitino.

Again, this is how the NBA works. It seems like everyone is connected. But this time things were getting messy. Bianchi let Johnny Newman walk as a free agent and Johnny signed with Charlotte. Mark Jackson was unhappy during the season and was suspended two games for "conduct detrimental to the club." Patrick wasn't happy and talks about a contract extension were going nowhere. Plus, we were losing and attendance was down.

Ironically, we had won four straight when ownership fired Bianchi in March 1991 and hired Dave Checketts, who had been the president of the Utah Jazz and the Denver Nuggets. Checketts was only thirty-five when he got the job, and he admitted, "I don't claim to be a terrific basketball personnel guy. What I claim to be is to make the decision on who is."

That meant Ernie Grunfeld, who had worked as an assistant coach under Stu Jackson, and then moved into the front office prior to the season, would have a more prominent role. There was a lot of change and uncertainty happening as we played out the end of the season. We finished at 39-43, and it seemed like we were trending in the wrong direction.

It didn't help that we failed to win a single playoff game, as the Chicago Bulls eliminated us in the first round in three games. Game 1 on April 25 set the tone for the entire series. We were trailing 65–36 at halftime and lost 126–85 as Michael Jordan scored 28 points in thirty-two minutes. In Game 2, we held them to 89 points. The Bulls held us to 79. We just couldn't hang with them.

The defining moment of the series, however, and really one of the defining moments in our battles with Michael Jordan, was in Game 3 at Madison Square Garden on April 30, 1991. It was a sequence that took place in the second quarter of our 103–94 loss.

Jordan caught the ball on the wing and was being defended by John Starks. Starks was in his first year with the Knicks. He had gone undrafted, and after spending thirty-six games with the Golden State Warriors and then being released by them, he bounced around the Continental Basketball Association and the World Basketball League. Then he had gotten an invite to the Knicks training camp in the fall of 1990. He was about to be cut on the final day, but he injured his knee in the last practice when he tried to dunk over Patrick. That injury may have saved his career. Since the Knicks weren't allowed under league rules to cut an injured player, Starks remained on Injured Reserve for a few weeks, and when he was healthy enough to play, the Knicks put him on the roster.

John had to fight like hell to make the NBA and stay there, and he never stopped fighting. He became a steady contributor off the bench and a great member of our team. He was competitive as hell. But he wasn't ready for Jordan in this moment. Jordan drove right around him.

Then I stepped up and I stopped him. Mike then dribbled back out, quickly spun around me, and drove along the baseline.

I did my job. I slowed him down. But Patrick was late on the rotation. Rod Strickland was late for practice and meetings, and Patrick Ewing was late on his help defense. He couldn't move. Patrick should have knocked Michael down. Instead, Michael dunked on Patrick and drew a foul. I'm not saying you have to commit a flagrant foul, but you have to put his ass down. You can't let him slash through you. It's mano a mano. I've gotten dunked on once or twice in my career. Patrick got dunked on all the time, by Michael, by Scottie. No way I'm letting them dunk on me. Michael's dunk was the play of the series and said a lot about the state of the Knicks and my former team, the Bulls.

Chicago and Michael didn't stop soaring that postseason. They swept the Detroit Pistons in the Eastern Conference Finals. In Game 4, Isiah Thomas and Bill Laimbeer led the Pistons off the court before the game had ended. They marched right in front of the Bulls' bench. That was a bitch move, but not surprising.

The Bulls reached the NBA Finals and knocked off the Los Angeles Lakers. My season was finished on the last day of April, and the Bulls went on to win their first-ever NBA title. That was tough to take. As an organization we needed to do something dramatic. Coach MacLeod was done, so we knew we would be getting a new coach. But what else could happen? Would they trade Ewing? Would they trade me?

7 | LIFE WITH RILEY

When I arrived in New York prior to the start of the 1988–89 season, part of my job was to provide protection for All-Star center Patrick Ewing, who was being hailed as the savior for basketball in the Big Apple from the moment the Knicks drafted him first overall in 1985. Things were moving along at a slow pace for both Patrick and the franchise. After my third season with the Knicks, and Patrick's seventh, the team still had not advanced out of the second round.

Now, heading into the 1991–92 season, the Detroit Pistons were wearing down after so many long playoff runs, and the Boston Celtics were aging and starting to fade away. Meanwhile, Michael Jordan and the Chicago Bulls were coming off their first title. Since we were both in the East, we would have to knock them off just to reach the NBA Finals. That meant we needed to improve from top to bottom, and that's exactly what Dave Checketts and Ernie Grunfeld set out to do.

Checketts went all in prior to the start of the season and made a big splash by bringing in a head coach who had championship experience, cachet, and Armani suits: Pat Riley. Thankfully, the powers that be also decided to keep both Patrick and me on the team.

Everything changed for the organization once Pat Riley was hired. Riley, who had spent the previous season working as an in-studio analyst for NBC's coverage of the NBA, was the biggest coaching name on the market. Riley became a legend as coach of the Los Angeles Lakers by leading them to four championships in the eighties. Those teams, featuring Magic Johnson, Kareem Abdul-Jabbar, James Worthy, Michael Cooper, and Byron Scott, became the Showtime Lakers.

The Lakers had two all-time greats—Magic and Kareem—and Riley maximized their talents. Their fast break was lethal, and even in those rare occasions when you were in position defensively to slow them down, Magic would simply wait for Kareem to set up in the post. You know the rest; he'd toss it into Kareem and watch the big man kill whoever was attempting to guard him, with his famous sky hook, the most unstoppable shot in the game. The Lakers high-flying playing style fit not only the personnel but also Hollywood and the celebrity crowds the purple and gold attracted to the Great Western Forum.

Needless to say, those Lakers were nothing like the team Riley was inheriting in New York. We were not flashy. We didn't have Magic, we didn't have Kareem. We were more like bouncers at a nightclub, in high tops. Riley adjusted his style to fit our personnel. That's what great coaches do. Riley knew what he had in Patrick and me, and his vision was for us was to be the toughest, best conditioned team in the NBA. Greg Anthony, who was on the Knicks from 1991 to 1995, once said of our teams in the early nineties: "We're either going to win the game or win the fight." That's about right.

If we were going to beat the Bulls, we were going to have to beat them down.

"I have the mentality of a butt-kicker," Riley once told Sam Smith of the *Chicago Tribune*. "That's where I come from, and those are the coaches I played for, and I didn't mind getting beaten up by them. That's what I responded to, and I don't know any other way."

The front office and Riley were putting together a team of physically and mentally tough players. One of the key moves was signing a no-name forward, Anthony Mason, over the summer. Mase was a six-foot-seven ball of muscle who could dribble like a guard. And Mase was hungry. He was a third-round pick of the Portland Trail Blazers and began his career in Turkey and then Venezuela. He'd spent twenty-one games with the New Jersey Nets and three with the Denver Nuggets, as well as brief stints in the now-defunct USBL with the Long Island Surf and the CBA's Tulsa Fast Breakers, where he averaged 29.9 points per game.

Mason was a New York guy who had attended Springfield Gardens High School in Queens and played his college ball at Tennessee State, the only state-funded historically Black university in Tennessee. With the Knicks, Mason was playing for his hometown team and knew this could be his last shot at making it in the league. He was exactly the type of player Riley craved. Mase was willing to run through a brick wall for Riley. He fit the style.

Mason and I hit it off right away. We were similar in both work ethic and how we approached the game. Me and our new six-foot-seven small forward, Xavier McDaniel, hit it off in a much different way. "X" or "X-Man," as he was nicknamed, had spent the first six and a half seasons in Seattle and then sixty-six games with the Suns before the Knicks acquired him on October 2, 1991, in exchange for Jerrod Mustaf, Trent Tucker, and two future second-round picks. In December 1989, when McDaniel was playing for the Seattle SuperSonics, we had traded punches at Madison Square Garden.

We were both chasing down a rebound and I pushed X-Man

out of way to get the ball. We both fell on the floor. X pushed me; I did what I do and pushed him back. Rod Thorn, our old friend and rule-maker from the league office, said that I pointed my "finger two or three times at McDaniel's nose. After one of them tipped his nose, McDaniel threw a left hook. After wrestling each other to the floor, they grappled around at the end of the court where a lot of punches were thrown."

It was the typical NBA fight; nothing crazy and over pretty quickly. We got fined $7,500 apiece and got suspended for one game. I was pissed off because at the time I had played in 323 consecutive games, the most among all active players.

"From the view of the NBA," Thorn said, "this was a very serious incident. There were a lot of punches thrown, and there was brawling at the end of the court. I think we were very lucky that either of the two participants were not seriously injured.

"We're very serious about curbing fights. We don't think fighting adds anything to the NBA. Our feelings are that heavy fines and/or suspensions will act as a deterrent against violence. We are now fining players for throwing punches, whether they land or not. We'll do anything we have to in order to curb violence."

One way of settling a feud with me and X-Man was to put us on the same team. The first day I saw him at training camp we spoke briefly, and that was it. He was on my side now, so it didn't make any sense bringing up our past. And honestly, I know he was glad about that. He wouldn't have lasted very long in a genuine fight with me. X had a reputation coming from the West Coast, but this was basketball in the Eastern Conference. So let's just say X marks the spot for physical basketball and it's in the East.

That being said, you put together a team with me, Xavier Mc-Daniel, Anthony Mason, and John Starks, and what you have is a group of guys that compete and don't take any shit from anybody. That's what Riley wanted. One of the first things he said to

McDaniel was "I want you to be physical. I don't want you to be Xavier McDaniel from the Phoenix Suns."

There was nothing wrong with what McDaniel did during his time with the Suns. Riley was simply challenging him. It was a smart way of saying, "You're no longer in the soft Western Conference. You need to become nasty."

That message was being heard loud and clear. Early in training camp Mason and McDaniel got into a fight during rebounding drills. Our assistant coach, Jeff Van Gundy, said they were "throwing haymakers." That's two big guys throwing punches.

"I was talking mad trash to him," McDaniel said.

The practices were high-intensity and physical, so things got heated quickly. Riley knew that. He wanted to see us compete. But he also wanted to bring us close together as a team. During a team meal Riley rolled a television into the dining room and ran the tape of me and X-Man fighting from 1989.

Riley showed the entire fight and then said, "Now we're fighting together."

That's Pat Riley. He was constantly pushing us, motivating us, testing us, and sending us subtle and not-so-subtle messages. I always said that playing for Pat Riley was like going from being a reserve in the military to training to become a Navy SEAL. It was boot camp. After a few days of practice with Pat Riley you're like, "So this is how the big boys work." Every practice was high-level and very strict. He was just different from any other coach I'd had. Always intense. He'd holler at you if you weren't working hard. No one wanted to get called out for that. He was a little lenient with Patrick, but no one really cared about that.

There were days where he'd give us a pop quiz during practice about how we were going to defend the pick-and-roll, defend a certain player, or what terminology we would use to communicate on the court. Other times, you'd be in your hotel room on a road trip at 2 a.m., and all of a sudden you'd hear a note slipped under your door. At two in the fucking morning it would be Riley sliding notes with a motivational message or just a reminder of what he expected. He tested us mentally and physically. He had the trainers check our body fat. He wanted us in shape. He wanted us to play through pain.

It wasn't uncommon for him to challenge a player right in front of the team. He walked into the locker room, and if a player had a sore knee or ankle and wasn't dressed for the game, that would get Riley going. Charles Smith had knee issues most of the time he spent with the Knicks. Charles could score, but he was always dealing with an injury. One night Riley walked over to Smith and very casually asked, "If I needed you to play thirty seconds tonight, could you give that to me?"

"Sure," Charles said.

"Then why the fuck aren't you in uniform?" was Riley's response. He may have been addressing Charles, but Riley was talking to the entire team. He pushed us and he wanted us to push ourselves.

He would also do some cool old-school things. There were road games when he made us dress in full uniform at the hotel. He wanted us to get off the bus and show up at the arena ready to play like we were all back in high school. Who does that?

Riles was pushing buttons and I responded to that. He knew what to expect from me. But there were times when he pushed a little too much. Everyone has a breaking point. The day after a loss, we were watching film and he said, "This is fucking ridiculous, Oak. You didn't do this right, you didn't do that right."

I said, "Coach, you're wrong. That's fucked up."

"Oak, are you talking to me?"

"Yes, I'm talking to you."

We went at it for about a minute. We were yelling. My thing was that the coach also needed to call out Patrick for all the mistakes he was making. He was fucking up just as much as anyone. Looking back, I know that's a little childish, but I wasn't having it that day. It got heated, but things settled down, and we talked. It's like you're driving 80 mph on a highway and don't get pulled over. You do it day after day and you get away with it. But then comes that one day when you finally get pulled over. Well, guess what, that film session was the day I pulled Pat Riley over.

We were all in a competitive environment. There was a lot at stake, and if you want to win, you need to commit yourself and make sacrifices. That's what we did under Riley.

I took that high-intensity, physical mentality that Riley was encouraging for the team *off* the court at one point during my time with the Knicks. It resulted in my first confrontation with security guards at Madison Square Garden, though the guards in question were not employed by MSG. They were employed by Al Haymon, a concert promoter best known as the boxing manager for Floyd Mayweather Jr. Al Haymon is also a Cleveland guy who attended Harvard and knew how to put together deals.

I was at a concert Haymon was promoting at the Garden with Johnny Newman, Pete Myers, Rod Strickland, and Mark Jackson, who was with his wife, Desiree Coleman. It was a show with multiple acts, including Heavy D and Guy. We purchased the tickets and had good seats, but after every act there was a fifteen- to twenty-minute break.

During the first break we had a lot of people coming up to us. That wasn't a big deal, but with five or six acts scheduled to appear, we figured we'd hang out in the tunnel just so we could chill. The Garden security guards knew who we were and allowed us to stand off to the side and not bother anyone. That wasn't good enough for one of Al Haymon's security guards, who asked to see our passes.

For a show like this, the promoter will occasionally bring in their own security force to complement the Garden security, who are always going to work and get paid because MSG is a union shop. When we tried to explain the situation to Haymon's guard, he said, "This is our house tonight. You need to leave."

You have to understand that a lot of these guys were from places like Compton. Al Haymon knew who to hire for security. I said something unfriendly back to the security guard, and the next thing you know, we had fifteen guards surrounding us. Mark wanted to get his wife out of there, which was understandable. The regular Garden security escorted us to the Knicks' locker room while the concert security guards were running their mouths. I just said, "You can't be that tough if you need fifteen of your guys."

Not too long after that concert we were playing in Dallas and I saw Deion Sanders, the Hall of Fame football player, sitting near the court. I looked over at Deion, and right next to him was the security guard who'd run his mouth at the concert. I'm telling you, I kept looking at the guy to make sure it was him. I even stopped at one point and looked directly at him. That was the guy.

Terry Davis, who played for the Dallas Mavericks and had attended Virginia Union, invited me out after the game to hang out with Deion. I was thinking, sure, I like Deion. Let's do it. Well, we showed up at this club and headed into a room where Deion was sitting. Guess who was there with him? Yep, the guy that was talking shit to me at Madison Square Garden.

I said, "You're the guy from the Garden, right?"

Deion asked, "What's the problem?"

The problem was that this motherfucker was threatening to beat up me and my friends, I told him.

I could tell the guy was getting nervous. He said he was only doing his job.

"And now I'm just doing my job," I said. "I'm going to kick your ass."

Deion was pleading with me not to do anything.

I kept at it though. "You were a big tough guy when you had fourteen friends with you. Now let's do it man to man with no one around."

He didn't take me up on that offer.

Terry Davis and I then walked out of the room, went to the bar, and ordered some shots.

I don't know if Pat Riley would have been proud of me or not, but there was no question that in me he had a player who was unafraid of confrontation, on or off the court.

We weren't a great defensive team before Pat Riley got to New York. He stressed defense and put that defense-first attitude in our heads. He didn't need to convince me. That was always my mentality. But as a team we played tougher and more disciplined now. Riley knew he could build an offense around a center—he'd done it with Kareem in Los Angeles. He did that in New York as well. Just about every play was called for Ewing. It didn't bother me: Patrick and John Starks got most of the shots. That's just the way it was.

But our calling card was defense and physical play. And we didn't disappoint. We lost our first two games on the road under Riley to a couple of crappy teams—Orlando and Miami—which isn't unusual for a team with a new coach and a new system. Eventually, we were clicking, and we finished 51-31 overall, with the league's second-best defensive rating.

In the first round we faced the Detroit Pistons. We had the chance to close the series out in Detroit in four, but when the Pistons forced a decisive Game 5 on May 2, 1992, you could feel the tension on our bench and inside Madison Square Garden. This was a series we had to win. With 8:12 left in the third quarter, we were holding a 1-point lead when Gerald Wilkins, who had just traveled and committed a foul, was taken out by Riley.

Wilkins was pissed. He was struggling—he had shot 1-for-9 in Game 3, and 1-for-6 in Game 4. With the crowd booing, he extended his arms and gave the home fans his middle fingers. Wilkins had an interesting explanation after the game. He told the media that he was responding to the Rodney King verdict in Los Angeles just three days earlier. That was an explosive few days after a California jury acquitted all four police officers of assault and acquitted three of the four of using excessive force on King, a Black man who was arrested for leading police on a high-speed chase. The verdict touched off riots in the Los Angeles area.

"That was for Rodney King," Gerald said. "That was for the verdict. It wasn't right what they did to Rodney, and it definitely wasn't right what they did to me. The crowd was against me."

In that moment after he put up his middle fingers, the fans were angry and frustrated with Wilkins, but Riley stuck by his guy. Wilkins returned to the game and responded with 9 points in the final five minutes of the third quarter. Wilkins finished with 13 points, but this was Ewing's day. The Big Fella produced 31 points and 19 rebounds, and X-Man added 19. The Bad Boys were history—we'd held them to less than 90 points in each of the five games, proving our defensive mettle—and now we had a date with that "Black Cat." (That's what NBA players called Michael, reason unknown.) He had the utmost respect from his peers and he had the backing of the league. He was the NBA's meal ticket, so beating him wouldn't be easy.

"If the league allows them to, they'll beat Chicago," Bill Laimbeer said after we eliminated the Pistons. John Salley said something similar to Ewing. Laimbeer and Salley were both right. When the Pistons were beating Michael Jordan in the playoffs they were allowed to be physical. The "Jordan Rules" said to hit Michael as much as you could. But that was also a younger Jordan the Pistons were facing. We were getting Michael as he was entering his prime and with one championship already in his pocket.

So instead of focusing everything on trying to stop Michael, we went after his sidekick, Scottie Pippen. Though it wasn't so much *we* who went after Pippen as it was Xavier McDaniel. That's what the Pistons had done with some success, that's what X wanted to do, and he felt there was no one on the Bulls to stop him.

Xavier said: "When Oakley came [to the Bulls], they stopped hitting Mike cuz they knew they would have to deal with Oak. When Oak left, who was that tough guy?"

The talk before the series was like pre-fight hype for a heavyweight boxing match. During the regular season we lost all four of our games against the Bulls, and yet we believed we had a mental edge. The Bulls couldn't mess with our heads or our bodies. Chicago's players knew this, so the Bulls did what they usually did: they whined. I mean, come on. Michael got all the calls and the Chicago Bulls were always whining. To this day, when he brings up the nineties, I tell him he got the calls. And yet Phil Jackson complained. Scottie complained, and before that 1992 Eastern Conference Semifinals series, Jerry Krause, the Bulls' general manager, was complaining.

"We're concerned about it getting crazy. I'm sure [NBA vice president] Rod [Thorn] will control it," Krause said. "I think if we play the way we play, clean and hard, then I think New York will play that way. But if they don't, if they want to make a mugging out of it, then I would be concerned."

The Bulls were right to be worried. The series opened on May 5, and we finally beat them at Chicago Stadium, 94–89. We led

25–16 after the first quarter and frustrated them all game. Michael scored 31, but Ewing was a monster: 34 points, 16 rebounds, and a one-game lead over Jordan in the playoffs.

It didn't last long. Chicago took the next two games. Then, with us facing a critical Game 4, Xavier McDaniel scored 24 points and got into Pippen's head. The New York crowd was eating it up as Pippen struggled to score 13 points on 13 shots. You knew the Bulls were concerned about Pippen's mental state because they started bitching as soon as the game ended.

"They were pushing our dribblers with two hands. That's football," Phil Jackson said. "I was also against the board play. I think the league has to take a serious look at this type of play. You could have called a foul on every play."

Phil had been an assistant coach under Doug Collins during my final season with the Bulls, and it was pretty obvious to me when I was there that he was eventually going to become the head coach, because Jerry Krause had found Phil coaching in the Continental Basketball Association and brought him onto the Bulls' staff. Jerry was a scout who liked to find little-known talents: players like myself and Scottie Pippen, and coaches like Phil Jackson. Even though Phil had played for the Knicks and won a championship in New York, he wasn't a well-known coach—I mean, he was in Albany, coaching for a team called the Patroons. But Jerry had uncovered another gem.

I like Phil. He's smart, he knows the game, and he's easy to talk to. Phil is a great coach, no question about it. But he was also always going to the papers and complaining about us. He was planting stories left and right to fuck with us. And that drove me crazy.

The whole thing seemed rigged. I would tell Michael, "You travel all the time and it never gets called. We're playing six against five." You tell me, who did the NBA want to see in the NBA Finals: Patrick Ewing or Michael Jordan? Everybody loved Michael. He talked to the media, he sold sneakers, and he was in every commercial. All Patrick was going to say in the locker room was to the ball boys: "Get me some ice for my knees and grab my robe." And when Patrick was interviewed by the media, all he ever said was "We need to play hard."

The Bulls always had the advantage because they had Michael. I just think it was disrespectful to us and the game to complain about calls when you didn't win. In the second half of Game 4 we locked up Chicago. The Bulls made just thirteen shots combined in the third and fourth quarters, and nine of those were scored outside of ten feet. Most of Michael's twenty-six field goal attempts were jump shots.

"Coach Riley told us before the game, 'Don't let them get into the lane,'" Starks said. "That's their whole game. Michael and Scottie penetrating, breaking you down, dunking and dishing off to guys like Horace Grant for layups."

Our strategy was working, and it had the Bulls confused and angry. Instead of giving us credit, Phil took his case to the officials during Game 4 and was ejected by referee Dick Bavetta. Afterward, Phil went after the league office. When the reporters asked Jackson about the Knicks' physical brand of basketball he said, "I think they like this style," referring to the NBA. Again, disrespectful.

All that bitching made its way into our locker room. Guys were pissed off. And Pat Riley said what needed to be said before we got on the plane and headed to Chicago for Game 5.

"I think what he's doing is insulting us, basically," Riles said of Jackson. "I was part of six championship teams and I've been to the finals thirteen times. I know what a championship demeanor is about. The fact that he's whining and whimpering about the officiating is an insult to how hard our guys are playing and how much our guys want to win.

"All we want is what they have. We are like they were a year ago. It's an insult, because he's not respecting the fact that this team is playing with as much heart as any team has ever played with. That's what championship teams are about. They've got to take on all comers. They can't whine about it."

We were fighting back, but all that whining from the Bulls worked. In Game 5, Michael attempted seventeen of the Bulls' thirty-eight free throws, while we attempted twenty-two free throws as a team, and Ewing fouled out in thirty-eight minutes. But we showed our heart in Game 6; we won it, and the series was now 3–3. For the first time in my career and for the first time in Patrick's career we were one win away from reaching the Eastern Conference Finals.

We were forty-eight minutes of solid basketball away from pulling off the upset of the 1991–92 season. Sure, it meant having to knock off the defending champs on their home court, but Pat Riley had us believing that anything was possible.

It was going to take our best game to win in Chicago, especially with Ewing hurting after suffering an ankle injury in Game 6. We needed a flawless performance, but it didn't happen. Everything about Game 7 on May 17, 1992, didn't seem right. It began during warm-ups as Xavier McDaniel was stretching and referee Jake O'Donnell asked to inspect X-Man's nails. X, like a lot of NBA players, kept his nails long. I have the scars on my arms, neck, and back to prove how common this was. But this was an odd request. You had to think that someone from the Bulls had complained to the league or the referees about it. The little games within the game were starting.

The league had assigned a veteran crew to officiate Game 7: O'Donnell, Hue Hollins, and Ed T. Rush. That's three good refs, sure. But in the first quarter Wilkins got called for two fouls while fighting Jordan for position twenty-two feet from the basket. That's a bad omen. "When Michael sees that kind of offici-ating, he's going to the basket," said Wilkins. "I knew. He knew. I knew he knew."

Michael attempted thirteen free throws and converted twelve. He also provided a mental spark for his teammates with two plays that involved Xavier McDaniel. Earlier in the first quarter, Jordan stepped in as X-Man was talking shit and nudging Pippen, who wanted no part of McDaniel. Jordan, though, wasn't backing down. He went nose-to-nose with Xavier, and when they were separated, Jordan glared at X-Man and screamed "Fuck you." NBC replayed the exchange in slow motion for those watching on tele-vision.

"He was showing that we weren't going to back down," Pippen said.

Jordan was just getting started. In the third quarter, he chased down McDaniel, prevented an easy layup, and stole the ball. The crowd in Chicago erupted. We were done. As Gerald said, Jordan did what superstars do; he scored 42 points in a winner-take-all game. Even Pippen played well, after struggling so much against McDaniel in the series, producing a triple-double—17 points, 11 rebounds, and 11 assists. In the end, he got the upper hand.

I had only 4 points with 10 rebounds in the 110–81 loss and averaged just 5.7 points and 7.1 rebounds in the series. It was a tough way to go out. I was working hard and defending, but it wasn't my best series. What are you going to do? In the weeks that followed, Michael and the Bulls defeated the Portland Trail Blaz-ers for their second straight championship. On my former team, they were building a dynasty in Chicago. On my current team, we weren't keeping pace.

In September, McDaniel signed a free-agent contract with the Boston Celtics. His agent, David Falk, who also represented Ewing, hadn't been able to work out a deal with the Knicks. None of it made sense. I'm certain Pippen and the Bulls were happy. We were so close, and after one season, X-Man was gone.

I still believed in what Pat Riley was doing. But I was starting to have doubts about whether we would get to the conference finals, much less win an NBA title. We were right in the middle of the Jordan era, and it felt like the entire NBA was just playing for second place.

8 | HIGH-STAKES BASKETBALL

There were several defining moments for the Knicks in the nineties, and perhaps the most memorable and painful three took place over successive postseasons starting in 1993. The three moments involved different teammates: Charles Smith, John Starks, and Patrick Ewing. The three moments in one way or another each ended our season. Ask any Knicks fan who lived through this era, and they'll remember those playoff failures like it was yesterday. You know how some fan bases get to relive those great championship moments? It could be a last-second shot or a champagne celebration in the locker room. Well, for Knicks fans a walk down memory lane is different. As Pat Riley once famously said, "There's winning and then there's misery."

I've got misery for you.

During the 1992–93 regular season, Riley's second as coach, we went 60-22. Only the 62-20 Phoenix Suns, led by Charles Barkley, the league's Most Valuable Player, won more games. Of course, the Chicago Bulls were still the Bulls. They won fifty-seven games, plus they had a championship pedigree and the best player in the world, Michael Jordan. Having just led the Dream Team to the Olympic gold medal in Barcelona, Michael's popularity was off the charts. He was a global brand now. But there was also a feeling that perhaps those deep playoff runs and the shortened off-season in the summer of 1992 due to the Olympics might have left him, and therefore the Bulls, vulnerable. Or at least that's what we were hoping.

Ewing was also in Barcelona for the Olympics that summer, as the front office was trying to figure out how to close the gap between us and the Bulls. It was a good off-season for the Knicks. For the first time I felt that the front office—Dave Checketts and Ernie Grunfeld—was willing to spend real money to upgrade the roster. It always seemed as if the other contending teams made moves for veteran players, but the Knicks, for whatever reason, shied away from doing that. But prior to the 1992–93 season, the Knicks acquired Rolando Blackman from the Dallas Mavericks. Then in September they executed a blockbuster trade by sending Mark Jackson to the Los Angeles Clippers in a three-team deal that also involved the Orlando Magic. We received Charles Smith, Doc Rivers, and Bo Kimble in return. The Knicks also drafted a promising North Carolina shooting guard, Hubert Davis, with the twentieth overall pick in the 1992 NBA Draft.

Charles Smith's scoring ability was needed and Doc's toughness and leadership were crucial. Doc was thirty-two years old when we acquired him and he had forty-nine career playoff games on his résumé, including forty-four with the Atlanta Hawks. Doc was a big, physical guard who adopted a Knicks/Riley mentality pretty quickly. His first season is probably best remembered for his part in a wild brawl with the Phoenix Suns on March 23, 1993. It started when Phoenix point guard Kevin Johnson set a dirty screen on Doc. It knocked Doc to the floor, and he immediately went after Johnson. In a split second the benches cleared and the brawl was on. John Starks and Danny Ainge got into it. Greg Anthony, who wasn't in uniform, charged out of the stands to punch Kevin Johnson.

It was a mess, and here's the crazy thing: me and Charles Barkley, despite our mutual dislike, were on the court together, but we weren't fighting. At least not each other. I was trying to pull guys away and ended up getting fined. In all, the NBA fined twenty-one members of the Knicks and the Suns a total of $160,500 for their part in the brawl. Anthony was fined $20,500 and suspended for five games. Kevin Johnson and Doc were both suspended two games. Barkley, Dan Majerle, Oliver Miller, and Ewing were the only players not fined. I told you Patrick didn't want to fight. And Barkley didn't want to mess with me.

That melee was a bonding experience for our team. It brought us even closer together. It was as if Riley had orchestrated the whole thing. We were the best defensive team in the league, and it was pretty clear that no one wanted to fuck with us. We had home court advantage in the East for the playoffs and we were on a roll; we took out the up-and-coming Indiana Pacers in four games and then advanced to the conference finals after beating the up-and-coming Charlotte Hornets in five games.

Most of us had never been this deep into postseason, though our excitement was tempered because we all had plenty of experience playing our next opponent, the Chicago Bulls. We knew better than any team the challenges we were facing. The series started on May 23, 1993, and we took Game 1 by the score of 98–90. In Game 2, Michael scored 36 points on thirty-two shots, but we hung on for a 96–91 victory. We were making things difficult for him and the Bulls. Meanwhile, our starters—me, Ewing, Doc, Charles Smith, and John Starks—all scored in double figures. Patrick scored 26, Doc 21, and I had a good night with 14 points and 16 rebounds.

We were playing our best basketball at the right time of year. Our winning streak was now at four and overall we had won seven of our last eight dating back to our overtime win to close out the Pacers in the first round. Being up 2–0 on Jordan and the Bulls with home court advantage was nice. But you never count your eggs before they hatch. We really hadn't done anything yet. The trick was finding a way to get those next two wins.

If we could somehow take one game in Chicago, we'd be in position to eliminate the two-time defending champs. This was our time. After Game 2, Dave Anderson, the award-winning columnist for the *New York Times*, reported a story that Michael was gambling in Atlantic City until 2:30 a.m. on the morning before the game.

Anderson wrote, "Jordan reportedly lost $5,000 playing black-jack in a private area in the baccarat pit, but that's not the issue. If he had won $5,000, it still wouldn't justify his being a two-hour limo ride from the Bulls' midtown New York hotel at 2:30 the morning of a big game.

"The issue is that arguably the best player in basketball history owes his teammates and coaches more dedication to what Jordan has called his 'driving force'—the Bulls' opportunity for their third consecutive National Basketball Association championship.

"If the Bulls are to win that third title, Michael Jordan must be what he is: basketball's Superman, larger than life and lighter than air. In the box score Tuesday night Jordan justified his reputation, scoring 36 points in the Bulls' 96–91 loss. But with more rest, might he have scored 46 points?"

I don't know, 36 points in a playoff game is not easy. And I didn't have a problem with Michael going to Atlantic City. That's what he does for relaxation. People do different things to relax. Shit, in my first year in Chicago we had guys drinking a beer or smoking a cigarette at halftime to relax. Pat Riley smoked at halftime. How does Michael relax? He gambles.

The trip from midtown Manhattan to Atlantic City in New Jersey is about 150 miles. Michael didn't deny taking a limousine with family and friends, including his father, James Jordan. Michael said he did it to relax and claims he left Atlantic City around 11 p.m. Monday and was in bed by 1 a.m. That's plenty of sleep before a game-day shoot-around.

With three days off between Games 2 and 3 the story was taking on a life of its own. You had media all over the country following the series. Jordan and the Bulls were a national story in newspapers across the country. This was the conference finals. A story like that created a feeding frenzy in the media.

When the Bulls returned to practice on Thursday, May 27, Michael had had enough. He abruptly cut off his group interview and called one reporter's question about the Atlantic City trip "stupid." He then challenged the media to identify the person who said he was in Atlantic City late into the night.

"Whoever says they saw me there at 1 a.m. or 2:30 in the morning, or whatever, I'd like to see them in person because I certainly will lay a lawsuit on them," Jordan said. "Where are they? Let me see one of them. One of them. Let me see one person say I was there at 2 o'clock and you have a lawsuit on your hands. You can even ask the casinos."

The media reached out to the Bally's Grand Casino, but a spokesman for the casino said it was against company policy to comment on guests. The *New York Times* had quoted anonymous Knicks fans who had courtside seats. They claimed they saw Jordan gambling after 2 a.m. Philadelphia radio stations were getting calls from anonymous people who said they also saw Michael at Bally's after 1 a.m.

"They're fabricating some things that certainly aren't true," Michael said two days before Game 3. "I'm here, I'm telling you where I was and that's it. That's the truth.

"I've always taken pride in laying my basketball skills on the line for this team, getting my rest so I can go out and play the game of basketball. That's what I'm going to do. It really hurt me that it was taken out of context when I'm just trying to do what I have to do to go out there and do what's best for this team."

On the Knicks we weren't really paying a lot of attention to the Jordan gambling story because none of us thought it was a big deal. And really, we didn't care. The media has a job to do, and there are always stories about how something away from the court could be impacting what happens on the court. And you had three full days off between Games 2 and 3. They were blowing the story up. Suddenly, the media was digging up old gambling stories about Michael. They wrote about Michael being a regular at the card tables when the Dream Team was in Monte Carlo prior to heading to the Olympics. In fall 1992, Jordan had testified in the federal drug and money laundering trial of James "Slim" Bouler that he lost $57,000 golfing and playing cards with Bouler during a weekend at Hilton Head Island, South Carolina.

It was getting crazy. The media need something to write and talk about. And everybody loved to write and talk about Michael Jordan. So Michael went gambling in Atlantic City the night before a game. He's a man. He can handle it. He probably wanted to do something different. Most of the time Michael just hung out in his hotel room during the playoffs.

Pat Riley didn't want us to fraternize with opposing teams, just like he didn't want us to help an opponent up off the floor. But me and Michael always talked on the phone. We'd go out to dinner on a day off during the playoffs. I feel I'm a grown man so I'm going to do what I want. As long as you take care of business on the court, it isn't a problem. When it was time to play, I played hard and I played for my team. You won't find anyone who will say anything differently. And really when it came to the Bulls and the Knicks it was more Phil Jackson and Riley bumping heads.

People can say this and that and complain that I was fraternizing—go ahead. I never let it affect me on the court. Michael was my friend but not on the court. Later in their careers, Magic Johnson and Isiah Thomas would kiss before games when the Lakers and the Pistons played. Maybe they wanted everyone to know they were good friends. But even Magic and Isiah eventually had a falling out. It happens.

Even though Michael was upset with the media coverage about his trip to Atlantic City, and he had a history of using anything to motivate him, the brewing controversy didn't translate into a great Game 3 for him on May 29, 1993, at Chicago Stadium. In fact, Michael didn't play well at all. He made just three of eighteen shots, and we still blew our chance to go up 3–0 in the series. Michael finished with 22 points because he made sixteen of seventeen free throws and Scottie Pippen scored 29 in Chicago's 103–83 win. Ewing scored 21, and the rest of the starters combined to score 23 points. We shut down Jordan and somehow we were down 19 at halftime and never made it a game. If you want to be a championship team, these are the games you have to win, and we didn't get it done.

On Memorial Day and with the media's focus squarely on Michael's struggles, Jordan had his breakout performance of the conference finals, scoring 54 points in Chicago's 105–95 Game 4 victory. Michael made an incredible eighteen of thirty shots and converted twelve of fourteen free throws. The Bulls attempted thirty-nine free throws compared to our twenty-six, which is also incredible. The Bulls were back in the series, but at least we still had home court advantage. Win two home games and we'd be heading to the NBA Finals. That was our mindset.

Getting that first win, however, was the key. And on June 2, 1993—a day that will live in Knicks infamy—we couldn't make a play in the final seconds and lost Game 5 97–94 in what a lot of people refer to as the "Charles Smith Game." In the closing seconds,

Charles had four chances under the basket to give us the lead, and all four times his shot was either blocked or altered by the Bulls. It was a demoralizing loss. You could feel the energy leave Madison Square Garden when the final buzzer sounded. Hope was exiting as well.

I'm not putting that all on Charles Smith. The Bulls smothered him. Also, both John Starks and Ewing missed a free throw early in the fourth quarter when Chicago was called for illegal defense. Those points matter as well. Doc Rivers was the player designated to shoot technical free throws, but he was on the bench when those calls were made. We went to the free throw line thirty-five times and made just twenty. That means we missed fifteen free throws in a playoff game that up until B. J. Armstrong's last-second dunk was a 1-point game. How are you going to put that on Charles Smith? This was a team loss. A bad team loss.

Everyone was at fault. Pat Riley never made adjustments to the Bulls trapping us full-court. I never understood why we never tried to trap them back. Change it up a little. Patrick scored 33 points, but he shot way too many damn fade-away jump shots when he could have passed the ball. And then on our final possession he got tripped up and threw the ball to Smith. If you're our number one guy, there comes a point when you have to outplay their number one guy. And when it was Michael vs. Patrick, it was always Michael who came out on top. In Game 5, Michael scored 29 points and had a triple-double. What does that tell you? There are A players, B players, and C players. Michael is an A player. Patrick is a B player. We never had a true A player on the Knicks.

In the span of five days we went from being up 2–0 to being down 3-2 in the series and needing a win in Chicago against Jordan just to keep our season alive. These are always the hardest games to win, especially on the road against the NBA's best player. Riley was desperately trying to use anything to get our minds off Game 5.

We didn't have a morning shoot-around prior to Game 6, and he had us dress for the game at the hotel, doing his old-school "come ready to play" thing. Riley fostered an environment of "us against the world." That was on full display on June 4, 1993.

Not only did we walk off the bus already in uniform, but we kept the locker room closed to the press before the game, which pissed off the media as well as the NBA. Riley didn't care and neither did we. Most players never talk to reporters before regular-season games, much less playoff games. Patrick never spoke before a game. And if you agree to talk to one reporter, it will attract more reporters. No one wants a scrum in front of their locker one hour before tip-off. And what could we say? "Yes, we fucked up in Game 5" and "I have no idea how we'll respond in Game 6."

The story was obvious: this was going to be our last game in Chicago for the season, and we needed to escape with a win to force a Game 7 back in New York. That's it. Was I confident? Sure. We were always confident when we took the court. The Bulls had Michael and he got the benefit of the doubt all the time from officials, but we believed we could win. Just do your job and live with the results. That's how I looked at it.

We managed to hold our own entering the fourth quarter, and with four minutes remaining in Game 6, we were trailing 83–80 with the ball. We went inside to Patrick, who got Bill Cartwright off his feet with a head fake. Patrick missed the shot as Cartwright banged into him, but no foul was called. I'm pretty sure Jordan gets that call. To this day I still tell Michael that a lot of bad calls went against us. Two bad calls can determine a playoff series. That missed call against Cartwright was big. Pippen then answered with a jumper as the shot clock was about to expire. It was a huge 4-point swing. Ewing and Starks both missed on our next two possessions, and after Michael drew a shooting foul on Doc, the Bulls crowd was standing and cheering as Michael began screaming in

Doc's face. Jordan made both free throws with ninety-four seconds left to put the Bulls ahead by 7. It was over.

"The first thing I would like to say is that we got beat by a great team," Riley said following the 96–88 loss. "Our players were so committed and all believed we could win a world championship. The misery and disappointment they will feel for a while will be overwhelming. Our players will have to realize there will be questions as to why we didn't get the job done. We can't take solace in this."

In the last four games of the conference finals Jordan averaged 32.5 points, 9 assists, and 6.5 rebounds. And for the third straight season the Chicago Bulls eliminated us from the playoffs en route to winning a title. If I had never been traded, that could have been me playing alongside Jordan and winning those rings. We'll never know. What we did learn is that the 1992–93 season took a lot out of Michael emotionally, starting with the Olympics and right through the playoffs, which included the story about his gambling in Atlantic City.

There was also a horrible family tragedy in Michael's life. A month after he won that third championship, Michael's dad, James, was murdered. That hit Michael hard. The best player in the world announced his retirement a few months before the start of the 1993–94 season. I felt bad for Michael. He was my friend and he was going through a rough period in his life. It was bad for him, the Bulls, and the NBA. Michael was their meal ticket.

But there is no denying that Jordan abruptly stepping away was good for the New York Knicks. This was our chance.

9 | RENO TO HOUSTON

With Michael Jordan momentarily retired from basketball and about to join the Chicago White Sox in spring training to play baseball, we felt we were the team to beat entering the 1993–94 season.

But navigating your way through an eighty-two-game regular season after a deep run in the playoffs can be mentally challenging if not exhausting. You want a good record for a home court advantage, but you also want to be healthy, sharp, and playing your best basketball heading into the postseason. Pat Riley, having coached championship teams with the Los Angeles Lakers, knew this better than any of us and understood when to push us and when to back off.

For example, we were in Seattle on January 28, 1994, and had a day off prior to our game against the SuperSonics. We got on the bus in the late morning thinking we were headed to practice. Instead, Riley took us to see the movie *Tombstone* at a local theater. When we arrived, Riley had popcorn, soda, and candy waiting for us on a table. He took care of the players. It was a good break. Sometimes changing the routine helps.

Riley went the extra mile for us after we lost 92–78 to the Phoenix Suns on February 27. The loss was a turning point in our season. The game against Phoenix included Charles Barkley slapping my face and me trying, and missing, to slap him back. Barkley didn't slap me hard. He knew not to throw a punch, but the fact that he gave me a slap made me want to smack his big round head. The whole thing was broken up pretty quickly, and neither of us was suspended. The league determined that since we didn't throw a punch we wouldn't have to miss a game.

I was still fuming, however. And Riley was frustrated. We had just lost four in a row and suffered our sixth loss in our last seven games. It was the worst stretch of Riley's three seasons as coach, and there was a sense that the team was starting to fracture. The true character of any team is revealed during losing streaks. Our lead over the Orlando Magic in the Atlantic Division had been cut to two games. We just weren't in a good rhythm, and Riley knew he had to do something.

Under normal circumstances, we'd get on the plane after a game and head directly for the next city. But we had a day off, and Riley's instincts told him we needed a diversion. We had no idea where we were going, but when the plane landed we knew we weren't in Sacramento. It turned out that after the game, Riley had asked our trainer, Mike Saunders, if it were possible to change our travel plans. He felt it was a good time for another team bonding excursion. Saunders consulted with the pilots and reported back to Riley that there were issues with getting us to Vegas, but they could get us to another gambling town in Nevada: Reno. This is why we all liked Mike Saunders. I don't know how, but he got things done. That's important for any trainer, but especially a trainer working for Pat Riley.

When we exited the plane, Riley handed each of us $500 to spend on food, beverages, blackjack, or whatever. It was a cool thing for him to do. We had the day to ourselves in Reno to get our minds off the losing streak and just off basketball in general. The best coaches know when to back off and give the players a mental break. Riley was the master at it.

The next day Riley was being evasive with the media concerning our whereabouts the night earlier. He told the beat writers that the plane got "diverted" and that it was a "sort of retreat." Riley also needed the chance to step back and take a longer look at the team and contemplate a lineup change. He took drastic steps.

"I think I've been about as patient as I can be," Riley had said after the loss to the Suns. "I really care about this team, especially the five or six guys that have been with us for two and a half years. I've always had a history of staying with guys, going up, going down. But I think somewhere, just in the best interest of the team, we're going to probably have to do something, just to get a different mix. Guys will have to look at it not as a penalty, but in the best interest of trying to change a few things and get some more energy out there. I don't think we're going to have any conflicts. The truth is out there on the court, and it's not very good."

Over the summer we had signed free agent Anthony Bonner, a former first-round pick of the Sacramento Kings. In December, Doc Rivers had torn his ACL and was finished for the season, so the front office went shopping for a point guard. Within a month, the Knicks traded Tony Campbell and a future first-round pick to the Dallas Mavericks for smart veteran point guard Derek Harper. Harper was a Chicago guy who came to New York when he was thirty-two, battle-tested, and ready to win. Bonner and Harper were both Riley's type of player.

Following our pit stop in Reno, ahead of our game against the Sacramento Kings on March 1, our last game of a West Coast trip,

Riley announced that Harper, Bonner, and Hubert Davis were replacing Greg Anthony, Charles Smith, and John Starks in the starting lineup. Our record at the time was 36-19, which is pretty damn good, but after the losing streak Riley felt something was missing.

The coach got the spark he was looking for.

We beat the Kings 100–88, with Ewing producing 28 points and 21 rebounds. Anthony scored 18 and Starks 10 off the bench. They didn't cry about being demoted. They accepted the challenge. It was not only a good way to end the trip but the start of the best stretch of our season. The victory at Sacramento was the first of fifteen straight wins, a new franchise record. We even lost Starks to injury after our fourth win in that streak—he needed arthroscopic surgery to repair cartilage damage in his left knee—but we kept on going. We were clearly the team to beat in the Eastern Conference. Nothing could stop us.

Our first-round opponents were going to be the New Jersey Nets.

The Nets' two stars were Derrick Coleman, a power forward who'd been drafted first overall in 1990, and point guard Kenny Anderson, the second overall pick the following year. Derrick made his one and only All-Star team in 1994, the same year I made my one and only All-Star team as well. That All-Star Game was played in Minneapolis and it was a mess. Bad weather caused a few of us to arrive only the day before the game.

There were a lot of future Hall of Fame players at the Target Center for that All-Star Game; the Western Conference roster featured Hakeem Olajuwon, Charles Barkley, Karl Malone, John Stockton, David Robinson, and Mitch Richmond. In the East we had Dominique Wilkins, Scottie Pippen, and three Hall of Fame centers: Shaquille O'Neal, Patrick Ewing, and Alonzo Mourning, although Mourning was injured and didn't play. Shaq started alongside Pippen and the Chicago Bulls guard B. J. Armstrong.

Meanwhile, Coleman and Anderson won the fans' vote and

started. It didn't seem right since the Knicks were a better team than the Nets. By the All-Star break we were 34-14, which was ten wins better than the New Jersey Nets. (And we ended up finishing the season with fifty-seven wins, tied with the Atlanta Hawks for most in the Eastern Conference.) But the All-Star Game is also a popularity contest, and at that time I guess Kenny and Derrick were more popular.

The coaches picked the reserves, and both Patrick Ewing and John Starks were named to the team. I made it as an injury replacement when Mourning couldn't play. The commissioner's office selects injury replacements, so at least somebody at the league office was looking out for me. With MJ about to start spring training, Scottie was thriving with Chicago. He scored 29 points with 11 rebounds in the All-Star Game and was named Most Valuable Player. I played just eleven minutes, the fewest minutes on either team, and finished with just 2 points and 3 rebounds. Those were the same numbers Coleman put up in eighteen minutes, so at least I could say I was more productive than the starting power forward.

This story didn't happen until ten years later, but it involved Coleman, and I just have to tell it. It was 2004 and I was with Derrick in Detroit at his restaurant there, Sweet Georgia Brown. I had traveled to Detroit for an O'Jays concert. One of my childhood friends from Cleveland is a member of the O'Jays, Eric Nolan Grant, and he'd invited me, so I'd driven over from Ohio. Eric was at Derrick's restaurant that night along with his O'Jays bandmate Eddie Levert, and some other celebrities, including Queen Latifah, Detroit mayor Kwame Kilpatrick, radio-show host Tavis Smiley, and Greg Mathis, the Detroit judge who had the television show *Judge Mathis*.

It seemed like a nice quiet night, but then Judge Mathis ran up a tab for $1,500 and didn't want to pay it. Mayor Kilpatrick said he'd chip in $500, but Judge Mathis said, "We'll have these rich NBA players pay it," meaning me and Derrick.

"Why you asking me to pay for it?" I told him. "Get the fuck out of here. You pay for it."

Things got heated. I had brought a female friend with me to the bar that night, and she was hanging out with Queen Latifah. Mathis was talking shit back to me, and said, "Even your girl left you for Queen." That took me over the edge.

I pushed him real hard. He started blustering and threatening me. "Don't let this TV show fool you, I'm from the street," Mathis said. "This is my town. You better watch how you talk to me. I've got a lot of friends here."

I told him, "I don't care where you're from. I'm a one-man army."

He was all talk, and didn't do anything.

Derrick was watching this all go down, and I thought he should have stepped in to back me up and put Judge Mathis in his place. I called Derrick a bitch and said: "This is your city. You should take care of this. This wouldn't happen to you in Cleveland, because I wouldn't allow it to happen."

A few years after that, Derrick and I were in California at Oprah's place for a fundraiser for Barack Obama. All of Hollywood came out, there were celebrities everywhere—including, of all people, Judge Mathis. Derrick was telling me, "Don't do anything here. This is Oprah's party." But there was nothing to worry about. I wasn't going to do anything. I just wanted to scare him. It didn't take much to do that.

When Judge Mathis saw me, he ran the other way.

Back in 1994, two months after the All-Star Game, I was facing my friends Derrick Coleman and Jayson Williams in the playoffs. Jayson, who had played at St. John's University in Queens, owned a club on the Upper East Side called Big Daddy's. It was a great after-hours place for the Def Jam crowd. You'd see Russell Simmons, Eric B. & Rakim, Ice Cube, Cuba Gooding Jr., Wesley Snipes, Martin Lawrence, and Tracy Morgan.

Between Games 1 and 2 of our first-round series, I walked in at 1:30 a.m. with Bruce Smith, the Hall of Fame defensive lineman from the Buffalo Bills. I had known Bruce for years and would attend his playoff games whenever possible. Jayson was there, and on this particular night the bartender lined up shots. I challenged Jayson and he took the bait. He was drinking shot after shot, but I wasn't. He thought I was drinking, but I tricked him. Bruce finally told Jayson, "You'd better get home. You have an early game tomorrow."

The game was Knicks vs. Nets, Game 2 of our first-round series. Jayson was feeling the effects of our night out and played only four minutes. I started and finished with 25 points and 24 rebounds. It was one of my best playoff performances. That was my advantage for not drinking.

We took out Jayson, Derrick, Kenny, and the Nets in four games. Derrick played well, averaging 24.3 points and 14.3 rebounds, but I held my own; I was second on the team in scoring at 16.3 points per game in the series and 14.3 rebounds.

Starks recovered from surgery and came off the bench in all four games. His knee seemed all right. So Riley then reinstated him into the starting lineup after we lost to the Chicago Bulls in Game 3 in the second round, a game best remembered for who wasn't on the floor in the closing seconds.

We had beaten the Jordan-less Bulls in Games 1 and 2 at Madison Square Garden, and in Game 3 we'd rallied from a 20-point fourth-quarter deficit to draw even at 102–102 with 1.8 seconds left. Phil Jackson called time out to set up a play for Toni Kukoc and not for Scottie Pippen, who was having an MVP-caliber season.

Pippen was so upset he refused to leave the bench, with the Bulls' season hanging in the balance.

A few years earlier, Kukoc, a six-foot-eleven forward from Croatia, was unwittingly caught in the middle of a feud between Bulls general manager Jerry Krause and Pippen. Krause elected to sign Kukoc while the Bulls were negotiating a contract with Pippen, who was bothered by the fact that Kukoc could draw a bigger salary the following season than him. At the Barcelona Olympics in 1992, Pippen and Jordan made it their business to shut down Kukoc as the United States beat Croatia 103–70. Kukoc, who said he had never faced defensive pressure like Pippen provided, scored 4 points on 2-for-11 shooting with 7 turnovers.

"That's like a father who has all his kids, and now he sees another kid that he loves more than he loves his own," Michael said to NBA TV during a documentary about the Dream Team, talking about Krause. "So we were not playing against Toni Kukoc. We were playing against Jerry Krause in a Croatian uniform."

That petty rivalry was renewed with 1.8 seconds remaining in Game 3 when Phil drew up a play that called for Pippen to inbound the ball to Kukoc, who would take the final shot. I get why Scottie would be upset. In his first season without Jordan, Pippen had averaged 22 points, 8.7 rebounds, 5.6 assists, and 2.9 steals as the Bulls won fifty-five games. Scottie proved that he was a superstar, he was the MVP at the All-Star Game, and he finished third in the season MVP voting behind Hakeem Olajuwon and David Robinson. But winning Most Valuable Player at the All-Star Game is not what everyone remembers about Pippen in 1994. It was sitting out the last 1.8 seconds of that Game 3. As Pippen was refusing to go in, one of his teammates said: "Pip, come on, get up. What are you doing?" But Pippen didn't move. Jackson replaced him with Pete Myers, who inbounded the ball to Kukoc, who hit a twenty-two-footer at the buzzer to beat us. A bad loss for us and a weird victory for the Bulls.

"Scottie Pippen was not involved in the play," Phil Jackson said after the game. "He asked out of the play. That is all I'm going to say about it."

Pippen would only say that he and Phil "exchanged words" and that he stayed on the bench. I thought Scottie had a right to be upset. He carried the Bulls all year long and felt he should get the ball on the last play. But he should have been on the court. For all he had done for the team, he owed it to them and himself to be out there. You have to be out there with 1.8 seconds left and your team in danger of falling behind 3–0 in a playoff series.

To his credit, Pippen bounced back in Game 4 with 25 points, and for the second straight season we were headed back to the Garden for a Game 5 against the Bulls tied at 2–2. But unlike the previous year, we caught a break in the final seconds of Game 5.

It was May 18, 1994, and we were trailing by 1 point late in the fourth quarter when referee Hue Hollins called Pippen for a foul as Hubert Davis shot a jumper just inside the three-point line with 2.1 seconds left. Pippen, Jackson, and the rest of the Chicago Bulls were irate. Phil was stomping around screaming, and Pippen looked at Hollins and said, "I didn't touch him."

On the TNT broadcast, Hubie Brown looked at the slow-motion replay and stated: "He definitely fouled him." Davis made his first free throw, and after Jackson called time out to ice the shooter and continue yelling at Hollins, Davis sank the second. Those free throws put us on the verge of knocking off the three-time defending NBA champs, who suddenly forgot that they once got all the calls when Jordan played.

"Have I ever seen a single call make a difference like that?" Pippen said. "No. Never ever. It cost us the whole series."

It really was bullshit to say that, since the Bulls had so many calls go their way over the years. For the longest time the Bulls benefitted from close calls late in the game. Now they wanted to complain? Too bad.

All that bitching wasn't doing the Bulls any good, because unlike previous seasons they didn't have Jordan to bail them out. Of course, we made things interesting by losing Game 6 in Chicago 93–79, but we took care of business in Game 7. We were the better team regardless of whether you thought we caught a break in Game 5. The 87–77 Game 7 win put us back in the Eastern Conference Finals, and it marked the first time I eliminated my former team. Ewing finished with 18 points and 17 rebounds, but my Game 7 was even better: 17 points plus a team-high 8 field goals and a team-high 20 rebounds in forty-six minutes. I could have played another forty-six. That's how good it felt to finally beat the Bulls.

Now all we needed to do was get four more wins and we'd advance to our first NBA Finals. Our opponent was the big and tough Indiana Pacers, who had an All-Star scorer in Reggie Miller and a huge front line. Rik Smits, the center, was seven-foot-four. The power forward and small forward were six-foot-eleven Dale Davis and six-foot-ten Derrick McKey, respectively. This was a classic 1990s NBA match-up. The Pacers also had six-foot-nine Antonio Davis coming off the bench along with backup shooting guard Byron Scott, who'd played for Riley in Los Angeles.

The series was similar to the 1993 Eastern Conference Finals. We won the first two at home and then dropped the next three, which included Ewing going 0-for-10 in Game 3 with 1 point and Miller putting us on the brink of elimination with a signature performance in Game 5 back in New York. Miller relished the idea of being the villain. In our first-round series against the Pacers in 1993, Reggie had baited Starks into head-butting him in Game 3, which earned Starks an ejection as well as a $5,000. The moment

Starks whacked Miller, both me and Patrick pushed him away and were cursing at him for fucking up. John's mother called Patrick and told him not to put his hands on her son again.

This is the type of chaos Reggie liked to create, and he accomplished that again on the night of June 1, 1994. The Pacers trailed by 12 entering the fourth quarter, and in the final twelve minutes Miller scored 25 points, including 5 three-pointers. After every shot he was either saying something or making a hand gesture at Spike Lee, our superfan who sat courtside. Some in the media and some of the fans blamed Spike for lighting a fire under Reggie. That's nonsense. We just couldn't stop him. We were outscored 35–16 in the quarter, and Miller finished with 39 points in the 93–86 victory. Reggie was always getting into it with someone. He and Spike were having a little fun. It wasn't a big deal.

Two nights later we were back in Indianapolis to play in front of one the league's most vocal and nasty crowds and try to save our season. Our number one fan, Spike, made the trip. We never make things easy, right? This was a make-or-break moment for the Knicks under Riley, and we responded with a 98–91 victory, our best road win of the Riley era. Miller scored 27, but Starks had a huge game, with 26 points. John was happy, Spike was thrilled, and the rest of us were pretty confident we'd take Game 7 on our home court.

Miller, who had scored 25 in the fourth quarter of Game 5, scored 25 in Game 7, while Ewing scored 24 points with 22 rebounds, including a crucial putback dunk with 26.9 second left after Starks couldn't convert a baseline drive. We defeated the Pacers 94–90 by outscoring them 27–19 in the fourth quarter. I had 14 points and 8 rebounds; the Davis boys (Antonio and Dale) combined for 10 rebounds. I did my job. Patrick did his, John did his, and Riley had gotten us to where we thought we should be. It was all coming together.

As a franchise, the Knicks were back in the NBA Finals for the first time since 1973, and I honestly believed we were good enough to sweep the Houston Rockets. You may think that sounds crazy because the Rockets had Hakeem Olajuwon, who had been the center for the University of Houston when Ewing and Georgetown won the NCAA title ten years earlier. We felt if Patrick could hold his own against Olajuwon, we'd take care of the rest. We weren't asking Patrick to hold his own against Michael Jordan, a shooting guard. This was center against center, and we liked our chances.

The series started in Houston, and after the Rockets beat us 85–78 in Game 1, we earned a split with a 91–83 victory in Game 2. With the NBA using a 2-3-2 format for the NBA Finals, we had the opportunity of winning the title in New York simply by taking all three home games. That sounded like a good plan, but the reality was that we weren't expecting a rookie to ruin things for us.

Sam Cassell, the Rockets' backup point guard, scored 15 points in Game 3, including the go-ahead three-point basket as well as four consecutive free throws in the final twenty-two seconds. It was a crushing loss because we had trailed by 14 in the fourth quarter, fought back, and went ahead 88–86 on a basket by Derek Harper with fifty-three seconds left.

The Rockets designed a play for Olajuwon, and we collapsed around him, forcing him to pass out of the double-team. The strategy was working. Hakeem scored just 21 points on 8-for-20 shooting. We dared someone else to beat us, and that's exactly what Cassell did.

"Dream [Olajuwon] created it all," Cassell said after his basket gave Houston the lead with 32.6 seconds left. "He had three guys on him. He made the pass. I made the shot."

It was a turning point in the series. Following a pair of timeouts, I inbounded the ball to Harper, but as Harper was about to throw a pass to Starks, Ewing was called for a moving screen. Patrick couldn't believe it, saying, "You can't make a call like that, especially at that point in the game."

But referee Jake O'Donnell stood by the call. He told a pool reporter afterward: "It was a judgment call. The play was a pick and roll. He moved his hip out and then he did it again. I'm not gonna let it be twice."

That was a critical sequence and very telling about both centers. Olajuwon made the pass that led to the game's biggest shot, while Ewing was called for the offensive foul that sealed the win for Houston. Your superstars have to make plays when it matters. That's what wins championships.

We got the series back to 2–2, as I had 16 points and 20 rebounds in Game 4. Then on June 17, 1994, we beat the Rockets 91–81 in Game 5 to take a 3–2 series lead. Patrick had 25 points, 12 rebounds, and 8 blocked shots. He was dominant. But all everyone was talking about after the game was O. J. Simpson. Why? Because that was the night of the O. J. Simpson car chase. While we were beating the Rockets, O.J. was hiding inside a Ford Bronco driving slowly on the 405 Freeway followed by Los Angeles police. NBC was using a split screen to show our game and the O.J. chase.

It was a surreal day and night because in the afternoon the Rangers, who we shared the Garden with, had their victory parade for winning the 1994 Stanley Cup. It was their first championship in fifty-four years. The Knicks drought was twenty-one years old. One win in Houston in either Game 6 or 7, and the wait would be over for both major MSG teams at once. June 17 was a night of celebrating in New York, yet the focus shifted to O. J. Simpson.

"A lot of people were not in their seats, and I didn't really know why," Dave Checketts said. "I couldn't tell exactly what happened, so I did what I did all the time, which was turn around in my chair to watch what was happening on the screen. I turned around, and all I could see was the white Bronco.

"At first, [Ernie] Grunfeld said, 'I thought it was a commercial.' Suddenly, no one was paying attention to the game.'"

There was a lot happening sports-wise around this time. Besides the Rangers winning the Stanley Cup and the O.J. chase, the FIFA World Cup was taking place in the United States. But on the night of Game 6 the focus was back on the NBA and the battle between the two All-Star centers.

Olajuwon made a season-saving play in the final seconds when Ewing set a screen on Vernon Maxwell, with the Rockets leading 86–84. Starks, who had scored 27 points and made 5 of 8 three-pointers, dribbled toward the corner near the Houston Rockets' bench. Olajuwon switched quickly and was able to close on Starks as he elevated from behind the arc. If John makes the shot, I thought, we're champions. But the shot didn't have a chance because Olajuwon managed to slightly deflect the ball, which fell two feet short. Rockets coach Rudy Tomjanovich ran off the court as if Houston had already won the title, but we still liked our chances because we honestly believed we were the better team.

There were two days off between Games 6 and 7, which is too long of a break to play one game against a team we'd already faced six times over the last two weeks. They knew us, we knew them. It was just a matter of which team could execute and make plays. On June 22, 1994, it all went horribly wrong for us. Starks shot 2-for-18 and missed all 11 three-point attempts. We never found our groove.

I didn't know John had missed sixteen of eighteen shots until the media was asking me about it after the game. What could I say? We felt like shit because we lost. I wasn't going to put it on John. He had a lot of good nights for us during the season. This was a bad night.

I felt Pat Riley had made a big mistake in the Rockets 90–84 Game 7 win. In the years that followed, Pat has admitted that he should have put Rolando Blackman, a savvy veteran, in the decisive game. Ro was a shooter, and if John was struggling, it made sense to me to give Ro some of those minutes. If he'd made a couple of shots, it would have taken the pressure off everyone. I know why Ro didn't play. Riley was punishing him because earlier in the play-offs Ro had defied Riley's request to not bring wives on the road. Why else wouldn't he play? It was one of the biggest mistakes of Riley's career. Riley knows it.

Derek Harper scored 23 points in Game 7 and might have been the MVP of the series had we won. I finished with 10 points and 14 rebounds, while Ewing scored 17 points on seventeen shots. For the series, Ewing averaged 18.9 and 12.4 rebounds compared to 26.9 points and 9.1 rebounds for Olajuwon. In Games 6 and 7 Patrick shot a combined 13 of 37 and scored 34 points.

Remember I said we needed to hold our own at the center position? In the last two games Olajuwon shot 21 of 46 and scored 55 points. Hakeem got it done the entire series. We needed Patrick to carry us and he couldn't carry us. Like I said, some guys are B players. And don't get me wrong: I know where I am. I'm the butcher cutting meat for people to buy it. That's my role. I'm not on the level of Hakeem or Michael Jordan. I'm not an A player. But guess what, Patrick wasn't on that level either.

As a team we never played a complete game against Houston, I'll admit that. But if you're the best player, you have to dominate three or four games. I know Patrick inside and out and I know what I saw. Hakeem dominated him like he wasn't a superstar. Patrick got us to a certain point but couldn't put us over the top. In the end the Houston Rockets were better. It didn't matter that we were in all four games that we lost. They got four wins. And we left empty-handed.

It was my best chance for a championship. I never got that close again.

10 | "THEY WILL CHOKE"

The worst summer for an NBA player is the off-season after you lose in the Finals. After the mental and physical grind of a long season that ended in disappointment, you have the shortest turnaround from your last game to the start of the next season. You try your best to enjoy the time off during an abbreviated summer, while, in my case, also trying not to think about losing to the Houston Rockets in Game 7.

During that summer of 1994 I did my usual thing and spent a few weeks in Alabama visiting relatives. I also made day trips to visit Michael Jordan in Birmingham, where he was struggling to hit a curveball for the Birmingham Barons, the Double-A minor-league affiliate of the Chicago White Sox.

There were a lot of theories going around that Michael left basketball because he was either being investigated for gambling or was told by the NBA to step away for a brief period because of his gambling. It wasn't that at all. He was going through a crisis in his life. His father had just died, murdered by two teenagers at a highway rest area in Lumberton, North Carolina. He needed a break from basketball, which he already knew he was great at. He wanted to try something different and was invested in proving he could make it as a baseball player.

When I was with him in Alabama, we didn't really talk about the NBA. And at no time did Michael tell me he missed basketball or hint that he wanted to play again. He was a full-time minor-league baseball player, even if it meant dramatic changes to his lifestyle, going from flying on private jets and team charters to riding the bus to different towns. Though of course that had become a luxury bus that was dubbed "the Jordan Cruiser." Michael, contrary to reports, did not buy the bus, but there was no question it was his name that allowed the rest of his team to travel in style.

My stance was always that it was Michael's life to live the way he wanted to. He knew I supported his decision, which at the time was to stay retired and keep playing baseball. It wasn't the reason I supported him, but there was a part of me that felt that him staying retired meant our window to win an NBA title was still open, and that if we didn't do it this year, it was never going to happen.

I'm not sure the rest of my teammates felt that way. It wasn't really something we talked about. We still had a lot going for us. We had a lot of experience without being an old team. Patrick Ewing turned thirty-two that summer and I would be thirty-one at the end of the year. You wanted to believe that we had learned from our mistakes and knew what it took to close out tight games in the playoffs.

After the quick summer break, players began arriving in New York in September for informal workouts and pickup games. Then camp opened in early October, and we spent the first week of it at the College of Charleston in South Carolina. That was all Pat Riley's idea. With the Lakers he did training camp in Hawaii, and he wanted to replicate that environment for the Knicks. Charleston is beautiful—a nice and quiet vacation spot for most people, with good food. For us, it was a place where we could concentrate on basketball and be as comfortable and relaxed as it's possible to be while doing two-a-day practices.

The front office didn't make any major moves during the summer, beyond acquiring athletic guard Doug Christie from the Lakers. We had two late first-round picks, and the front office selected Monty Williams out of Notre Dame with the twenty-fourth pick and Charlie Ward twenty-sixth overall. Charlie was a natural leader; he had just won the Heisman Trophy as a quarterback at Florida State. Monty and Charlie both had potential, but we weren't anticipating either helping us much as rookies. They spent most of their time working with our assistant coach, Jeff Van Gundy, and our strength coach, Greg Brittenham, showing up early and staying late, learning what it takes to be a professional, the Riley way.

As our season got started, injuries and lineup issues fast became problems for the team, and resulted in us underperforming the first two months. Patrick Ewing's knees continued to bother him, as they always had, though to his credit he always played through pain. Our new guard, Doug Christie, had an ankle injury that ended up limiting him to just twelve games over the course of the season, so he couldn't make the kind of difference we'd been hoping for. In December, Doc Rivers, who had fully recovered from his torn ACL but was playing behind both Derek Harper and Greg Anthony, asked to be released. I thought Doc could have helped us for one last run, but he left and eventually signed with the San Antonio Spurs. And I was playing with a dislocated toe, the one next to my right big toe, from the start of the season. My foot was throbbing with pain every time I ran. Nike even made me a sneaker with a specially inserted orthotic, but it didn't do much to reduce the pain. It kept getting worse and worse, and after I scored 20 points in a 107–104 loss to the Chicago Bulls on Christmas Day, I'd had enough. Playing with the injury wasn't doing me or the team any good. I didn't feel I would make it through the season without surgery, and my goal was to be healthy for the playoffs, so after the loss in Chicago I made the call to get the surgery over with.

When we lost to the Bulls on Christmas, our record was 12-12. On top of the injuries and lineup issues, you could tell we had a hangover from losing Game 7 to the Rockets. But over the two months that I was out recovering from the surgery, we went 22-6. Our rookie Monty Williams worked his way into the lineup and started fourteen of those twenty-eight games during my absence. Instead of Riley taking the team to Reno to change our fortunes in 1994–95, it looked like me being out of the lineup for two months was what got us going in the right direction. I was okay with that because I wanted us to win, and I knew that once I was healthy our team would be even better.

My big return was set for February 26, 1995, against the Phila-delphia 76ers. Riley played me twenty-one minutes off the bench. It felt good to be relatively pain-free, and I could tell my teammates were happy to have me back. In our next game, against the Orlando Magic, I returned to the starting lineup.

My comeback, however, was just slightly overshadowed by the return of the guy who'd decided his time in baseball was over. In March, Michael Jordan stunned the sports world when he announced that he was ready to rejoin the Chicago Bulls after being away for one and a half seasons. Had I thought he was retired from basketball for good? No. But like I said, I didn't have any reason to believe that he would return so soon. I didn't think he'd come back in the middle of the season, that's for sure.

Being away for more than a year hadn't hurt Michael's popularity. In fact, his absence had made the fans miss him even more. You know that NBA commissioner David Stern and the league's television partners were thrilled by the news of Michael's return. Having Air Jordan back in the game would be a big ratings boost for the NBA. Meanwhile, it was going to make the Eastern Conference that much tougher. Between the Knicks, the Indiana Pacers, the Orlando Magic, the Charlotte Hornets, and now Jordan back with the Bulls, our road back to the NBA Finals would be challenging.

Michael's season debut was March 19 against the Pacers in Indiana, and of course the game was televised nationally. Just like that, Michael became the story of the 1994–95 season. The Bulls lost, and he scored 19. Everyone was quick to judge him and his potential. "He's lost his legs" or "he's lost a step" is what you kept hearing that first week. What did everyone expect? The guy hadn't played a competitive basketball game in nearly two years and only had a few practices. Even someone as great as Michael Jordan needs time.

As it turned out, he just needed a few days. In less than a week it went from "he's rusty" to "he's back." That's Michael. Things reached an absurd level when Jordan beat the Atlanta Hawks on a last-second shot. Three days later, he was set to return to Madison Square Garden.

The anticipation for a regular season game was unlike anything I can remember in the NBA. Ticket prices for scalpers were increasing with each passing day. You have to understand that players love playing at the Garden for so many reasons, and fans are willing to shell out to see it. The crowd is knowledgeable, they understand the game, they're vocal, and you have celebrities sitting courtside. The Garden also uses theater lighting, which creates the feeling that you're performing on a stage. Michael Jordan, who was born in Brooklyn before moving to North Carolina as a little kid, was built to play at Madison Square Garden.

As you would expect, it was a playoff-type atmosphere around New York City on March 28, with Jordan back in town. There was a buzz in the arena. The celebrities came out in full force. Of course, Spike Lee was carrying on. It hadn't felt this way at the Garden since Game 5 of the NBA Finals, the night O. J. Simpson's slow car chase hijacked the moment. Nothing was going to steal the spotlight from Michael, though.

Wearing a new number, 45, Jordan played a lot like the guy who'd worn number 23 and had beaten us every time we met him in the playoffs. With just four games and eight practices under his belt, Michael put on an epic show. For a regular season, it has to rank up there with the greatest performances of his career. Michael scored 55 points, which at the time was the most ever against the Knicks at MSG. (That record was later broken by both Kobe Bryant and Carmelo Anthony.)

Jordan made twenty-one of thirty-seven shots and began the game by making nine of eleven shots and scoring 20 in the first quarter. I always felt that in just about every game we played against Jordan, we waited too long to trap him. I'd rather have had his teammates shooting open three-pointers as opposed to Michael going one-on-one and hitting mid-range jumpers and getting dunks. We didn't trap the Houston Rockets enough in the NBA Finals. We allowed them to come down, set up, and get the ball to Olajuwon in the post. We were repeating the mistake with Jordan.

By halftime Michael had scored 35 points, but we were up 56–50 and in control of the game, having led by as many as 14. We weren't aggressively double-teaming Jordan. The idea was to double him late and make someone else beat us. Plus, there was always the possibility that he would naturally wear down in the second half since he'd only been back for ten days.

Of course, that didn't happen. Michael added 20 points in the second half, including a short jumper with 25.8 seconds left to give Chicago a 111–109 lead. John Starks tied it with two free throws, leaving Jordan 14.6 seconds to mess with us one last time. A few possessions earlier, Patrick had blocked Jordan's shot. So we started running Ewing at him again. This time with Ewing providing the double-team, Michael didn't shoot. Great players make great plays, and in this moment Jordan passed to a wide-open Bill Wennington for the game-winning dunk.

It was a stunning finish to a wild night that I think left some of the guys a little rattled in the locker room. Jordan was back, and maybe some guys felt we would never beat him. I didn't feel that way. I was confident that we were winning the Eastern Conference again. After the game, a reporter asked Jordan if this game was a statement to the Knicks and the NBA that he was officially back.

"I just let my game go, let my game come to me," he said. "I forgot how to make a statement."

Pat Riley refused to give Jordan, Phil Jackson, and the Bulls the satisfaction of thinking it was more than just a game in March. All he said was "The implications? We have to look at it as a regular-season game. We have to get ready for the playoffs."

Riley was right. We won our next four games, and eight of our next nine overall. Jordan beat us in March, big deal. That month only matters in college basketball, not the NBA. Plus, we finished the regular season with a 55-27 record, and the Chicago Bulls were on the other side of the playoff bracket with the Orlando Magic, whose 57-25 record was the best in the conference.

The way I looked at it was we were either getting the Bulls or the Magic in the conference finals; Michael and Scottie or Shaquille O'Neal and Penny Hardaway. On the one hand you had Michael still trying to get himself into basketball shape, and on the other hand you had an inexperienced Orlando team. If it turned out to be Orlando, Shaq was going to bully Patrick, but we had a lot of big bodies to throw at him. Plus, Shaq wasn't a good free-throw shooter. We weren't worried.

Nor did we worry about our first-round opponent, the Cleveland Cavaliers, my hometown team, which had originally traded me to the Chicago Bulls on draft night in 1985. The Cavs did well to make the playoffs, considering that Brad Daugherty, their All-Star center, had been forced to retire following the 1993–94 season due to recurring back pain. Daugherty, who had been Jordan's teammate at North Carolina, had formed a lethal pick-and-roll duo with point guard Mark Price. They were the John Stockton–to–Karl Malone tandem of the Eastern Conference.

But without Daugherty forcing Ewing to work on the defensive end, the Cavs didn't stand much of a chance. In our 103–79 Game 1 victory I scored 19 points and grabbed 11 rebounds. Cleveland's starting five—Price, John "Hot Rod" Williams, Tyrone Hill, Bobby Phills, and Chris Mills—combined to score just 29 points. That's terrible. The Cavs found a way to win Game 2, but all it did was prolong the inevitable; we won both of the next two games in Cleveland and advanced out of the first round for the fourth straight year.

We were very familiar with our second-round opponent, the Indiana Pacers, a team we had eliminated the previous two seasons. The one difference this year was that the Pacers had added our old teammate Mark Jackson. Jackson could run an offense, get people in the right spots, and set them up. And with Reggie Miller and Rik Smits, he had two offensive weapons.

In Game 1, Smits outscored Ewing 34 to 11 and Miller outscored Starks 31 to 21. And yet with less than twenty seconds remaining, we were in control. We had a 6-point lead, which should have been enough cushion to close it out. But then disaster hit, just like it had two years earlier in Game 5 against the Chicago Bulls. Somehow we managed to blow a game that we had no business losing.

It started with Miller hitting a three-pointer, followed by Miller stealing an inbound pass and hitting a game-tying three. The second three was the result of Anthony Mason trying to inbound the ball. As Mase attempted to throw the inbound pass to Greg Anthony, Miller shoved Greg just enough to make him fall down, but not enough for the referees to make the call. Miller dribbled to the three-point line and shot.

"I knew immediately I easily could have gone in for the lay-in, but I wanted to tie it up and that's what I did," Miller said.

In all the confusion, we didn't call time out. Instead, we made a successful inbound pass to John Starks, who was fouled by Sam Mitchell because Sam thought the Pacers still trailed by 1 point. Think about how lucky we just got. We screwed up, but the Indiana Pacers matched our screwup with a foul. And then things got really crazy. Reggie Miller started telling Mitchell not to worry about it "because these motherfuckers will choke." John heard it and started yelling back at him.

Starks should have been more focused on his free throws. That season Starks shot 73 percent from the free throw line. He had made both free throws he'd attempted earlier in the game. So what happened when he went back to the line with 13.2 seconds to go? John missed. Reggie again started saying to Mitchell: "I told you that motherfucker would choke."

You could feel the tension inside the building. It was only Game 1, but it felt like our season was on the line.

"You can look in John's eyes and he just wasn't as comfortable as he normally would be," Mark Jackson said. "And Reggie being Reggie, he got under his skin. I don't know if it played a factor, but I know it made for good TV."

All John had to do was make the second free throw to give us the lead. He missed it. Ewing grabbed the rebound, missed a short putback, and when Miller came down with the rebound, Starks made another huge blunder by fouling with 7.5 seconds left. Years later, Mitchell told NBA.com, "I remember looking over at the

Knicks bench and Pat Riley could have turned every color in the rainbow. He just couldn't believe it."

That's how we all felt. Miller, who up until that point had made twelve of thirteen free throws, converted both and gave Indiana a 107–105 lead. On our last possession Greg Anthony slipped and we never got a shot off. Miller had scored 8 points in 8.9 seconds to beat us in Game 1, and we had no one but ourselves to blame.

"You know, you never heard Madison Square Garden that quiet," Smits said. "Everybody was in shock."

In a seven-game playoff series, when you lose a game you should have won it is devastating mentally. You need four wins to advance and that should have been the first one. Instead, we managed to fall behind 3–1 in the series. In Game 5 we saved our season with a 96–95 victory at home that included me putting up 13 points with 13 rebounds. In Game 6, back in Indianapolis, Ewing scored 25. I chipped in with 19. It was our biggest road win of the season. We held Reggie Miller to 4-for-13 shooting to bring the series back to New York for a Game 7 on May 21, 1995.

This is why home court advantage is so important. We had lost Game 1 to the Pacers at MSG, but we felt they wouldn't beat us twice in New York. We entered the fourth quarter trailing by five, rallied, and found ourselves behind 97–95 with five seconds left. We had a sideline inbound play: Derek Harper passed to Ewing, who caught the ball one step inside the three-point line. With Starks standing behind the line and screaming for the ball, Patrick drove past Derrick McKey and then avoided Dale Davis, who was in the paint trying to draw a charge.

As the clock was about to expire, Ewing had a finger roll at the basket that he should have made ninety-nine out of a hundred times. But nothing seemed to break right for us on the nineties Knicks. Not against the Bulls in 1993 or against the Rockets in 1994 or against the Pacers in Game 7 in 1995. Ewing's finger roll rimmed out and our season was ending one month earlier than it had in 1994. We came back from 15 points down and couldn't finish the deal.

"I thought we were going into overtime," Patrick said. "I just laid it up. I thought it was going in. I was watching to see it go through the net. I was stunned. I was stunned.

"I thought I made a great play to get to the hole. I probably should have tried to dunk it. But I took off too far to dunk it. They pay me to take that kind of shot. Today, unfortunately, I didn't come through."

It wasn't my best game, either. I finished with 9 points and 6 rebounds, and I missed three of ten free throws. I have to take responsibility for my role. And while Ewing did have 29 points and 14 rebounds, that last moment will live with him forever.

That miss ended the Riley era in New York. The Knicks wouldn't give Riley the power that he wanted going forward, so he faxed in his resignation and joined the Miami Heat as their head coach and president. I had heard he was also upset that management never reimbursed him for the time he gave each player $500 of spending money for our trip to Reno a year earlier. He felt the front office didn't understand the value of that trip.

I wasn't mad at Riley for leaving. Coaches get fired all the time. This was his decision. He wanted control. Gregg Popovich had control in San Antonio. Doc Rivers later had it with the Los Angeles Clippers. Riley should have been granted that same power. The Miami Heat lured away our coach with a five-year, $40 million contract that included an ownership stake.

I feel that Pat Riley never got the chance to really change the Knicks the way he wanted to. When you have a guy like Riley, you're looking to win every year. None of these mom-and-pop organizations will hire Riley because they won't spend the money to do whatever it takes to win. Pat wants to do everything first class.

If you don't share his philosophy, then he is not the right coach for you. The Knicks are a corporation. They should have realized what they had when they hired him and made it work.

When Jordan returned in March 1995 I thought it would come down to the Knicks and the Bulls in the playoffs. It was meant to be, right? Instead, Orlando eliminated Chicago in the second round and made it to its first NBA Finals before being swept by Hakeem Olajuwon and the Houston Rockets. Unlike the Rockets, we failed to take advantage of Jordan being away. Our coach was leaving for Miami to build a franchise, and our championship window felt like it had been nailed shut.

11 | GOING HOLLYWOOD

The NBA is a celebrity-driven league. All the actors, singers, and rappers like being associated with NBA players, and a lot of us players want to be actors, singers, and rappers. Shit, I'm not an actor and I've been in three movies: *Space Jam*, *Forget Paris*, and *Pastor Brown*. Unfortunately, no Academy Award wins for me though—or NBA Championships either, for that matter.

The crossover between the NBA and celebrity culture started back in the mid-eighties, when commissioner David Stern began embracing the league's relationship with the entertainment world, and then really accelerated in the nineties.

A-list Hollywood stars became regular fixtures at games, particularly in New York and Los Angeles. In the nineties, you'd see Denzel Washington sitting courtside in both cities. Chris Rock was becoming big, and he'd be around a lot. And of course, you had Jack Nicholson in L.A., and Spike Lee in New York.

I became friends with Spike as soon as I got to the Knicks. He was always shooting movies around the city and would invite a bunch of the guys from the team to visit the set. I came away with an appreciation for the moviemaking process: it might not be a hard job for the actors, but those shooting days are long.

Jungle Fever, which was released in 1991, was especially cool for me because it starred my friend Halle Berry. I got a chance to watch her film a few scenes. Halle is a Cleveland girl. Over the years we became real close: I'd see her in Chicago, New York, and L.A. But as she became a bigger star, winning an Academy Award for Best Actress and all that, we spoke less and less. We're still cool, but she went on with her life and I went on with mine.

Also starring in *Jungle Fever* were Wesley Snipes, Annabella Sciorra, Samuel L. Jackson, and John Turturro. Turturro was in a lot of Spike's movies, including *Do the Right Thing*. He was good buddies with Spike. Turturro would sit next to Spike at games if Spike didn't bring his wife, Tonya, or one of his kids or his other good friend Al Palagonia. Al was a former stockbroker turned actor who was in Spike's movies *Summer of Sam*, *He Got Game*, and *25th Hour*, and eventually got into the private jet business. Spike hung around with the right people.

Robert De Niro was always a big deal around New York. I ran into him at his Manhattan restaurant once, Tribeca Grill, when I was there with Jayson Williams of the New Jersey Nets and a few other friends. De Niro, the man himself, came to our table, said a few nice things, and then told us to order anything we'd like. I wasn't really that hungry, and being a picky eater as I've mentioned, whatever they put in front of me I sent back. I could tell that the waiter was getting nervous. Finally, the chef came out and asked me exactly how I would want the food cooked. I told him I just like things cooked a certain way. I'm a chef myself.

At the end of the meal, they gave us dessert on the house and it looked pretty good. I took a couple bites and then started coughing. I'm allergic to peanuts, and I was thinking they might have been in the dessert. Jayson claims that I wasn't just coughing, I was choking, and at the same time I was doing that, I was also grabbing the waiter by the neck and choking him. Jayson loves telling that story. About 70 percent of the stories Jayson tells are not true, but I'll hand it to him—they're funny. I was coughing, not choking, and I gave the waiter a hard time, but I wasn't grabbing him by the neck or anything like that.

Every Sunday, especially after home playoff games, a bunch of us would head over to Chaz & Wilson's Grill on West 79th Street. There was always a good crowd there: Mary J. Blige, Jamie Foxx, Prince. I was there with Jayson Williams so much they thought we owned the place. The China Club was the spot on Monday night. Models, actors, and athletes all went to the China Club. In the summer of 1995, Anthony Mason was involved in an altercation there, and one of the New York newspapers said he was "A Bull in a China Club." You'd see Lawrence Taylor with a lot of Giants and Jets players. There'd be singers and rappers like Kid 'n Play, LL Cool J, and Heavy D. We all traveled in the same circles. It was one big party. I would go to LL's apartment in Queens to hang out with him from time to time before he became a big Hollywood star. I even had a cameo in the music video for his song "Back Seat (of My Jeep)." We filmed it at a drive-in movie theater on Long Island.

Then, in the summer of 1995, I was asked to be a presenter at the Source Awards in New York, during the height of the East Coast–West Coast rap wars. I presented an award to the Notorious B.I.G. at the show, which was held on August 5 at the theater that's connected to Madison Square Garden. It's now called the Hulu Theater; in 1995 it was called the Paramount; but before naming rights and sponsorship deals became such a big deal, it was known as the Felt Forum. The Felt Forum hosted boxing matches and the NBA Draft, including the 1985 draft when I was a first-round pick. I didn't attend the actual draft in 1985, I watched with my coach in

Virginia, but in August 1995 I was right there, inside the theater, for one of the more memorable award shows of all time.

I'll give you a little background on why there was bad blood between the East and West Coast rappers before the Source Awards. On November 30, 1994, the West Coast rapper Tupac Shakur had been robbed and beaten at gunpoint in the lobby of Quad Recording Studios in Times Square. When he tried to fight off his attackers, he was shot. Tupac underwent three hours of surgery at Bellevue Hospital.

I didn't know him that well, but just a couple weeks before he was shot, on November 4, 1994, I had run into Tupac at Roseland Ballroom in Midtown Manhattan. It was the twenty-fifth birthday party for East Coast rapper-producer Sean Combs, aka Puffy. Tupac was balling out, having a good time. There are photos from that night of me and Tupac together. There are also photos of Tupac and Puffy together.

Not long after he was shot, Tupac was sent to prison for an unrelated issue. In a 1995 interview with *Vibe* magazine, done from prison, Tupac accused Puffy, along with Notorious B.I.G. and record executive Jimmy Henchman, of setting up the robbery.

Tupac was with Death Row Records in Los Angeles, which was run by Suge Knight. On the night of the 1995 Source Awards, Suge had about a hundred friends with him in the audience, most of them gangbangers from L.A.

When Suge went up to accept the award for Soundtrack of the Year for executive producing the music for the movie *Above the Rim*, he said: "I'd like to tell Tupac keep his guard up, we riding with him." Suge then insulted Puffy, who was known for being closely involved in the projects he produced. "Any artist out there that wanna be an artist, stay a star, and don't have to worry about the executive producer trying to be all in the videos, all on the record, *dancing*—come to Death Row!"

That set the tone for the night. When Puffy performed, he told the audience, "I live in the East, and I'm gonna die in the East." He was followed by Snoop Dogg, a West Coast rapper, who asked the crowd: "Ain't got no love for Snoop Dogg, Dr. Dre, and Death Row?"

There was a lot of tension, a lot of smoke. I'm still surprised that no fights broke out in the theater. Puffy did make an effort to calm things down. He won an award and said he was proud of what Suge and Death Row had accomplished. "This East and West . . . it needs to stop," he said.

I have to be honest though, in the East–West rivalry, I thought the East lost that night. As I saw it, a bunch of guys from Los Angeles came in, talked shit, and the New York guys didn't do anything about it. If I'd been a New York rapper, I wouldn't have stood for that. I would have told the Los Angeles guys to come get their award and go home.

After the show, I went out to get something to eat. I had no interest in attending any after-parties. There were too many guys beefing and it had nothing to do with me. I figured that something serious could be about to go down.

I was right and wrong. As far as I know, things were quiet that night. But they didn't stay quiet forever.

On September 7, 1996, Tupac was shot four times while he was stopped at a traffic light in Las Vegas. He and Suge, who was also in the car, had just attended Mike Tyson's fight against Bruce Seldon at the MGM Grand. Two bullets struck Tupac in the chest. He died six days later.

Five months after that, on February 23, 1997, I saw Biggie outside a club in L.A. The Knicks were in town to play the Lakers. I was surprised to see someone of his stature just driving around without any security, especially out west. It was the last time I saw him.

On March 8, Biggie presented an award to the singer Toni Braxton at the Soul Train Music Awards at the Shrine Auditorium in L.A. Some people in the crowd booed Biggie. He wasn't on home turf. After midnight that night, he was stopped at a traffic light when a car pulled alongside him. One guy got out and started shooting. It was similar to what happened to Tupac. Biggie was twenty-four when he died. Tupac was twenty-five.

We played the Bulls later that day, March 9, 1997, and I still remember a reporter from the *New York Daily News*, David Cummings, asking a bunch of us players for our reaction. I told the truth, as usual: I was shocked but I wasn't surprised. I had seen how tense things were at the Source Awards less than two years earlier. I wasn't the only one who had a feeling that this was not going to end well.

The mid-nineties were a tumultuous time for the superstars of the rap world, but in the NBA, things were heating up in a good way.

The sport was being marketed around individual superstars. Of course, no one was a bigger star than Michael Jordan.

So it was only natural that Michael went Hollywood after returning to the NBA in March 1995. The Bulls lost to the Orlando Magic in the second round of the playoffs that year, but you could tell that Michael was on the cusp of taking over the league once again. And in the summer of 1995, he started filming the movie *Space Jam*. There was only one condition: the studio had to find a way to let him play basketball every day.

Warner Bros. finally settled on building a facility on the studio lot for Jordan. A court from Long Beach State University was shipped to the studio, and Jordan's personal trainer, Tim Grover, set up a weight room as well. All of it was put under a huge tent. That summer "The Jordan Dome," as it was being called, hosted some of the best pickup games of the last 25 years. I had a cameo in the movie and was involved in all the games.

On most days, Michael filmed scenes until 6 p.m., and then he'd head to the court. We'd play until ten, and then Mike would be back on the set by 6 a.m. Michael, Reggie Miller, Dennis Rodman, Alonzo Mourning, Charles Barkley, Patrick Ewing, Grant Hill, Rod Strickland, Tim Hardaway, and Glen Rice were just some of the guys who played. We played every day. If you lost, you would have to wait for two or three games before you could get back on.

There were always Hollywood celebrities coming to the Jordan Dome to watch. It was like an NBA Finals game with Celebrity Row. I'm talking about the big names: Halle Berry, Arnold Schwarzenegger, Kevin Costner, Queen Latifah, and LL Cool J.

Everybody played at a high level because Michael was running the game and there were all those stars watching us. And it was especially fun, because it was basketball as we'd grown up playing it. There were no referees. I remember telling guys, "No ticky-tack fouls. No bitch-ass calls. Just play." For the most part we were all on our best behavior. There were no fights—just good basketball. Michael invited a few guys from UCLA, including Tracy Murray, who eventually played in the NBA. Kris Johnson, whose dad Marques played in the NBA, also came over. One night, NBA player Cedric Ceballos showed up and was complaining that Kris Johnson was playing on Mike's team. He was bitching that the game was only supposed to be for NBA players. But Mike liked Kris, and he didn't want to hear any shit from Cedric, so Mike set out to dominate Cedric in the game. Of course, Mike came out on top, and got Cedric with a few dunks. When Michael played pickup, it was like Michael Jackson performing. The games were an event. Michael ran the game, ran his mouth, and everyone was enjoying it, on the court and off. Michael was using these runs to get back into basketball shape after being knocked out in the second round and watching the Orlando Magic carry Horace Grant, our old teammate in Chicago, on their shoulders. Yes, the Orlando Magic gave Michael more than enough to motivate him for the 1995–96 season. Jordan wanted to prove something and that was bad news for the rest of the NBA.

With Michael at the top of his game, the Bulls went on to set an NBA record by winning seventy-two regular season games during the 1995–96 season. Shit, they only lost ten times! The Bulls were better and bigger. They had added seven-foot-two center Luc Longley during the 1992–93 season, and the following off-season they added Ron Harper, a solid guard who could defend multiple positions. With Jordan officially back, they also decided to take a chance on Dennis Rodman, who was known for making hustle plays and had won championships in Detroit. Rodman was also an asshole, but the organization probably felt that the combined pull of Jordan and Phil Jackson could control him to some degree.

Rodman came late to the party. I don't get why everyone finds Dennis interesting. Even in *The Last Dance*, the documentary about the nineties Chicago Bulls, Dennis was made to look better than Scottie Pippen. The Bulls had already won three titles before he arrived. You had Batman and Robin already in Chicago. *The Last Dance* was trying to make one of the villains into the real Robin. That makes no sense.

Rodman and I were never friends. That became even more clear after I retired, when I ran into him during an event at the Gansevoort Hotel in Miami Beach. He was wearing his usual outfit: shades, a scarf, and makeup. He sort of joined a conversation that I was in, during which I said that I would be heading over to my restaurant in South Beach later that night. I had become part owner of a place called Red, the Steakhouse. Rodman said he'd meet me over there.

A few hours later I was at the go-to place in Miami, Prime 112, and I was talking with the owner, Myles Chefetz. The manager of Red called to tell me that there was a problem at the restaurant: Dennis was walking around trying to be funny by eating food off customers' plates.

I told Myles, "I need to take care of a problem," and went to my place. When I looked in the window, I saw Dennis sitting at a table bothering some people. This motherfucker, I thought to myself. I walked in, made a straight beeline for him, and said, "What the fuck do you think you're doing?" I didn't even hesitate. I grabbed him by the shirt and threw him out.

Not long after that, I received an appearance fee to attend the opening of a strip club in Manhattan. Lawrence Taylor and O. J. Anderson, two former New York Giants, were also there. Dennis came strolling in out of nowhere, saw me, and it was clear he was trying to avoid me. L.T. waved him over and Dennis reluctantly made a brief visit. He was wearing a dress. Why? I have no idea. I wasn't going to fight him. All I said to him was "Which bathroom are you using tonight?"

As much as I dislike Dennis, there's no question that the Bulls continued their championship winning ways after he joined the team, even if he gets too much credit for it.

The transformation of the Knicks wasn't as impressive. The front office replaced Pat Riley with Don Nelson, an innovative coach who, like Rick Pitino, preferred to play small lineups and shoot three-pointers. Nelson had once coached our general manager, Ernie Grunfeld, in Milwaukee. Nelson's teams with the Golden State Warriors featuring TMC—Tim Hardaway, Mitch Richmond, Chris Mullin—were as explosive as any team over the last thirty years. We didn't really have that type of personnel in New York, but that wasn't going to stop Nellie.

Right from the start Don Nelson and Patrick Ewing didn't seem to be on the same page. Patrick wasn't featured in the offense like he had been under Riley. Nellie didn't want to just run plays for Ewing in the post. Plus, he decided to make Anthony Mason the point guard so Mason could exploit mismatches. Mase was versatile: he was built like a football player but had quick feet and was agile. That's why Nelson loved him. He was taking Derek Harper off the ball and letting Mason run the offense. It worked because Mason was a good passer and he found the open man.

While Mason was enjoying a bigger role in the offense, Ewing and John Starks were at odds with our new coach. The tension between John and Nelson rose to the surface when the *New York Post* quoted John's sister and grandmother complaining about how the coach was making life miserable for John. When the story hit the newsstand, Starks confronted the reporter, Thomas Hill, after practice at our training site on the campus of Purchase College in Westchester, New York.

"Don't you ever call my family again!" he yelled.

John was shouting at the reporter when in reality his issue was with Nelson. For so many years the core of the team had been me, Ewing, and Starks, but now Nelson felt it was time to move away from John and Patrick. There were whispers about Nelson wanting to trade for Tim Hardaway or shoot for the stars and make a play for Shaquille O'Neal, who was entering the final year of his contract. Imagine a Ewing-for-Shaq swap? It was worth a try, but I don't think that had any realistic chance of happening.

Nelson didn't have a problem with me, and I didn't have a problem with him. I did what the coach told me, because if it didn't work, they were going to fire the coach anyway. I always tried to do right by the head coach.

There wasn't much pressure or focus on Nelson early in the season, because the fans and the media all had their attention on December 19, 1995, the night Riley would return to Madison

Square Garden. For all that Riley did for the organization, the fans just couldn't forgive him for leaving and joining the Miami Heat. The newspapers were calling him "Pat the Rat," and when he walked onto the floor, he was greeted by a loud chorus of boos. Pat then encouraged the crowd to keep showering him with vitriol and even blew kisses.

"I embraced whatever the fans had to offer," Riley said after we beat the Heat 89–70. "I spent four years here and I think they know what I put into this and we were very successful. I've always embraced the fans here and what they had to offer me. I would just take it for what it is, and I wanted to show my appreciation back to them, regardless of what was being said."

Everyone at some point needs to confront their past, and Pat was relieved to get that game over with. Nelson had had a similar experience sixteen days earlier when the Washington Bullets came to Madison Square Garden. The Bullets' young budding star was Chris Webber. Nelson and Webber had been together for one season, in 1993–94, with the Golden State Warriors, and even though Webber played well and the Warriors made the playoffs, Webber was unhappy. He wanted to play on the perimeter and Nelson wanted him in the post.

Webber had an opt-out clause in his contract and threatened to leave if the Warriors didn't fire Nelson. Nelson offered to quit, which only made Webber more upset because he felt it was a public relations stunt. Ultimately, the Warriors traded Webber to the Washington Bullets for Tom Gugliotta and three future first-round picks.

Webber was reunited in Washington with his former Michigan teammate Juwan Howard, and the three of us got into it on December 3, 1995. They were talking a lot of shit, and after we beat them 107–83. I told the reporters that it was "young guys talking. They don't have respect for me, I don't have respect for them.

"I only have a few friends in the league, because the league is full of bull," I added. "It's not about talent anymore—so many teams have talent, but they're not going anywhere. It's about marketing and individual things. Like the Washington Bullets. They have good players, but they're not going anywhere."

Webber said our problems started when I elbowed him. I don't remember that. But when we met four weeks later in Landover, Maryland, I do remember that Webber told the media that I was on my way out. "If he doesn't win a championship this year, he'll never win one," Webber said. "Me, I got nine more tries maybe." Webber also said that I wouldn't try to bully him or Juwan Howard. That's true, because I didn't "bully" anyone. I just went out and played, and when necessary, threw a punch.

On December 29, 1995, we played the Bullets without Ewing, who had twisted his ankle the night before in a home loss to the Cleveland Cavaliers. We were trailing 114–112 in overtime when me and Webber dove for a loose ball. He hurt his shoulder on the play and had to leave the game. Washington beat us 127–120, ending a fifteen-game losing streak to the Knicks. I guess they were feeling pretty good about themselves, because afterward Webber was accusing me of being dirty and intentionally trying to hurt him. That shit got back to me real fast.

As I was walking to the bus, I saw Webber standing in the hallway with a small group of people. I walked right up to him and said, "Motherfucker, you ever say anything about me and I'm going to fuck you up." And that was it. He didn't do anything. I walked into his crowd. That was his chance.

I wasn't trying to hurt him. It's a loose ball. It was a basketball play. If I'd been trying to hurt him, I'd have hurt him. But I guess we're cool now. A few years ago I cooked for Webber at an event at his place in Atlanta. It wasn't like I was worried about him jumping me and beating me up. It wasn't like that. But as far as that game was concerned, I wasn't trying to hurt him. Don Nelson didn't put a bounty on Webber. It was just a physical play in the game and he got hurt.

I should know. A few weeks later, on February 14, 1996, we were trailing the Charlotte Hornets by 33 points when I dislocated my thumb against the backboard after fouling Robert Parish. I had surgery the next day and was sidelined from February 15 until March 26. By the time I returned, things had changed dramatically. We had a new coach. Ewing and Starks had led a mutiny, which resulted in Nelson being fired, with a record of 34-25, on March 8, 1996. It's crazy to think about now, but the front office fired a guy who was nine games over .500. The standard for the Knicks in the nineties was different; a 34-25 record wasn't good enough.

12 | NEW YORK TIME'S UP

Dave Checketts and Grunfeld replaced Nelson with our assistant coach, Jeff Van Gundy, who had been initially brought to the Knicks by Stu Jackson but really made a name for himself under Riley. We were all happy for Jeff and figured it would work because Riley's way of doing things had worked in the past. It also meant that Patrick would again be featured in the offense, and the days of Mason being the point forward were over. Of course, Mason was not happy about going back to the Riley way.

Jeff lost his first game at Philadelphia, but two days later we recorded our best win of the season by taking out Jordan and the Bulls at Madison Square Garden. It was a huge moment for Van Gundy to beat a team that would finish 72-10, but it was also a good moment for Ewing and Starks, two players who had felt lost thus far during the season.

In many ways it was a transitional year for the Knicks. In the span of ten months we were on our third coach. Also, the front office began trading away players in order to clear cap space for the free-agent summer of 1997. That meant Charles Smith, Doug Christie, and Monty Williams were traded for players with expiring contracts. The plan was to use those expiring deals to get under the salary cap and pursue free agents starting July 1. And the free agent class of 1996 was deep and talented. Management was looking ahead, but as players and coaches we had to focus on the present. Did it feel like the front office was giving up on the season? Yes. But what was I supposed to do about it? It's not like they asked me what I thought about the plan.

I had my own problems to worry about, namely staying healthy. First it was my thumb and then on April 9, in the first quarter of our game against the Boston Celtics, I was hit by friendly fire. Patrick hit me with an inadvertent elbow that gave me a cut below my right eye that required six stitches. But it felt worse. My vision was blurry and I had considerable swelling. An X-ray revealed that I suffered a fracture of the orbital bone.

Dr. Scott said a CAT scan would determine if there was any displacement of the fracture fragments. It was the kind of injury where if you're not careful you can lose an eye. If surgery was necessary, it would likely end my season. If surgery wasn't needed, I would wear a mask and would return for the playoffs that were scheduled to begin on April 25.

I wasn't crazy about wearing a mask, but if that's what it would take to allow me to play, I was willing to try it. Van Gundy was looking to have the interim tag removed from his job title, so he was definitely in favor of me playing with a mask. Maybe I could be a superhero. Super Oak. How does that sound?

"He's going to have to play with a mask if he plays, that's not even a question," Van Gundy told the media. "The question tomorrow is whether the fracture is displaced. With Charles, he'll do all he can do to get back on the court. But we're not going to push him. If he's comfortable, we'd love to have him. If not, we've just got to go on.

"Even if the X-rays come back negative, he has a lot of swelling. You can't fit him with a mask until the swelling goes down. It's not like he'll get X-rayed tomorrow and practice Wednesday. It won't be that quick."

Reggie Miller had suffered a similar injury a year earlier that required surgery and knocked him out of the first round of the playoffs. When the reporters asked me if I was worried that I could be facing a similar fate, I told them: "I can take more than Reggie."

They laughed, but I was being serious. With the season ending on April 21 and our first playoff game scheduled for April 25 in Cleveland, Van Gundy took us back to Riley's favorite spot, Charleston, South Carolina, to prepare for the postseason. I avoided surgery and was cleared to begin practicing with a mask. I gave it about fifteen minutes before I tossed it aside. I couldn't play with that thing. It bothered me and it felt like a target, as if I was daring someone to elbow my face.

I think my presence in Charleston let the rest of my teammates know that despite a coaching change and despite making trades to clear roster space, this was not a throwaway season. As the lower-seeded team, we won Game 1. I scored 17 points in thirty-four minutes, and we went on to sweep Cleveland in three games. That set up a date with MJ and the Chicago Bulls in the conference semifinals.

We had handed the Bulls one of their ten regular season losses, but the idea of winning four times in a seven-game series didn't seem realistic. Sure enough, Jordan set the tone with 44 points in Game 1, and we came back to New York down 0–2 and playing back-to-back home games on May 11 and 12. NBC wanted those weekend games with Jordan on their network, and we made it a series by winning Game 3 in overtime.

That meant we avoided the sweep, but the Bulls took the next two games and closed out the series in Chicago on May 14 with MJ scoring 35. That same night back in the Bronx, Dwight Gooden of the New York Yankees threw a no-hitter. We couldn't beat MJ, but he was upstaged on the back pages of the New York tabloids by Gooden.

To take two games from Jordan and the Bulls that season wasn't a great accomplishment, but it was something. That Bulls team was special. Within two months, Jordan won his fourth title in six years. Meanwhile, the Knicks front office was again left searching for a plan that could end the Bulls' dominance.

Reggie Miller was a free agent in the summer of 1996, but the front office decided to sign the younger shooting guard Allan Houston. On that same day, we signed free-agent point guard Chris Childs and also traded Anthony Mason to the Charlotte Hornets for Larry Johnson, one of the best scoring forwards in the league, even though he was dealing with back issues.

I didn't want to see Mase go. I felt he could still help us win. He knew the system and he made us tougher. Patrick Ewing had something to do with Mason being traded because Mase would talk shit to Patrick every day. He always had something to say about Patrick. Mase would tell Pat that he was not a leader and get on him for never throwing the ball out of the post. Mase always said what was on his mind.

As for Larry Johnson, a few months earlier we played a physical game against the Hornets that nearly escalated into a brawl. I had my hand around L.J.'s throat and he was doing the same to me. It happens.

"I remember my mother asking me before training camp started,

'Will you and Charles be able to get along?'" Johnson said. He told her, "We're cool now. We're on the same team."

That was my philosophy as well. We're teammates now so it's cool. When Xavier McDaniel joined the Knicks, we put our differences aside. You don't have to be best friends in order to do your job. That's true with every job. A lot of people don't get along but they still work together. As long as things don't get personal, it's fine. And if the unfortunate thing came to pass, and things got personal with X-Man or Larry, I liked my chances.

But Larry and I became friends. We were both trying to win. That's all that mattered. Our team in 1996–97 was talented and close-knit. Ewing was still an All-Star. John Starks embraced his role as a backup and became Sixth Man of the Year. L.J. sacrificed his scoring to do just about everything else for the team. Houston was one of the better shooting guards in the league. And the point guard combination of Childs and Charlie Ward proved to be solid.

The million-dollar question was: Did we have enough to finally knock off the Chicago Bulls? We were definitely better than the 1995–96 Knicks, and every bit as good as the 1993 team that took a 2–0 series lead against Chicago before dropping the next four games. During the 1996–97 season, our first meeting with the Chicago Bulls wasn't until January 21, 1997, which gave us plenty of time to mesh as a unit. We entered the game with a 28-11 record while the Bulls, coming off a season where they went 72-10, got off to a 35-4 start. They were 105-14 in their last 119 regular season games. That's remarkable.

What's also remarkable is what Van Gundy said about Jordan on a Chicago radio station a few days before the game. It's not like Michael needed added motivation, but Jeff provided some by essentially calling Mike a con man.

"His way is to befriend [his opponents], soften them up, try to make them feel he cares about them," Van Gundy said. "Then he goes out there and tries to destroy them. For some reason, league wide, it's important to be liked by him, and I don't know why. There's such a mystique about him that everybody wants to be like him, play like him, make as much money as he does. And be able to do all the off-the-court things he does. You see him every game, he smiles at guys, pats them on the ass, then goes out and kicks their ass. Then they hug him after the game like it was some great thing that he scored 45 points on them.

"I admire him for it. He uses everything he has to his advantage, whether psychological or physical. He cons them by inviting them to his movies. He cons them with the commercials. He pretends to enjoy guys, like them and befriend them, and all he wants to do is win."

I thought Jeff was out of line. And I didn't know what he was talking about. I was in a movie with Jordan. So were Larry and Patrick. Was he trying to say that I wouldn't compete against Jordan because he's my friend?

I do believe that Jeff wanted to play mind games in the media the way that Riley and Phil Jackson did for all those years. Jeff said what he felt he needed to say, but I didn't agree with it. And it made a lot of people in Chicago upset. Jeff was public enemy number one in Chicago, and that night the Bulls beat us 88–87. How did Michael respond? He scored 51 points. Michael will use anything to motivate him. This was easy.

When the Bulls moved into the United Center, both team benches were on the opposite side of the court from their respective locker rooms, so after games the teams had to cross paths to exit the court. On this night, Jordan walked past Jeff and called him a "little fuck." He then told Spike Lee to tell Jeff to "shut up." I think Jeff's reply, maybe not in that moment, but afterward, was that the Bulls beat us by only one point. It didn't matter that Jordan had a great game. What mattered was that we were in the game.

We split our four meetings against the Bulls that season, including a 103–101 victory on April 19, 1997, the final night of the regular season. Often in the last game on the season, playoff-bound teams rest their star players. That wasn't the case on this night. Jordan played thirty-nine minutes, Ewing forty. Jordan "only" scored 33 points as we improved to 57-25 and prevented the Bulls from winning their seventieth regular-season game. The feeling was that we would eventually meet again, so we didn't want to give away a game, even on the final night of the regular season.

That game was a good launching point for us, because we swept Anthony Mason and the Hornets 3–0 in the first round. Then we beat Pat Riley's Miami Heat 88–79 in Game 1 of the second round on May 7, for our seventh straight victory overall. The Heat tied the series at 1–1 in the second game in Miami with an 88–84 win, led by Alonzo Mourning and Tim Hardaway, but they couldn't hang with us at Madison Square Garden. We took both home games and returned to Miami with a 3–1 lead and fully expecting to travel to Chicago two days later for Game 1 of the Eastern Conference Finals.

We never made it to the Windy City. More misery was in store for the Knicks.

On May 14, we lost Game 5 to the Heat 96–81. In the last two minutes we trailed by 12, and I set a hard pick on Hardaway at midcourt that leveled him. Alonzo Mourning retaliated by pushing me, and when I pushed back, referee Dick Bavetta ejected me. I was in the locker room when Charlie Ward fouled Hardaway with 1:53 to play. The game was basically over. Miami was ahead 88–74, but after Hardaway's second free throw, P. J. Brown nearly tossed Ward into the front row to ignite a bench-clearing brawl. Or more precisely, our bench cleared.

Charlie was trying to box out a much taller player in P. J. Brown, and Brown felt that Charlie was going after his knees. As soon as the game ended, Pat Riley made his case in the media like he had so many times before when he was coaching the Knicks and we were facing the Chicago Bulls in the playoffs. This time he was talking about his former team and his former assistant coach.

"I wasn't coaching Charlie Ward when he took P. J. Brown's legs out from under him," Riley said.

The fallout was a worst-case scenario for us. Brown was suspended two games while Ward, Ewing, Starks, Johnson, and Houston all received one-game suspensions for leaving the bench. Since there was an NBA rule that required teams to dress at least nine men, they split the suspensions: Ward, Ewing, and Houston were suspended for Game 6, and Johnson and Starks would be forced to sit out Game 7. Because Charlie was involved in the original fight, he was automatically suspended for Game 6. The suspensions for the four remaining players were determined, by league rules, alphabetically. These quirky rules really hurt us, because I'm convinced that having Patrick, John, and myself together for one game would have been enough to defeat Miami.

The rule about leaving the bench area is fucked up because Patrick wasn't even close to the scrum. He stepped one foot onto the court. And if you look in recent years, the rule has changed a little. The league doesn't always suspend a player for being one foot on the court. That ruling turned the series in Miami's favor. The league had it out for the Knicks.

Everyone knew the Knicks and the Bulls were the two best teams in the East that season. I don't care that Miami won four more regular-season games. We kicked their ass in the first four games of our playoff series. Game 5 ruined us. Our crowd was electric for Game 6, and even though I finished with 18 points and 12 rebounds, we lost 95–90. We got Patrick back for Game 7 on

May 18, and he scored 37 points, but Miami took a 25–14 first-quarter lead and we never recovered. We lost 101–90 and never got the chance to challenge Jordan and Chicago. They eliminated Miami in five games and went on to win their fifth title.

Maybe it's difficult for some to appreciate the mental toll it takes to lose a series you believe in your heart you should have won. I felt that way in 1993, 1994, and I definitely felt that way against Miami in 1997.

Every time your season ends, you want to believe that next season will be better, but there are no guarantees. We were returning the same core group for the 1997–98 season, but on December 20, Patrick fractured his right wrist when he used his hand to break his fall in a game against the Bucks in Milwaukee. He jumped to catch a lob pass but was fouled in midair by Andrew Lang, lost his balance, and landed awkwardly. The doctors said it was the type of injury you normally see happen to a driver in a car crash.

Ewing was finished for the regular season, and I became the team's new starting center. Even though I wasn't being paid nearly as much as the regular starting center, I held my own. I played in seventy-nine games that season, missing two due to suspension and sitting out the final night of the regular season to rest for the playoffs. We went 43-39, and as the seventh seed we faced the team we wanted to see, the Miami Heat.

The series went like you would expect. We lost Game 1 but got the split in Miami when Houston, Johnson, and Starks combined for 71 points in our 96–86 victory. We held Mourning to 7 points in Game 3, but with Voshon Lenard scoring 28 and Tim Hardaway 27, the Heat escaped with a 91–85 victory.

We needed to win Game 4 at home to force a winner-take-all Game 5 in Miami, and we were in control, leading by 5 with twenty seconds left, when another fight broke out that changed the series. This time it was Larry Johnson and Mourning, two former teammates in Charlotte who had left on bad terms. Now, in front of our bench, they were squaring off and throwing punches. I immediately grabbed hold of Mourning to serve as—what else?—a peacemaker. Seriously, that's what the league wants the players who are already in the game to do. If you're on the bench, stay on the bench. If you're in the game, break up the fight. I was just following the rules.

As I was trying to pull Zo away, Jeff Van Gundy fell and was holding on to Mourning's leg. It was crazy. And it was funny. Riley escorted Mourning off the court, and it looked like Riley was making the same face he had made in 1995 when Reggie Miller scored 8 points in 8.9 seconds. He looked sick to his stomach because he knew Alonzo would be suspended for Game 5. L.J. also couldn't play, but the loss of Mourning was comparatively much bigger.

On May 3, we went down to Miami Arena and crushed the Heat, winning 98–91 in a game that never felt that close. I had 18 points, 13 rebounds, and even got up for a dunk late in the second half. I didn't get many of those. It was a big moment for us, to upset a higher-seeded team without our All-Star center.

We advanced to face the Indiana Pacers, who had home-court advantage, and we still didn't have Larry for Game 1, because he was serving a two-game suspension. We lost that game. Ewing, who hadn't played since December, returned for Game 2 on May 7. When you haven't played for nearly five months, it's impossible to show up in the playoffs and think you can make an impact. Ewing shot 3-for-11 in twenty-seven minutes, and the Pacers defeated us 85–77. Honestly, Patrick hurt us more than he helped us; he shot 20 for 56 in the series, which we ended up losing in five games.

For the fourth straight season we were eliminated in the second round. We were still a good team, but losing in the second round wasn't going to cut it. When the results don't change, the players change.

Six weeks after we were eliminated by the Indiana Pacers, I received the call from Ernie Grunfeld saying that I was being traded to the Toronto Raptors. After ten years with the New York Knicks, my services would no longer be needed.

13 | BARKLEY AND HIS BIG MOUTH

There are three players that basketball fans seem to naturally associate me with. The first two are obvious: Michael Jordan and Patrick Ewing. I was teammates with both Hall of Fame players, and I spent the best years of my career with them. Michael Jordan has been my friend since 1985. I made it to the NBA Finals with Patrick and made the All-Star team with him in 1994.

The other player I always seemed to be connected to is Charles Barkley. And I'm not too crazy about that.

I'll admit we do share some common ground, starting with our first names and the fact that we both have ties to Alabama. Barkley is from Leeds, Alabama, which is approximately 160 miles northeast of York, where my grandparents lived. I'm better looking, but we both wore number 34. He's ten months older than me, and we played the same position, power forward. Who knows, maybe we clash because we're so much alike.

I'll also keep it real with you—Charles Barkley is a great player. The man could shoot and dribble and he was explosive. In fact, for his size you could make the case that he's the number one power forward of all time. See, I can say nice things about him.

When it comes to power forwards, Kevin McHale had a lot of skill, Tim Duncan is an all-time great, and Karl Malone was great, too. But Karl flopped a lot. Dennis Rodman got rebounds, but he couldn't score, and I don't put him up there with Barkley, McHale, Duncan, and Malone. Rodman was also afraid of me: when he was with the Detroit Pistons and I was on the Bulls, he was one of those guys who waited for me to leave before he started hitting Michael.

When I first got into the league, Barkley and I had mutual respect for each other. Barkley handed out a lot of compliments early on. He said that I went after rebounds like they were "raw meat." He called me the strongest player he'd ever faced. (That statement was made before Shaquille O'Neal came into the league.)

Even after a little dustup we had when he played for the Sixers and I was with the Knicks, things weren't so bad. Barkley said he wouldn't mind playing with me and Ewing in New York. He called us good friends and said that "we're going to remain good friends long after our careers are over."

It's a nice thought, but that's not exactly how things turned out.

How did things go wrong with me and Charles Barkley?

Let's start with his big mouth. It always gets him in trouble. This is more recent, but it's a good example: In 2017 he went after LeBron, calling him a whiner. When LeBron heard it, his response was "What makes what he says credible? Because he's on TV?" I chimed in with a tweet that Barkley needed to "stop drinking at work." A few years ago, Barkley criticized Michael in his role as owner of the Charlotte Hornets. That was a big mistake, because today Barkley isn't close with Michael anymore and that bothers him. Well, that's too bad. I'm sure he misses smoking cigars and playing thirty-six holes of golf with Michael, but those days are over. That same mouth of Barkley's, the one that pissed off LeBron and hurt his friendship with Michael, played a role in my problems with him as well. We all know that Barkley's job is to talk, and TNT pays him a lot of money to do just that. But there comes a time when the man needs to shut up.

The first time me and Barkley got into it was on March 24, 1987, in Chicago when I was on the Bulls. There was some pushing and shoving. Coach Doug Collins stepped in and got me over to the bench. It wasn't really much. And no one was at fault. The NBA is physical, and sometimes players reach their boiling point. That's perfectly understandable.

In 1988–89, my first year with the Knicks, we swept Barkley and the Philadelphia 76ers in the first round of the playoffs. The series was physical, and after the three-game sweep Barkley said that I should be charged with "assault and battery." Why, because we beat his ass? It was a typical series. A lot of shit happens. Get over it.

Things changed a little when Barkley got traded to the Phoenix Suns after the 1991–92 season. It meant I only faced him twice a year; once at home, once on the road. He gave me a cheap shot—a slap to the face in 1994—during a game in Phoenix, but it wasn't anything hard. Neither of us got suspended by the league.

Our biggest on-court fight took place during a preseason game on October 25, 1996, when Barkley was with the Houston Rockets. It started when Barkley's teammate Clyde Drexler drove down the lane and came up short on a floater as my teammate Patrick Ewing contested the shot. I was guarding Barkley, who got inside position and grabbed the rebound. He wasted no time trying to score on a putback, but Patrick recovered and blocked it. Barkley grabbed the rebound over his right shoulder, but I was also in position to grab the ball. He was a little off balance, and as I yanked to wrestle the ball free, his momentum caused both of us to fall backward. He landed pretty hard on his back and immediately got up and approached me.

On a play like that—two guys falling hard to the floor—you always have to be prepared for the fallout. Barkley tried to shove me, and I responded by throwing a punch, which luckily for him didn't connect. We were quickly separated. Patrick and Mario Elie, the Rockets' forward, grabbed me while our two New York Knicks that had been added to the roster just a few months earlier, Larry Johnson and Allan Houston, restrained Barkley.

"There is no question what happened, punches were thrown," the late John Andariese said on the Knicks telecast for MSG Network.

"I would think the call would be that they both would have to be ejected," said Marv Albert, the Hall of Fame broadcaster.

Marv was right about that. By 1996 the NBA had outlawed fighting, and the veteran referee, Joey Crawford, threw us both out. This was long before replay review. It was an automatic ejection, and Joey, a no-nonsense guy from Philadelphia, didn't take shit from anyone.

On the MSG Network telecast, Andariese took my side. When Marv Albert said that Barkley wouldn't appreciate what happened because he had back issues, John responded by saying that the way Barkley jumped to his feet to go at me showed that his back was feeling just fine.

"I can understand Charles Barkley's point of view," Marv said. "The play was over. He took him down. That's a little over the edge."

A little over the edge. That's one way of putting it. When you make your living in the NBA fighting for rebounds and diving on the floor for loose balls, sometimes you have to be a little over the edge. Not everyone is the superstar. I once told the New York writers covering the team that I was like a butler in a mansion. I did the dirty work. I cleaned up and made sure everything was all right. That was my job description. That's what I got paid to do.

Barkley was a typical wiseass after the game, telling reporters: "They tell me people on steroids have mood swings." The reporters tried to bait me into a war of words. All I said was that Barkley has been talking since he came into the NBA and he hadn't stopped since.

I ended up with a two-game suspension and Barkley got one. NBA commissioner David Stern wasn't happy with our behavior. He said, "The more things change the more they stay the same." That's a cliché, but with us it was pretty accurate.

That night in Houston was our last on-court scuffle. We only faced each other three more times before Barkley retired after the 1999–2000 season. He was yelling shit from the sidelines in a few games. He mentioned some bullshit about steroids, then he said to some reporters in Houston: "I told [Oakley] 'I'm going to keep torturing you until you apologize.'"

I wasn't going to apologize for anything. I wasn't the one talking. He was the one running his mouth. He was trying to insult me and get cute with reporters. He made it personal. That's what led to our infamous altercation inside a Manhattan high-rise office building in 1999. I had recently been traded away by the Knicks, but New York was still my city. That was my home turf.

When I was traded to the Toronto Raptors for Marcus Camby on June, 24, 1998, it was only the start of what would be an eventful time, not only for me, but for all NBA players. Six days later, the league imposed a work stoppage. It was the beginning of the 1988–89 lockout.

NBA commissioner David Stern wasn't playing around. He shut down teams: no trades and free agent signings until the owners and the players worked out a deal on how to divide roughly $2 billion in annual revenue. The NBA and the owners were ready to kill the season completely, and a lot of the younger players were afraid of losing their money. The NBA figured they could break the Players Association, and we started to show cracks early on. Our leverage was also significantly decreased, because even though he didn't officially announce it until January 1999, everyone pretty much knew that Michael Jordan was going to retire for the second time in six years, after Phil Jackson resigned as head coach of the Bulls the day before I was traded to the Raptors.

In October 1998, with the lockout ongoing and the start of the season well delayed, we held a Players Association meeting in Las Vegas. Patrick Ewing was the head of the association. He spent most of the off-season at the negotiating table, which was admirable but ended up taking a toll on him physically, since he didn't have time to stay in shape. It's not crazy to think that the Achilles injury he suffered in 1999 once we finally got back to playing was the indirect result of that. In so many ways Patrick was hurt the most by the work stoppage.

Our meeting in Vegas was at Ceasars Palace, and in retrospect, the whole thing wasn't a smart choice. It's difficult to get fans to feel badly for players when we're hanging out on the strip. Two weeks later, Kenny Anderson, who was playing for the Boston Celtics, told the *New York Times* that things were so tough "I might have to sell my Mercedes." We were not winning the public relations battle.

That same month, October, the Players Association decided to bring in the heavy artillery into a meeting with the owners. Michael Jordan wasn't yet retired, technically, and he was one of about one hundred players in the room. In a now-famous story, Jordan got into it with Abe Pollin, the late owner of the Washington Wizards, who was seventy-five at the time. Pollin talked about struggling financially to keep his team. Michael finally said, "If you can't make it work economically, you should sell your team."

It got real heated. Pollin got angry, and I swear it looked like he was about to call MJ every name in the book. Even Jerry Colangelo, who owned the Phoenix Suns, looked at him and said, "What are you doing?"

It was a stressful time for everybody, and I got dragged into it when the Players Association decided to play a charity game in Atlantic City in December 1998. They were trying to get as many big names as possible to raise money, mostly guys from the Dream Team. Of course, they wanted Michael to come, but he didn't play. Barkley did show up. As usual, he started running his mouth. The New York reporters all made the trip, and they were eating up everything Barkley said. Knowing that me and Barkley didn't get along, the media asked him for his thoughts on the Knicks trading me to Toronto for Camby.

"That's an upgrade," Barkley said.

Barkley then approached Patrick and said in front of the reporters: "[Oakley] was a hard worker, right? That tells you all you need to know about his game when all people can say is that he works hard."

Those quotes were in every New York newspaper: the *Daily News*, the *Post*, the *Times*, *Newsday*. Those comments got back to me quickly, and I didn't appreciate it. If he thought he was tough, he should have been tough enough to say it to my face instead of insulting me to the media.

So I waited for the day in January when we were going to vote on the collective bargaining agreement at the GM Building in Manhattan. Things nearly got out of hand the night before. Jayson Williams, who was playing for the New Jersey Nets, was worried that players might be getting screwed in the deal by David Falk, the agent who represented Patrick and Michael. Jayson was concerned because a lot of players with positions in the union, including Alonzo Mourning and Juwan Howard, were all represented by Falk. He wanted to make sure we were getting a good deal for everyone as opposed to a deal that was just good for Falk. I was with Jayson, 100 percent.

The night before the vote, I was at a club in the city with Jayson and we ran into Juwan and Alonzo. It was a crazy night. Derek Jeter was there and a couple of guys from the New Jersey Devils, Jason Arnott and Patrik Elias. Jayson ended up having words in the bathroom with Juwan and Alonzo. Jayson swears that the two hockey players, who were his friends, took their teeth out and were ready to fight. I don't know if that's true, but everyone was on edge.

Jayson's plan for the next day was to recruit some local players as well as some stars, including Hakeem Olajuwon, to make sure we had a voice in the room. We were told to wear suits and meet at a hotel across the street from the GM Building early in the morning, ahead of the vote. Of course, Anthony Mason showed up late wearing a black mink coat with his number 14 on the back. Jayson went crazy. We wanted to look professional and send the right message to the league, the owners, and Falk's people.

"We look like superheroes," Jayson was saying as we walked across the street. The first person we saw was Miami Heat forward P. J. Brown, who I had battled against for three straight seasons. Jayson gave him a big hello and hugged him. But I had my game face on. I told Jayson, "Don't shake this motherfucker's hand. He's the enemy."

There were a little more than three hundred players inside the GM Building for the vote, but one of the people I encountered right away was, guess who, Charles Barkley.

He was leaning against the wall outside the conference room where the meeting was taking place. There were a few players standing between us: Derrick Coleman, Anthony Mason, Hakeem Olajuwon, and Chucky Brown, but I was only focused on one person. I wanted payback for the comments he'd made about me to the media.

"I see Oakley coming, so I'm looking at Oakley, and it looks like he's looking at me," Chucky Brown later said. "Barkley's standing right over [there]. Oakley and I had gotten into something on the court. I'm thinking I don't want to fight this dude, but if I gotta do it I gotta do it."

I didn't want Chucky Brown. I wanted the other CB. I felt Barkley had it coming to him, and all these years later I still feel the same way.

"What was this shit you were saying?" I told him.

Barkley didn't respond. He just looked at me. Here was his chance to insult me face-to-face and he stayed silent. I didn't. I slapped him with an open right hand. I told him to "keep my name out your mouth," and that "the next time you say something about me you better have gloves on because there is only one Charles in this town."

Barkley didn't do anything. Nothing at all. And that was it.

The meeting went on, we voted on a new contract, and Charles Barkley kept quiet in the back of the room.

To this day, Barkley denies that we got into it. Years later he was quoted saying, "We never had a confrontation in public." What? Over one hundred people witnessed it.

He also goes around saying that he doesn't understand why I hate him over something that happened twenty-five years ago.

"Every two years, somebody will play me an interview of him bashing me and I kind of just laugh," Barkley said.

Though I stand by my actions that day, today the way I see it is that it happened in 1999 and it's over. I did what I felt I needed to do. We have been civil around friends in the time since. In 2015, I was in Atlanta when the Hawks presented Dominique Wilkins with a statue. Dr. J, Julius Erving, was there. Karl Malone, Bernard King, Clyde Drexler, Kevin Willis, Dikembe Mutombo, and even the former heavyweight boxing champion Evander Holyfield. I actually spoke to Barkley at the ceremony. We sat at a table and spoke. It was the right thing to do for 'Nique, as I call Dominique.

"We went to it," Barkley told the media a few years ago. "Dominique Wilkins got a statue and we sat at the same table and talked the whole time."

Maybe I'm mellowing just a little. I wasn't calm back in 1999, especially with the NBA season in jeopardy. But that day we reached an agreement to end the lockout and play a shortened fifty-game season. It would begin the first week of February. And it was going to be a much different season for the NBA, as well as for myself.

Michael Jordan was retiring yet again, and I was leaving the country.

14 | FIVE MINUTES FOR FIGHTING

There were a few problems with being traded to the Toronto Raptors. After the initial shock wore off, the trade itself didn't bother me. I was thirty-four, ten years older than Marcus Camby. Younger doesn't always mean better, but I understood what the Knicks were trying to do. Getting traded is part of the business. I'd been through it before, and it was out of my control. Why fight it?

The first problem was actually entering the country. Canada traded for me, but the country wouldn't let me in.

When I drove to the Canadian border in January 1999, after we reached the deal to end the lockout, I didn't have the necessary paperwork. Border patrol started asking me all kinds of questions. I told them I was moving to Toronto to play for the Raptors and that the NBA's fifty-game lockout shortened season was about to start. But they wouldn't listen. All they knew and saw was that I was this big Black guy in a BMW that was filled with clothes, and I didn't have the proper documentation.

After a few hours of debating at the border, I called my business manager at the time, Billy Diamond, and told him: "I'm turning around and going home." Billy told me not to go that far, so I drove to Buffalo to find a gym to work out, while he called Glen Grunwald, the Raptors' general manager. Within twenty-four hours, I had my papers and the border police waved me in. I stayed at the Royal York Hotel in downtown Toronto at first, until I found a permanent place, and that's where I discovered the second problem: no ESPN.

I couldn't find basketball highlights anywhere. The only thing on television in Toronto was hockey. Every day and night it was the same thing; hockey, hockey, hockey fights, more hockey, and a few French-language programs.

I felt out of place. I could see that Toronto was a world-class city, but it didn't feel like the NBA to me. I wasn't sure how it would work out.

Thankfully, it didn't take too long for me to fall in love with the town, the culture, and the people. The fans in Canada were great to me and still are today. I've spent a lot of time in Toronto since retiring, and the Raptors organization invited me back for the 2019 NBA Finals. The city and the franchise had come a long way. I never would have thought it was possible twenty years earlier.

The Toronto Raptors had entered the league at the start of the 1995–96 season as an expansion team. By the time they acquired me, they were building a team around two young budding stars, twenty-year-old Tracy McGrady and twenty-two-year-old Vince Carter. Tracy had come right from high school and was taken with the ninth overall pick in the 1997 NBA Draft. Vince, who had played for Dean Smith at North Carolina, was the fifth overall pick the following year. In fact, Vince was drafted on the same day the Knicks traded me to the Raptors for Marcus Camby.

My main job with Toronto was the same one I'd had in Chicago and New York: protect the stars. The guy Vince was being compared to, Michael Jordan, was dead serious all the time, but Vince liked to play around a lot, which was refreshing. (If you watched *The Last Dance*, you would think Michael joked around, but that wasn't the case. It was Michael's show, so you saw what he wanted you to see.)

We also had a few good veterans on that team: Dee Brown, Doug Christie, and Kevin Willis, who like me was a power forward entering his thirteenth season in the league.

We had a terrific coach in Butch Carter, who was not related to Vince Carter. He is, however, the older brother of Hall of Fame wide receiver Cris Carter. Butch was a tough coach who knew X's and O's. He's one of the best I've been around. We had all these team meetings before training camp, and I had one with the veteran players where I told them we had to do everything we could to make this work around Tracy and Vince.

In the last thirty years, the best one-two punch in the NBA has been Michael Jordan with Scottie Pippen. I would rank Shaquille O'Neal and Kobe Bryant second. Vince Carter and Tracy McGrady had the potential to be in that class. They got along great, and Butch knew how to keep both of them happy.

Our season opener was February 5, 1999, and eleven days later the Raptors visited Madison Square Garden. I was looking forward to seeing my old Knicks teammates. The New York media was wondering if I would cry like the former New York Ranger Mark Messier did in 1997 when he returned with the Vancouver Canucks for his first game back in the Garden. They liked my response: "I'm six-foot-nine; he's only six-four. He won a Cup for them. I just brought the Knicks a glass of water."

The fans were incredible. They gave me a huge ovation when I was introduced, which meant a lot to me. Ewing told the media that I'd watched his back for ten years, which was true. I still didn't shake hands with any of the Knicks before tip-off, because that wasn't my thing. I did, however, instinctively look to the Knicks bench for the coach to call a play at one point in the first quarter when the ball went out. I looked directly at Jeff Van Gundy and held up my hand for a play. Jeff laughed as he turned toward the Knicks trainer Mike Saunders, who also noticed my mistake.

The Knicks did something embarrassing as well. The team decided to play a video tribute to me, not while I was on the court, but instead while I was in the locker room at halftime. Someone said that Van Gundy didn't want it to get in the way of the preparation for the game, whatever that means.

"It was embarrassing," I told reporters after the game. "They should have done it before the game. I appreciate it, but do it professionally. They always talk about being professional. I didn't see it. It was for the fans, not for me. It was special for the fans. I'll see it one day."

We lost to the Knicks 95–85 and began the season with five straight defeats. We still finished a respectable 23-27. It was a seven-win improvement over the previous season, which was saying a lot, given that the team had played thirty-two more games that year.

The Knicks also had a rough regular season, finishing eighth, but made up for it in the playoffs when they went all the way to the NBA Finals before losing to the San Antonio Spurs in five games. I went to a few playoff games at the Garden, and they showed me on the giant scoreboard. All I ever got from the New York fans was love.

Even after trading me, the Knicks still had a veteran team. Our stars on the Raptors were young, and young guys have to learn how to win—they rarely pick it up right away. So that off-season we added Antonio Davis and Dell Curry, two more solid veterans. Dell would always have his wife, Sonya, and their kids hang around after practice. There were plenty of times when the eleven-year-old Steph Curry played Vince Carter one-on-one at the end of practice. Even back then Steph was hitting half-court shots. I should have known something big was going to happen to him because he was doing incredible things as a kid. His shot was gold.

We could have used Steph when we faced the Knicks in the first round of the 2000 NBA playoffs, at the end of my second season in Toronto. We'd had a great regular season, finishing 45-37, and it was the organization's first-ever trip to the playoffs, which was exciting and a huge accomplishment. We even had a chance to win both Games 1 and 2 at Madison Square Garden, but we failed to make plays down the stretch. We ended up getting swept. Things got worse for us that summer when McGrady left as a free agent and signed with the Orlando Magic. He was trying to create a super team by joining forces with another free agent, Grant Hill.

It was a big loss because Vince was becoming a star. At the 2000 All-Star Game in Oakland, Vince set the league on fire with that great performance in the slam dunk contest. After that, his confidence grew. As a team we were getting better. Young kids, especially in Toronto, were now following basketball because of Vince. We had the full support of not only the city of Toronto but really all of Canada. Even the hockey crowd appreciated us because we had a bunch of big, physical players.

We were developing a reputation as a team you couldn't push around. We hadn't accomplished anything significant yet, and it would be difficult to without the talented Tracy McGrady, but gaining a reputation as a tough unit was still important for our young team and young franchise, and I'd like to think I had something to do with that.

It was the summer of 2000, ahead of my third season with the Toronto Raptors, and I was hanging out in Washington, D.C. I called this woman whom I had been seeing. I'll just leave it at that. She was living in Charlotte, North Carolina. As we were talking on the phone I heard a voice in the background yelling, "Who are you talking to?"

I then heard this guy's voice scream: "Tell that nigga you don't want to talk to him. Get off the phone, woman!"

All I said was "Who is that?"

She told me it was her friend "Jeff."

That's all I knew: that it was a guy named "Jeff." He was now screaming at her to hang up the phone. I had no idea who Jeff was, but I was already thinking that maybe Jeff and I should have a little talk. So I jumped in my car and decided to take a trip to Charlotte. It's about a four-hundred-mile journey from D.C. to Charlotte, which is nothing for me. I drive everywhere, especially during the off-season.

I arrived at my friend's house in Charlotte at approximately 12:30 a.m. to see if "Jeff" was still hanging around. I wanted to give him an opportunity to speak to me face-to-face. My lady friend told me Jeff had left, which was definitely good for Jeff but bad for me. When I was later informed that this "Jeff" played in the NBA, I put two and two together and realized it was Jeff McInnis, the Los Angeles Clippers' twenty-four-year-old point guard. Charlotte was his hometown, and he was there for the off-season.

This was good news for me, because I had two games—one home and one away—against Jeff and the Clippers next season. The Clippers were scheduled to come to Toronto on December 1, and thirty-two days later we would play them at Staples Center.

For those who may not know this, normally for a game that starts at 7 p.m. or later, both teams will hold a short practice in the morning, which we refer to as a shoot-around. It usually takes place at the arena, though depending on the availability of the court, opposing teams may practice at a local gym. In today's NBA, a lot of teams have so-called "sleep doctors" or "sleep advisors" who feel that allowing players to get a full night of uninterrupted sleep is better than getting them up at 9 a.m. for a 10 a.m. shoot-around, so they no longer have a morning practice. Sounds ridiculous to me, but whatever. When I played for the New York Knicks, Pat Riley would have intense shoot-arounds. We would tape our ankles and sometimes go for as long as ninety minutes to two hours and then play the 7:30 p.m. game.

On December 1, 2000, the Raptors and the Clippers were each scheduled to hold a shoot-around at Air Canada Centre. The Clippers were scheduled for 10 a.m., and we had the court at 11 a.m.

I had a habit of walking out onto the court at 10:55. I would roll the ball on the court as a way to say "get the fuck off our floor." On this day, I was a little late. It was 10:57 when I made it to the court. I saw Jeff McInnis sitting there, which was perfect. I gave him a chance to make an exit before the clock struck 11, or in his case, midnight. So at 11:01 I made a straight beeline toward McInnis and punched him. One shot. That did the trick.

Lamar Odom, who was a good player on that Clippers team and is something of a B-list celebrity for having married Khloé Kardashian in 2009, said to me, "You just hit my best friend."

"Fuck your best friend," I told him. "You want some of this?"

That's when all hell broke loose. Both teams were on the court, separating me from McInnis and Odom. There were no more punches thrown. But I got in trouble. The NBA did a quick investigation and announced before the game that I had been suspended for a total of three games without pay and fined $15,000. I was making $5.89 million that season in U.S. dollars, so that punch and the suspension cost me $220,000.

Alvin Gentry was the Clippers coach, and he was the one who informed the league about the fight just minutes after it happened.

"It was an incident that needed to be dealt with," Gentry said. "We tried to do it the proper way by just calling the NBA office and letting them handle it.

"You have to give hats off to Horace Balmer [senior vice president of NBA security] and Stu Jackson [senior vice president of NBA basketball operations] because they did handle it the right way. I have to think that at some point if it wasn't handled properly . . . somebody might have gotten hurt. I am not saying that we would have intentionally gone out there to try and hurt somebody, but if you have those two guys on the court. . . . Jeff McInnis is a very proud guy and a very competitive guy."

Alvin Gentry told the league the story and that was good enough. A few years later, after I had been traded, I ran into Alvin and cussed out his bitch ass. He was a straight pussy for doing that.

With me home watching the game and Vince Carter out for a third straight game with a left quadriceps injury, I thought we were in trouble. But the Clippers blew a nine-point lead in the final 1:22 of regulation, and we outscored them 11–2 in overtime. Jeff had a bad morning and worse evening; he went just 3-for-13. Our point guard, Mark Jackson, my old teammate from the Knicks, crushed McInnis. Mark had 20 points and 15 assists. My replacement, Kevin Willis, who was still going strong at thirty-six, finished with 19 points and 7 rebounds.

In the *Los Angeles Times*, McInnis was quoted saying that my Raptors teammates were asking him if he was okay because "they knew it wasn't right." Whatever. McInnis accused me of punching him while wearing a big ring on my finger. That's ridiculous. I certainly got fined an equivalent amount of money by the NBA to what would have purchased an expensive ring in Manhattan's Diamond District, but no, I was not wearing any jewelry when I punched McInnis. That was a clean shot with a bare fist.

The crazy thing is behind the scenes McInnis told a friend of mine that he knew some gangbangers and they would get me back in Los Angeles. But at the same time, he told reporters to call his attorney about the incident. A lawyer? Hilarious.

On December 5, Peter Vecsey of the *New York Post* wrote: "This isn't funny. McInnis has sworn revenge, told teammates he plans to get even with Oakley when the Raptors are in L.A. Jan. 2 for their rematch. The kid from Charlotte says he's going to have some gang members 'mess up' Oakley."

I had no idea if he had a gang or was in a gang, but he was certainly talking all this shit to me ahead of that meeting thirty-two days after our incident in Toronto. He said, "When you come to L.A., I've got people there. They're coming after you." A lot of guys talk shit. But I was ready for anything. I brought my own gang to Los Angeles for the rematch. I had seven of my friends wear black suits. I told them just "be yourself and don't say anything to him. Just wait for me." We lost the game, but in the fourth quarter McInnis got hurt, went to the locker room, and never came back. The game ended, I showered, and walked to the bus. Nothing happened.

One month later I did bump into Lamar Odom during All-Star Weekend in Washington, D.C. The Players Association books a hotel every year for players who aren't in the game but want to attend the festivities. I was waiting for the elevator at the hotel, and when it stopped on my floor, the door opened, and there was Lamar with maybe five other guys. I stepped on. He looked at me, and I said right to him, "Somebody needs to get off. You can wait for the next one."

He didn't say a word back. He just walked off the elevator. I was in, and he was out. That was that.

Like I said, some guys like to talk shit. And some guys run and hide. But I eventually catch them.

It was that same 2000–2001 season when my feud with Philadelphia 76ers forward Tyrone Hill became public and eventually played out during our second-round playoff series with the Sixers.

A lot of players, myself included, like to gamble: cards, dice, dominos, you name it. After practice we would take wagers on trick shots from half court or seated in the front row. It wasn't crazy money. A few hundred dollars here, a few thousand there. It's fun. It's a way for teammates to bond, build chemistry, and make a little money—if you're good at it. Or maybe I should say if you're lucky. Some guys are; other guys, not so much.

Tyrone Hill was neither good nor lucky.

Tyrone was a little like me, a power forward from the state of Ohio. He attended Xavier University in Cincinnati and was a first-round pick of the Golden State Warriors in 1990. He went eleventh overall. That was the year when Derrick Coleman went first and Gary Payton was the second pick. Toni Kukoc was a second-round pick. Out of the fifty-four players drafted in 1990, only Gary Payton was inducted into the Hall of Fame. Tyrone Hill had a solid career. He averaged 9.4 points and 8.6 rebounds over fifteen NBA seasons. He was a good role player who made the All-Star Game once and was on the Philadelphia 76ers in 2001 when Allen Iverson carried them to the NBA Finals. Iverson was named league MVP, but the Sixers lost to Shaquille O'Neal and Kobe Bryant in the NBA Finals. That Sixers team had Iverson, Dikembe Mutombo, and a few more role players, like George Lynch, Eric Snow, and Aaron McKie. Hill earned $51 million in his career, which is pretty good. It was also the reason we had an issue.

It started in the summer of 1999, when me, Tyrone, and a few other guys were playing cards and dice in Atlanta. I knew Tyrone a bit through his former Cleveland Cavaliers teammate Bobby Phills. Tyrone and Bobby were on that Cavs team that the Knicks swept in 1996. Tyrone was losing big, and he asked me if I could lend him some money. So I gave him $20,000 and figured he was good for it. For the 1999–2000 season his salary was $6.4 million. For the

2000–2001 season he was scheduled to make $7.4 million. He could easily cover $20,000. Or at least I thought so.

A year passed and he still hadn't paid me back. He hadn't called me or written me. I wasn't looking for interest on the original $20,000. I'm not a loan shark. I just wanted my $20,000. I decided I'd waited long enough, and was going to be more proactive.

It was October 2000 and we were in Chapel Hill, North Carolina, for a preseason game against the Sixers. The game was a big deal because Vince Carter had played for Dean Smith at UNC. Philadelphia 76ers head coach Larry Brown had been a Tar Heel under Dean Smith as well.

There was a lot of focus on Vince at this time. "I'm not here to put on a show," he said before the game, in his typically humble way. "I'm here to get better and to win. I've learned not to get caught up in that."

Well, Vince put on a show. He scored 38 points and had a windmill dunk that brought the house down. He gave the fans what they wanted. And if Vince was the main event, you could say that I had been the warm-up act.

Before the game, all I was thinking about was Tyrone Hill and getting my money. When both teams took the court about ten minutes before tip-off, I decided to join the Sixers layup line. It looked strange to some, but preseason NBA basketball can be casual at times. Old friends and teammates tend to have short conversations before games. Tyrone was never my teammate and he definitely wasn't my friend. Eventually we were standing nearby each other and I could tell Tyrone was trying to avoid me.

"Where's my money?" I asked him.

"Dawg, I don't have it. I'm going through a divorce—" he started telling me.

I interrupted him and shot back: "Divorce? Who married your ugly ass anyway?"

So we got into it. I shoved him in the face with both hands. Everybody rushed over to separate us and we were ejected.

Former NBA player Brendan Haywood, who spent most of his career with the Wizards and the Mavericks, was a college player at the time at UNC and was there to watch the game. The way he describes it is that he saw me walk through everyone on the 76ers team, and they "parted the way like the Red Sea. [Oakley] walked over to Tyrone Hill with his finger pointed. When Tyrone pushed Oak's finger out of the way, he slapped the fire out of him. He slapped him in the face like Charlie Murphy in the Dave Chappelle show. So, I know Oakley don't play. Especially if you owe him money or with any type of disrespect."

Not only did I not get my money, I was fined $1,000, which made it a losing effort. But I wasn't giving up.

The Sixers and the Raptors were both in the Atlantic Division, which meant we'd have two home games and two road games against them during the season. Our second trip to Philadelphia was January 21, 2001, and on that night somebody sent flowers to me in the locker room. It's not uncommon for fans to do that. With the flowers in my locker, I took out a piece paper and wrote a note to Tyrone telling him that I was still here looking for my money. I had the ball boy deliver the flowers and the note to the Sixers' locker room. According to the ball boy Tyrone got the flowers, read the note, and took off. I didn't have my money, but I think he was starting to get the message.

When the Sixers came to Toronto for the next game, on April 3, I made sure I was on the floor for the morning shoot-around. I arrived at around 10:55, as I liked to do, spotted Tyrone, and hit him in the face with the basketball. Larry Brown got nothing out of Tyrone Hill that night—he was 0-for-6 in thirteen minutes and we won by 15. But I got a $10,000 fine plus a one-game suspension. I was *losing* money in the process of chasing Tyrone for my money.

And my coach, Lenny Wilkens, wasn't happy. "If it's a personal thing or something that needs to be settled, it shouldn't be brought to the court," Wilkens said. But I didn't care. It was worth it. I did what I thought was right.

Then, as fate would have it, we drew Philadelphia in the second round of the 2001 playoffs. We advanced by beating the Knicks in the first round, after trailing 2–1 in the series. It's true that the Knicks weren't really the Knicks anymore: Ewing had been traded to the Seattle SupersSonics in September 2000 in a blockbuster four-team deal, and Larry Johnson had injured his back in March, so he wasn't available for the series. But that didn't make it any less sweet. As an organization, it was our first-ever playoff series win, and against the team that had swept us the year before. Personally, what made it special was winning the series in Game 5 at Madison Square Garden. I never beat the Bulls in a playoff series after they traded me, but I got some revenge against the Knicks in 2001.

Our expansion franchise was now four wins from reaching the Eastern Conference Final. Philadelphia had home court advantage and they were the clear favorites, but we felt we had a shot. Vince was already a star. It wouldn't be easy, but winning a second-round series the year after Tracy McGrady left as a free agent was an accomplishment we thought we could achieve.

This was a good time for us. We had eliminated the Knicks. And I was getting my money.

A few games into the series the media got wind that me and Tyrone had a problem that ran deeper than just a basketball rivalry. On the morning of Game 5, with the series tied at 2–2, reporters asked me questions about our relationship. They said that every time we played the two of us would talk shit. One guy asked me if I was playing mind games.

"There are no mind games," I told the reporters in Philadelphia. "He's playing mind games with me. He owes me. That's his own mind. I don't play mind games. I'm for real. Like I told him, he better be glad it's the NBA playoffs."

They had heard rumors that Tyrone owed me money—a lot of money—so they bit on my statement that "he owes me."

"If it's ten, twenty, thirty dollars, he owes me and that's what it's about," I told them. "He's trying to say it's about something else. That's dumb. . . . I gave him many chances. He knows what's up."

I heard after the fact that Larry Brown found out why I was after Tyrone and told Tyrone to pay me. Maybe I owe Larry Brown some money, because we split Games 5 and 6, and then before Game 7, Tyrone came to my hotel to finally settle our financial disagreement.

I called him a "coward," and I asked, "Where my interest at?" just to see his reaction. But he did pay me and apologize.

On the morning of our Game 7 against Philadelphia, the biggest game in the franchise's history, Vince Carter was in Chapel Hill, North Carolina, for college graduation.

Vince had left school after his junior year and completed his undergraduate work over the summer of 2000. But he had already missed walking with his graduating class in 2000, and he could have waited another year to attend the ceremony.

"This is a special time for me, an important time for me," Vince had said about going to Chapel Hill on the morning of Game 7. "Now that this day is here, I'm feeling better and better about it. This is something I had to do for me, regardless of what other people say about it, because it's something I wanted to do, something I had to do.

"It's something I'm going to accomplish on top of playing in Game 7 and I think I'm mentally prepared for both."

According to the Associated Press: "About 20 minutes into the nearly two-hour ceremony, Carter got up, high-fived [former teammate Brendan] Haywood and was whisked away to [Raptors owner Larry] Tanenbaum's waiting jet for the flight to Philadelphia. He missed most of the speeches, including ESPN sportscaster Stuart Scott's commencement speech, and was not there for the ceremonial turning of the tassel."

Vince got back to Philadelphia on Larry Tanenbaum's plane about five hours before the game. A lot of guys were not happy about it, including Antonio Davis, Chris Childs (my old teammate whom we acquired from the Knicks in February for Mark Jackson), Muggsy Bogues, and me.

We lost Game 7 88–87, with Vince scoring 20 points on 6-for-18 shooting. He missed a desperation jumper at the buzzer that would have won it for us. I'm convinced we would have won if Vince hadn't gone to North Carolina on the day of the game.

As I said at the time, Vince is still our brother. It was important to him and his life. He made the right decision for him, but it wasn't a team decision. He came in, played a good game, but it's like a band member off-key. You know the difference.

The Sixers went on to beat the Milwaukee Bucks in the Eastern Conference Finals before meeting Shaq, Kobe, and the Lakers. Philadelphia won Game 1 on the road, but the Lakers won the next four for their second straight championship. Vince had a long and successful career. He played until he was forty-three, and his career ended when the NBA shut down during the coronavirus pandemic. But he didn't have much playoff success. He made it to one Eastern Conference Finals, with the Orlando Magic in 2010. His second most successful playoff run was with us in 2001, the year he graduated.

I was thirty-seven when we lost to Philadelphia in Game 7. I had 11 points and 10 rebounds that night and held Tyrone Hill to 6 points and 4 rebounds. I didn't realize it at the time, but it was the last playoff game of my career. It wasn't, however, my last run-in with Tyrone Hill.

The playoff series in 2001 should have been the end of it, but we still had a beef. A few years after I retired, we were back playing pickup in Atlanta, the same city where our problems started in 1999, and my team was killing his team, 10 to 4. He called "ball," meaning he was calling a foul on me.

"Fuck you," I said.

He said a few choice words back, and before you know it, I had hit him about three or four times. He called the manager of the gym and then the police showed up. There was soon a warrant out for my arrest. We eventually ended up in court, and the judge said that Tyrone was complaining of being bullied by me. Bullied? The judge didn't know what to do. My lawyer and his lawyer were trying to reach an agreement. The court was threatening me with one night in jail if we couldn't reach some type of understanding. They gave me a fifteen-minute recess to think about it, and the whole time I was telling my lawyer, "I can spend a night a jail. I know what jail looks like. I'm built for this."

In the end, I didn't spend a night in jail. Instead, I was issued a restraining order that required me to stay "500 feet away from Mr. Hill," as the court put it.

A few months later I was with Michael Jordan in Miami for South Beach Bike Week, and standing closer than five hundred feet from me was Tyrone Hill. Mike knew our history, generally speaking, and right away he issued a warning.

"Oak, please don't go near that man. Please," Michael said.

I told him not to worry. "I can't," I said. "He's got a restraining order against me."

"Restraining order?" Michael asked.

He couldn't believe it.

He just looked me and shook his head.

15 | THE REASON THEY CALLED ME OAK TREE

Two months after the Toronto Raptors lost Game 7 to the Philadelphia 76ers in the Eastern Conference Semifinals, I was kicked out of Canada. All right, it wasn't really that dramatic: on July 19, 2001, I was traded back to the organization where my career began, the Chicago Bulls. But there was a good amount of drama in Canada in the months leading up to it.

There were reports coming out that I wanted to be traded. That is false. I never went to management and told them to get me out of there. There were stories that the Washington Wizards wanted to acquire me now that Michael Jordan had unretired for a second time and was playing for Washington, where he was also a part owner of the team. But I never wanted to leave Toronto. It was the organization that decided to get rid of me, because I was outspoken and said some things that bothered the front office about Vince Carter and our head coach, Lenny Wilkens, during our 2001 playoff run.

We ended up winning that first-round series against the Knicks, but Vince shot 5-for-21 and scored just 20 points in Game 3, which we lost. He just about disappeared in the fourth quarter. When the reporters asked me if there was too much pressure on Vince, all I said was "All the plays go through Vince, so it's not too much focus on Vince. It's been there all year. You can't shy away from it now. This is the time you've got to step up and be a man about it. When they went to play for the Dream Team, he went. All twelve of us didn't go. When they do a commercial, we don't go, he goes. It's one of them things."

What was wrong about that? I stand by the idea that if you're the face of the franchise, it's up to you to deliver in playoff games. But of course, everybody focused on just three words: "be a man." And with two days off between Games 3 and 4, the story gained momentum. The media was having a field day.

"We should be supportive of our teammates, not critical," Lenny Wilkens said about me. "We need to tell them when they're not doing the job and encourage them. Oak's heart is in the right place, he may not say it right, but his heart is there."

Damn right my heart was in the right place. I said what I said to help the team, and help Vince. I never had a problem with Vince Carter. He visited my house all the time to watch television. I bought him clothes. I taught him how to be a pro. Vince and I were cool. This was the NBA Playoffs. What I was saying was that he needed to be the guy to carry us. He needed a little nudge, that's all. I felt it was important for Vince to understand that if we were going to advance out of the first round, it would be because of him.

When a small group of reporters from New York approached me prior to Game 4, I asked them: "What'd you think about what I said about Vince? Think I was too hard on him?"

They all said it wasn't a big deal, though I'm not sure any of them would have disagreed with me in that moment, out of fear that I would get upset. After all, this was a win-or-go-home scenario. Everyone in our locker room was on edge, which can be a good thing in the playoffs. It can make you dig to bring out your best.

And guess what? In Game 4, with our season on the line, Vince scored 32 points to force the series back to New York. And then, in the fifth and decisive game, on May 4, he played all forty-eight minutes and scored 27 points. The young guy came through for us. This was the biggest moment of his career up until that point. In the final minutes of Game 5 Vince made two crucial plays: he put back his own miss to give us a 4-point lead, and later he picked up a loose ball and assisted on Alvin Williams's jump shot, which sealed the win.

The first playoff series victory in the franchise's history led to a short trip down the New Jersey Turnpike to Philadelphia for Game 1 of the Eastern Conference Semifinals two days later. The momentum from the win against the Knicks carried over: we beat the Sixers 96–93 with Vince scoring 35 points in forty-seven minutes.

So you tell me, did the comments I made help or hurt the team?

Lenny Wilkens had replaced Butch Carter as the Raptors' head coach before the start of the 2000–1 season. Lenny Wilkens is a household name in NBA circles. He grew up in Brooklyn, attended Providence, and became a Hall of Fame point guard playing for the St. Louis Hawks, the Seattle SuperSonics, the Cleveland Cavaliers, and the Portland Trail Blazers. He was a nine-time All-Star and was named to the NBA's fiftieth anniversary all-time team. Lenny is also in the Hall of Fame as a head coach. He won an NBA Championship as the head coach of the Seattle SuperSonics in 1979. He then coached for some of the other teams he'd played for—the Trail Blazers and the Cavaliers—as well as for the Hawks, before coming to Toronto. He finished his career up with the Knicks, and retired with 1,332 wins and 1,155 losses. To me that's 1,000 wins and 1,000 losses. You're basically a .500 coach. Butch is a better coach than

Lenny Wilkens in my opinion. But Butch wanted more power, the ability to have some say in personnel, so the front office got rid of him after our loss to the Knicks in the 2000 playoffs. That was a mistake. If Butch were in the league today, he'd be a top five coach. Butch had a good read on our team. He did well to build everything around Vince Carter and Tracy McGrady, while also leaning heavily on the veterans. The players liked Butch. We had his back because he had our backs. He got our teams prepared for every game, and he was very good coming out of time-outs. I still don't understand why Butch can't get another chance. The same is true of my former teammate Mark Jackson, who coached the Golden State Warriors for three seasons starting in 2011. Mark's record is 121-109. How is it that some guys get second chances, but Butch Carter and Mark Jackson don't? It doesn't make sense.

By the time Lenny got to Toronto he was sixty-three years old. I didn't feel his heart was in the job. His battery was so low he couldn't jump a car. Lenny was on vacation in Toronto. He had done okay as a coach in Cleveland, Atlanta, and Seattle, but when he got to Toronto he was taking it easy. If we went on a road trip longer than five games, by the end of the trip he would just tell us "try your best." There wasn't a lot of preparation. I've been in the league and I've been around some of the best coaches. It's important to run defensive drills and learn different schemes. Pat Riley was a real student of the game. Jeff Van Gundy was Riley's protégé. Butch Carter was the same way. Wilkens was not.

We weren't prepared coming into our first-round series against the Knicks in 2001, and when we lost Game 1, a few of us, including myself and Antonio Davis, made those feelings public.

I told reporters that I was certain Jeff Van Gundy was preparing the Knicks better than Wilkens was preparing us. I said that Jeff was watching tape, drawing up plays, and "we didn't do that." I added: "I know the game and I know what that coach [Van Gundy] means over there and how hard he works." Then I directed a comment toward Wilkens: "Don't be mad and jealous because I'm speaking the truth."

Wilkens told the media that he wasn't offended, but I know the front office wasn't happy about it.

Antonio Davis then backed me up. "This is the first time I've gotten to the playoffs and there weren't meetings, with video, and two practices a day," he said. "In Indiana, as soon as we knew who we were playing, the next morning they came in, they broke down film, broke it up with the small guys in watching video and the big guys out on the floor. And then we switched. It took all day but that's the type of preparation we felt we needed. . . . We all knew our game plan."

Another thing that bothered me was that usually when you play the last game of a playoff series on the road, the coach will tell the team to pack enough clothes for their next series. It's a way of telling the players that you expect them to win. After we eliminated the Knicks, Lenny didn't really have much to tell us about Philadelphia. The series was starting in less than forty-eight hours. Either he hadn't thought we'd beat the Knicks or he just wasn't prepared for the Sixers. Maybe it was both. In fact, I drew up five plays for us to work on before Game 1. Lenny didn't appreciate that. We upset the Sixers in Game 1, and had a 14-point lead in Game 2, but Lenny sat me for a long time in favor of Jerome Williams and Keon Clark. I played twenty-eight minutes in Game 2 and was a plus-6 for the game. Every other player on our team was a minus.

Lenny was one of those guys who was going to give guys their usual minutes no matter what was happening in the game. I don't like that. My feeling was, if the other team's starters played forty minutes, ours should play forty minutes too. It's not about keeping guys happy. It's about trying to win every game and never letting up. I loved Pat Riley, but he made the same mistake. When the Knicks played the Bulls, the only times we got hurt were when we subbed and put our bench against their starters.

What I said about Vince needing to play better didn't make the front office happy, but I'll always believe it was criticizing Lenny during the 2001 playoffs that ultimately got me traded. Was I out-spoken as a player? Yes. But when I spoke, I did so because I wanted to help the team.

The Raptors and Lenny Wilkens didn't understand that, and decided it wasn't the case, even though we got to Game 7 of the second round. So they made a deal with Bulls general manager Jerry Krause and traded me to Chicago, where my career had started. That's why I keep telling people I never had a problem with Krause: he had a reputation as an elite talent evaluator, and he was responsible for bringing me to Chicago twice in my career. He also helped me get paid, because my contract in 2001 included an 11 percent trade kicker on top of my salary of $6.5 million. Jerry Krause was always loyal to me and I was always loyal to him.

"Oak's always been a joy to me because of the kind of person he is," Krause said on the day I returned to Chicago. "Charles is a natural born leader. He'll be great with our younger players. They're going to have to follow him because he will demand it and he'll get it done. He wants his teammates to play as hard as he does, and he's disappointed when they don't."

Unlike the Raptors, however, the Chicago Bulls were not a contending team. Not even close. And they weren't well coached. Lenny Wilkens was going through the motions in Toronto, but at least he had an impressive résumé. My new coach in Chicago, Tim Floyd, had no business being the NBA at all.

A lot had changed with the Chicago Bulls since my three sea-sons there in the 1980s. They had moved into a state-of-the-art practice facility, the Berto Center, in the early nineties, and they had then demolished Chicago Stadium and moved across Madison Street into the United Center in 1994. It was a much bigger building, and early on Michael Jordan complained that the sight lines affected his jump shot. After the Orlando Magic eliminated the Bulls in the second round of the 1995 playoffs, Jordan, on his way out of the arena, walked past the media room and said softly into the microphone, "They should burn this place down." Thirteen months later, Jordan was celebrating title number four at the United Center. He learned to play and dominate in the new building.

Both the United Center and the Berto Center were decorated with something else I didn't see when I played for the Bulls: six championship banners. If I had never been traded from the Bulls to the Knicks, I could have been a part of those teams. Okay, maybe they wouldn't have won six. Maybe they would have won more. Bill Cartwright, the center the Bulls acquired from the Knicks, was a solid player. He could score, rebound, and defend. But it also helps to have Michael Jordan. As long as he was healthy, no one was stopping the Bulls in the nineties. The Bulls had drafted Horace Grant and eventually moved me out. You can't argue with the results, but I know they would have been at worst the same, and at best better, if they had just kept me.

When I returned to Chicago prior to the 2001–2 season, the days of championships, playoff basketball, Michael Jordan, Scottie Pippen, and Phil Jackson were long gone. In the years after winning the 1998 championship on Jordan's last shot against the Utah Jazz, the Bulls had declined beyond recognition. They barely resembled an NBA team. Tim Floyd was the head coach handpicked by Krause to replace Jackson, a coach who had won six championships. Floyd was a college coach who had never coached in the NBA. He was inexperienced, and the roster he inherited lacked NBA-ready talent.

All the Bulls did during Floyd's first three seasons was lose. Starting with the lockout-shortened season in 1999, Floyd and the Bulls went 13-37, 17-65, and 15-67. The guy had won forty-five games over three seasons! I was realistic about the team I was going to. It was a rebuilding situation, and Krause obviously wanted me to be a veteran presence. I understood.

Over the summer the Bulls had also made a deal for Greg Anthony, my former teammate with the Knicks, who, after our loss to Indiana in 1995, had been selected by the Vancouver Grizzlies in the expansion draft. He eventually landed with the Portland Trail Blazers and was with the Blazers in 2000 when Portland blew a double-digit lead to Shaquille O'Neal, Kobe Bryant, and the Lakers in Game 7 of the Western Conference Finals.

Other than me and Greg, the Bulls had a lot of young players, including Ron Artest, Brad Miller, Marcus Fizer, Ron Mercer, and Fred Hoiberg. Jamal Crawford was entering his second season but got injured and played just twenty-three games. In the draft, with the second and fourth overall picks, Krause had selected two high school players, Tyson Chandler and Eddy Curry.

That was the same draft when Michael Jordan, who was now running the Washington Wizards, drafted Kwame Brown first overall. It was historic because Kwame was the first high school player to be drafted first. Michael probably gained a greater appreciation for the job Krause had done back in the eighties for the Chicago Bulls, because picking talent isn't easy. Kwame Brown was a bust. The third pick of the 2001 draft was Pau Gasol. The last pick of the first round was Tony Parker.

I didn't agree with Krause's decision to draft two young guys in Tyson and Eddy. Why take two guys out of high school in the top five who play the same position? I thought that was dumb. But I understood what my role was, and I was going to help out the rookies. Sometimes, that meant defending them.

Marcus Fizer was only in his second year in the NBA, but he

was always giving Tyson and Eddy a hard time. One day at practice he took it too far and I told him to stop messing with them. We got into it.

I told him: "If you keep talking shit to me, I'm going to slap you in the mouth."

"Fuck you, Oak. I thought you're supposed to be a leader," he said.

"I am. That's how you lead. You let people know they can't fuck with you."

I was trying to teach him what it meant to be a team player in the NBA, a young player, and where the line was drawn. But from the start, I could tell that Bulls team was a lost cause. Some people thought Ron Artest was the problem, but he wasn't, and it wasn't a mistake drafting him. People were speculating things like that he was off his meds in Chicago. But I didn't see any kind of unhinged side of him. All I saw was a guy who worked hard on his game, and played hard. He lived ten houses away from me and we got along. The real issue with the Bulls was that there just weren't enough veterans around to teach the younger guys, including Ron.

We lost our first two games of the season and got our first win on November 3, 2001, against the Knicks. I started, and scored 6 points with 8 rebounds, while both Anthony and Mercer scored 17.

But only two games later, our season imploded in Minnesota, where we faced a good Timberwolves team. The score after the first quarter was 34–14. By halftime we were trailing 68–36. The final score was 127–74. It was a disaster. Minnesota made 52 of 81 shots. We just sucked. When you lose by 53, it's beyond embarrassing. In fact, it was the worst loss in the franchise's history.

If you didn't know it then you knew it now: the Michael Jordan Bulls were officially dead.

"We couldn't beat a snappy junior high team with this group

tonight," Floyd told the media afterward. "What you saw was a pathetic effort—the young guys were pathetic, the old guys were pathetic. If we don't want to bring effort, 50-point losses are what should happen to us."

The reporters couldn't wait to tell me what Floyd had said. When they did, I felt I needed to stand up for the young guys, including the two rookies who had only been in the NBA for five games. A year ago, Tyson Chandler and Eddy Curry were in high school. Now they're being called out by a guy who to me wasn't an NBA coach. Early in the first half Floyd had subbed out all five players on the court at once. That's bullshit.

"You can't put five young guys in for five veterans," I told the Chicago media. "That ain't going to work. You don't make a move like that early in the season."

I was seething. I was upset that we lost. I was upset that I was part of a five-for-five substitution, and it annoyed me that Floyd decided not to play me in the fourth quarter. Nor did I understand why he canceled our morning shoot-around before the game. We clearly needed the extra work before facing Minnesota. Looking back, it's kinda funny to remember the reporters trying to write down everything I was saying. They couldn't keep up. I was on a roll.

"If we're not trying to win or get to the playoffs, we might as well just play young guys, sit everybody else on the bench, and get blown out by 50 every night," I said. "He's the coach. I'll express it to him. That's how I am, like it or not. They can trade me, but I'm going to speak my mind."

It became a big story in Chicago, and the team had no other choice but to penalize me. Jerry Krause hit me hard. He had the title of vice president of basketball operations, and he used that power to kick my ass where it hurts most: the wallet. I was fined $50,000 for what they called "conduct detrimental to the team."

"Charles's comments were completely inappropriate and out of line," Krause said.

Honestly, I don't regret anything I did. I was trying to show guys on the team, especially young guys, that you have to be accountable. Jerry Krause took Tim Floyd's side. I can't be mad at him. Jerry Krause brought me into the league, drafted me, and treated me like one of his kids. Sometimes your kids need to be spanked. But let's not avoid the real issue; we had a substitute bus driver coaching the team.

The following day we had practice back in Chicago and I got into it with Floyd. We were in a team meeting and he was wearing out the young guys, even though Tyson had only played twenty-two minutes and Eddy eleven in the loss. All I said was "These guys didn't lose the game. Talk to the starters."

When we sat down for a one-on-one meeting, he looked and me and said, "They said you're a tough guy to coach."

What was that supposed to mean? I didn't give a fuck what they said, whoever "they" were, and I also felt it was a lie. I told him "I'm still going to be Oak." In other words: I'm going to work hard, give everything I have, and I'm going to speak up when I think it's appropriate.

Tim Floyd came in trying to be the next Phil Jackson, which was impossible. He didn't have the talent or the respect of the players. It was different for Phil. He came up in the CBA, spent one year as an assistant under Doug Collins, and then took over. Most of the players didn't even know that Phil once played for the Knicks. As an assistant coach he was real quiet. He'd run us through drills and mostly kept to himself. It takes time to learn the league and gain the trust of the players. Phil went about it the right way. Everyone thinks he arrived as Dr. Phil. No, he was just Phil the coach. He knew his role, did it well, and grew with the job.

The media loved the story of me and Floyd going at it, because here you had a struggling coach and a player who wasn't afraid to stand up for himself. When the beat writers asked me about my issues with Floyd, I didn't back down.

"If Tim challenged our effort, you have to challenge the way he does things, too."

I told them I wasn't going to pull a Scottie Pippen and apologize for what I said. That wasn't going to happen. In another month I was turning thirty-eight years old. Maybe I was getting too old for the game. The situation was getting ugly. Floyd got his shots in as well. At one point during practice, he challenged me to coach the team. He knew he was losing the locker room, so the way he fought back was to go after me.

"I don't need any player's approval," Floyd said. "Not Charles Oakley or anybody else. . . . Guys that typically speak out usually are putting up big numbers. And I haven't seen those numbers from our guy."

My job isn't to put up numbers, so I don't know what he was talking about. The job of the coach is to prepare the team. He wasn't doing that. Look at the record.

That loss to Minnesota was part of a losing streak that included seven straight games on the road. We were traveling all over the country to get our asses kicked: Denver, Los Angeles, Sacramento, Golden State, Milwaukee, New York, and finally New Jersey. The losing streak reached ten with a 100–68 loss to the Nets on November 27. It wasn't even December yet, but at 1-12 our season was already over. After the Nets loss, K. C. Johnson of the *Chicago Tribune* asked me to sum up the road trip, and I gave him an answer that made him laugh.

"This ain't like a flat tire you can pull over to the side of the road and fix and keep on riding," I told him. "This is a blowout with no spare and nothing's open for a hundred miles. So we gotta do some walking."

By early December the Chicago newspapers were reporting that Floyd was stepping down. Krause and Floyd both denied it, but you could sense that change was imminent. Floyd said something about how the media expected him to quit but he wasn't a quitter. He said he would continue to try and make the team better. It was just words and empty promises. On Christmas Eve, the Bulls and Floyd decided to part ways. His record as head coach of the Chicago Bulls was 49-190.

"I have really tried to give my best effort and sometimes that's not enough," Floyd said. "I think it's going to provide hope for a lot of people that maybe this next coach could be the guy who can help the Bulls go to where they ultimately need to be."

Our assistant coach, Bill Berry, served as the interim coach for two games before Krause hired Bill Cartwright as the full-time coach. The player I had been traded for by the Bulls back in 1988 was now my new coach. I was happy for Cartwright. There were still some things that needed to be changed, but it wasn't going to happen overnight. Bill knew that and management knew that.

Cartwright coached the final fifty-five games of the season and went 17-38. Considering Floyd's record in Chicago, Cartwright did well. Our best win came against Cartwright's old coach, Phil Jackson, and the defending champion Los Angeles Lakers, on January 12, 2002. The game, a 106–104 Bulls overtime win, featured a fight between Shaquille O'Neal and Brad Miller that referee Danny Crawford called "a nasty situation." Of course, I made sure to get involved in that.

Shaq was big and powerful. And sure, he was tough. But there's a reason they called me "Oak Tree." I was hard to move, too. I didn't give easy layups. I liked playing against Shaq. People said he was a man among boys. Well guess what? I'm a real man. Most of the time Shaq was an 18-wheeler going up against a Volkswagen. He was seven-foot-one, 340 pounds. I'm also an 18-wheeler. You see the highlights of Shaq dunking on people and throwing the ball at them. Man, he knew I'd hit him in his big-ass head if he tried that on me. He knew he couldn't get away with some of that shit. It's like what Karl Malone said: "When you play the Knicks you worry about Oakley and Anthony Mason."

On the night of January 12, me and Brad Miller both fouled Shaq hard a few times and Shaq finally had it. He went after Brad from behind and threw a wild punch that barely missed.

I'm like FedEx. I'm always going to deliver. I jumped right in and went after Shaq. The whole scrum was right in front of our bench. Shaq was pulling Brad's jersey so tight that he was choking him. Brad ended up without his shirt on. I was grabbing Shaq and saying to him, "Are you serious?"

He was disrespecting me and my teammates. You ask anyone I've played with if I'm a good teammate, and they'll tell you. I don't play games. Shaq was wrong for doing what he did.

The league suspended Shaq for three games, Brad got one, and somehow I got two games. The first was for a flagrant foul and the second was for what I was told was accumulating too many flagrant-foul points. Who knew I led the league in "points"?

What I never liked is that Shaq was always complaining that he wasn't getting enough calls. A year earlier he said, "Now that I have a championship ring, let me say this: If I feel someone is trying to hurt me, I will take action. Foul me hard under the basket and I've got something for you. One day, somebody's going to foul me hard and I'm going to go crazy. I don't think the league knows that. I don't think they know that I will fight."

But that wasn't much of a fight. He was trying to hit Brad when Brad had his back turned.

"There's only so much a person can take as far as physical abuse," Kobe told reporters. "I'm not saying fighting is an option; it's a last resort.'"

Shaq really wasn't a fighter. But during the 2001–2 season, the Lakers—behind Shaq and Kobe—won their third straight title, and suddenly people were mentioning Kobe in the same breath as Jordan.

Me? My one season in Chicago was a disaster. I was one and done and heading to Washington to join my friend Michael for one last ride.

16 | THE LAST WALTZ

The biggest snowstorm to hit the East Coast in years wasn't enough to stop Michael Jordan's fortieth birthday party in Washington, D.C., in 2003. Everyone from Jay-Z, Beyoncé, and Michael Keaton, to Jasmine Guy and Robin Givens attended the party thrown by Michael's wife, Juanita Jordan, on February 15, two days before Michael officially hit the big four-oh.

The bash was held at Residences at the Ritz-Carlton in D.C.'s West End. It was a nice, expensive location with a doorman and full-time security. The place offered hotel services like housekeeping, room service, valet parking, and access to the Equinox Sports Club and a spa. There were plenty of power brokers, diplomats, and politicians among the residents. Two former Senate majority leaders, Harry Reid and Tom Daschle, once lived there, as did the director of the Kennedy Center, Michael M. Kaiser.

The building's most famous resident, however, was Michael Jordan. His presence gave the place cachet. In January 2000, Michael announced that he was joining the Wizards as a part-owner, with the title of president of basketball operations. This was Michael's chance to prove to Jerry Krause that Jerry wasn't the only executive who could build a winner.

Seventeen months later, the biggest move Michael had made was signing Michael Jordan. He was announcing that he was returning to play competitive basketball again and that he would donate his salary to victims of the September 11 terrorist attacks. Michael's first year with the Wizards didn't go well. The team finished 37-45 and failed to reach the playoffs. Michael lasted just sixty games and was finished for the season after tearing cartilage in his right knee.

Jordan didn't want to go out that way and decided to run it back. He announced that he was returning to play one final season with the Washington Wizards in 2002–3. That summer, in 2002, we were playing pickup in Chicago and Jordan asked me what my plans were for the season. I was a free agent and told him I didn't have a team but I wanted to play and I was ready to play.

Before you know it, I was back with Michael, living in the same swanky apartment building as him, after signing a one-year contract with the Wizards for the veteran's minimum of $1 million. I lived in a small suite; Mike owned an entire floor. Patrick Ewing was also living at the Ritz, after having retired as a player following the 2001–2 season. My last season with Ewing in New York was in 1997–98. His last season in New York was in 1999–2000, when the Knicks lost in six games to the Indiana Pacers in the Eastern Conference Finals. In Patrick's last game the crowd was groaning each time he touched the ball. They were growing tired of him, and apparently Patrick was growing tired of them.

In September 2000, the Knicks traded Patrick to the Seattle SuperSonics. It was one of those rare deals that didn't benefit either the Knicks or the Sonics. Patrick spent one season in Seattle alongside Gary Payton and Vin Baker and then finished his career with the Orlando Magic, who were coached by our former Knicks teammate Doc Rivers.

"This is one of the hardest decisions that I've ever had to make. I'm still torn," Ewing said when he retired. "It took me forever to say that I'm retiring from playing. I've been playing basketball so long, and I still enjoy doing it."

Ewing's next goal was to get into coaching, and with Michael's help, he landed a job on the Wizards' coaching staff which also included John Bach, Larry Drew, and Brian James. The head coach, of course, was Doug Collins, my old coach from the Chicago Bulls. By signing with the Wizards, I was reunited with Doug as well as two former teammates, Jordan and Ewing.

It was a little weird having Patrick as a coach because it was such a different role for him. Patrick was learning the ropes and understanding that there is a difference between being a player and being a coach. Me and Mike would go out to dinner after just about every game, and Patrick wanted to join our party. He was constantly asking us where we were going for dinner, and Michael was always giving him a hard time.

"You're a coach, you can't hang out with the players," Michael would tell Patrick. Man, it was nonstop. Michael would pick on Patrick like a tooth. Pat would get real salty at times. To me, it was funny.

Patrick did get an invitation to Michael's fortieth birthday party midway through that season in 2003. It was the place to be and been seen in D.C. The Ritz ballroom was transformed into "Club Jordan" to accommodate the three hundred guests. There were rumors that Juanita had tried to convince Michael Jackson to provide the entertainment, but settled for Funkmaster Flex, who had the party kicking. The party was catered, but Michael also wanted me to cook a few things for him.

The only downside to scheduling a party in February and inviting people from all over the country to come to Washington is you're taking a chance with the weather. As the day grew closer, there were reports of a major storm hitting the city. No one knew how big.

When the weekend of the party arrived, the entire East Coast was crushed by what meteorologists called the "Presidents' Day Blizzard." New York City and Boston got walloped with record-breaking snow. In D.C. we got over a foot, which for some reason the weathermen described as a "glancing blow." The storm's impact closed everything down and ultimately stranded the guests who had come from out of town at Michael's party.

From what I remember, only one person got out before the airport closed. I don't know how he pulled it off, but somehow he attended the party and avoided the blizzard. It was Donald Trump.

The future president of the United States was there with his future wife, Melania, and managed to have his private jet leave that night from Reagan National for Palm Beach, Florida. Trump came to a lot of our games when I was playing for the Knicks. I'd see him at all the big fights, but I had never cooked for him before Michael's party. Not a lot of people can say they cooked for Oprah, Michael Jordan, and the future president, all in one night.

When the *Washington Post* gossip reporter contacted Trump after the party, he was complimentary of his hosts, saying, "I never met Juanita before but she did a wonderful job with the party, and there was just great affection for Michael." And of course, when Trump was asked about his stealth exit, he bragged about being the only guest to beat the blizzard.

"We just missed it," Trump said. "We stayed until about twelve o'clock and got out of there just in time. There was a little snow, but about twelve minutes after we left, everything was just inundated. It wasn't a problem for us, but an hour later it was obviously a disaster."

As you can tell, he hasn't changed one bit.

Michael Jordan, on the other hand, had changed. He was still a great player, but at thirty-nine going on forty, he couldn't carry the Wizards like he had once carried the Bulls. No one was expecting a championship in Jordan's final season, but a playoff appearance was a realistic goal. At least that's what we thought. Maybe the problem was that Michael was still our best player even at his advanced age. Did guys defer to him too much? You can make a case for that being true. But Michael only wanted to win. He wanted what was best for the organization, but the roster was flawed.

Kwame Brown, whom Collins and Jordan drafted number one overall straight out of high school in 2001, was in his second season and still only twenty years old. Kwame was mostly used as a backup that season and averaged a modest 7.4 points and 5.3 rebounds per game. He did appear in eighty games, which ended up being a career high for him.

Larry Hughes was a talented wing player who was entering his fifth season. Jared Jeffries was a rookie from Indiana who in April 2002 had lost to our other rookie, Juan Dixon of Maryland, in the NCAA championship game. Brendan Haywood, the center out of North Carolina, was in his second season, and Etan Thomas was a power forward out of Syracuse. Tyronn Lue was a point guard who had won two championships as a player with the Lakers. Thirteen years later, Lue would coach LeBron James and the Cleveland Cavaliers to the NBA title.

We also had Christian Laettner, who had played at Duke and been Michael's teammate once before, on the Dream Team in 1992. You can guess which player Mike liked to get on. There was always some Duke-UNC debate going on. When the Dream Team was in Barcelona, there was a Ping-Pong table at their hotel, so of course Michael organized a tournament. The guy always needs to challenge someone at something. Jordan and Laettner met in the Ping-Pong tournament final, and the young kid from Duke won.

The way I heard it, Michael was so upset that he had the hotel order a Ping-Pong table for his room so he could prepare for a rematch. Maybe Michael just wanted Christian around on the Wizards for some Ping-Pong revenge.

Jordan had also signed Bryon Russell, whose most memorable NBA moment was defending Jordan's last shot with the Chicago Bulls. It was Game 6 of the 1998 NBA Finals in Utah, and after Jordan stole the ball from Karl Malone, he calmly dribbled over mid-court for his signature finals shot.

The dramatic sequence included the Jazz making the horrible decision of electing not to run another defender at Michael. Instead, it was Russell on Jordan, and we all know how that turned out. Michael used a crossover dribble and a push off to free himself from Russell before making the championship-clinching shot. It is one of the most memorable shots in NBA Finals history.

Of course, that shot came up constantly during the 2002–3 season in Washington. It's as if Michael wanted Bryon Russell around just to talk shit to him about that moment. This is what Michael does.

Russell would always say that final play in 1998 was a foul, and Michael's response was "If they didn't call it, it wasn't a foul." Come on, we all know it was a charge. It was a blatant push off. But in the last two minutes of the game some people get the calls, some people don't. And since Bryon Russell is Rodney Dangerfield compared to Michael Jordan, he didn't get any respect.

But Russell knew what he was getting himself into. Michael wanted to sign him and Russell came to Washington to play. It's similar to the attitude some football players take with Tom Brady. If you can't beat him, join him. Who wouldn't want to play with Michael in the final year of his career? That's something you'll have for the rest of your life. It was a great opportunity for any NBA player.

Actually, there was one guy who joined Michael Jordan but did so kicking and screaming: Jerry Stackhouse.

In July 2002, the Wizards acquired Stackhouse from the Detroit Pistons in a six-player deal that featured Richard "Rip" Hamilton heading to Detroit. Rip was a rising All-Star, while Jerry, who'd played for Dean Smith at North Carolina, had made the All-Star team twice and had just helped the Pistons win fifty games, an eighteen-win improvement from the previous year. Michael was eager to add an experienced player who was averaging 21.2 points in his first seven seasons. That was the highest among any player taken in the 1995 draft.

The Wizards were excited about the trade, but Jerry wasn't crazy about it. "I'm just disappointed . . . because I have to leave my home," Stackhouse said at the time. "I have to leave a fan base that has grown with me since I've been here and who have been just unbelievably great for me. It's not easy, but at the same time it comes with this business and I understand that."

Stackhouse's instincts were spot-on. He was frustrated playing with Michael. I think that when he got to Washington he thought they were going to pass the torch from Mike to him. But Mike still had the brand. It was still about Michael. Stack was good, Mike is the G.O.A.T. It's fine to want to be the man and take over, but he couldn't do that on the same team with Michael. Even though Jordan began the season as the sixth man, and only was forced back into the starting lineup because of injuries on the team, he was unquestionably the center of gravity.

All these moves Michael and Doug Collins made during the off-season didn't have an impact. The Wizards finished with a 37-45 record and in fifth place in the Atlantic Division, identical marks from the year before. A lot of the young guys were unhappy, and at different points during the season Stackhouse, Larry Hughes, and Kwame Brown publicly criticized Collins, which was also interpreted as criticism directed at Mike.

The season was becoming a circus, and on April 14, Michael's last home game in Washington, everyone got to see it for themselves. The night began with Jordan receiving a U.S. flag from Defense Secretary Donald Rumsfeld and included a video tribute to him at halftime. It was a nice start and a messy finish. After we lost 93–79 to the Knicks, Collins couldn't hold back any longer and he ripped into some of my teammates.

"I've had guys curse at me in the locker room this year, show no respect,'" Collins said. "It was insidious. It won't happen next year. Trust me. I treat people with dignity. I expect the same thing in return."

I have no idea if Doug was referring to Kwame, Stackhouse, or Larry Hughes, since I didn't hear any of that myself. It didn't much matter because our season was ending two nights later in Philadelphia. Michael agreed with Doug, saying that the conduct of some of the players was "definitely a concern" and that it was something "we have to address."

"Some people believe I prohibited this group from growing up," Michael said after scoring 21 points in thirty-seven minutes in his final home game. "I'm not buying that. Next year's going to be a test for some of these guys to understand at forty years old what I gave to the game the last two years."

On April 16 in Philadelphia, Michael played his last-ever NBA game. It was game number 82 for the season. The forty-year-old Jordan was the only player on our team to have appeared in every game. So don't ever think that Michael wasn't invested in the team. He tried to push himself and his teammates to the limit. It just wasn't meant to be. The Sixers won the game easily, 107–87, with Allen Iverson putting up 35 points.

Michael's final numbers in the box score represented some milestones from his career. He scored 15 points, one for every season he played in the NBA. He also made six shots, one for every title he won in Chicago.

"Michael can't carry a subpar team to the playoffs at age forty," Doug Collins said. "If Michael were twenty-five, we would have made the playoffs. This team never mixed; it never fit."

It was a bittersweet ending to a legendary career. Stackhouse decided to sit out the final game, seemingly out of protest of all the retirement ceremonies surrounding our famous teammate. He admitted to wanting no part of what he called the "Michael Jordan farewell tour."

"It says a lot about him that he's been able to play all eighty-two games," Stackhouse added. "But we're a young team, we're an athletic team, and this year we've played a little more of a slowed-down pace. Having Michael in the lineup had a lot to do with that, and next year we'll come in and reassess."

Years later, Stackhouse reiterated that he never wanted to be part of the trade to become Michael's new sidekick. He had no interest in being the Scottie Pippen of the Wizards to an aging Michael Jordan.

"Honestly, I wish I never played in Washington and for a number of reasons," he said. "I felt we were on our way in Detroit before I got traded there. It was really challenging to be in a situation with an idol who, at this particular point, I felt like I was a better player [than]. . . . It just kind of spiraled in a way that I didn't enjoy that season at all. The kind of picture I had in my mind of Michael Jordan and the reverence I had for him, I lost a little bit of it during the course of that year."

Michael probably agrees more than you might think. My sense is he feels it was a mistake to come out of retirement and play for Washington. He thought he could turn the Wizards around, first as an owner and executive, then as a player. And even after retiring from playing for good, after the 2002–3 season, he still believed he could make the team a success as an executive. But Wizards majority owner Abe Pollin, the same guy who had gotten into a nasty shouting match with Michael during the 1999 labor dispute, had other plans. On May 7, 2003, just a few weeks after Michael's final retirement, Pollin made a power move on the greatest player in history.

He fired Michael.

"It was an atmosphere on edge," Pollin said few months after the firing. "It was not a healthy atmosphere to produce a happy organization or a winning team."

Like a textbook mob hit, Michael never saw Pollin coming.

"I agonized over it for days and nights, thinking, What is it that I have to do?" Pollin said. "I'm going to think very hard about these decisions and make the best decisions that I think are best for the franchise."

Jordan's exit from the Bulls was perfect: a last-second shot to win a sixth NBA Championship. His exit from the Wizards was a bloody mess. A losing record, upset players, and a final stab in the back by a business partner.

"I'm pretty sure everyone would like to see me get the game-winning shot in the finals," Michael had said before his last game in Washington. "To some degree, that is a dream ending. But to a competitor, sometimes, not being as successful is also a great send-off. To know that you have to move on to do other things and do it in other ways, that's how I'm looking at this."

Michael Jordan could have been speaking on my behalf as well, since I was nearing the end of my career. I was thirty-nine. I'd played forty-two games in my one season with the Wizards, and made only one start. My last game with Washington and my final one playing next to Michael, had been back on March 18, a 94–90 overtime loss to the Detroit Pistons. I played just six minutes.

My one-year contact with the Wizards was up at the end of the season. The summer went by, then training camp, and then the start of the 2003–4 season, and I was still unsigned and unsure if I had played my last NBA game. My desire to contribute to a team was still strong, but the last thing I wanted to be was the guy at the end of the bench, just clapping. If I was going to be in uniform, I wanted to play.

The Houston Rockets finally called me in March 2004 and signed me to a ten-day contract.

It had been ten years since they beat me and the Knicks in the NBA Finals. Then they'd won again the following year. But in 2004, much like when I rejoined the Bulls, this Houston Rockets team was in a rebuilding mode. My former Knicks coach Jeff Van Gundy was now in charge of the Rockets. Jeff had brought along two former Knicks assistants, Tom Thibodeau and Steve Clifford, who both eventually became NBA head coaches. The roster included Mark Jackson, my former teammate in New York and Toronto, who was now serving as the backup point guard. The Rockets' young stars were Steve Francis and Yao Ming, the seven-foot-six center from China who was the top overall pick of the 2002 NBA Draft.

The team seemed to be on the right path, but their future didn't include me. After appearing in just seven games, I was released when power forward/center Kelvin Cato was activated from the injured list. In my final NBA game, April 2, 2004, against the Denver Nuggets I grabbed the last two rebounds of my career.

Could I have made it on a team somewhere as one of those veterans who was on the end of the bench and collecting a paycheck? Sure. But I felt it was time to move on. I didn't have any regrets. That chapter in my life was over.

I walked away ranked seventeenth all-time in rebounds. I had been one of the top ten rebounders in the league during five of my NBA seasons.

My work was done.

17 | TWO KINGS

Michael Jordan was my teammate with the Chicago Bulls and the Washington Wizards, and my opponent in some epic playoff series when I played for the New York Knicks. The one constant since we first met in 1985 is that we've always remained friends.

That stayed true after my retirement in 2004. That year, Michael bought a superbike motorcycle team called "Michael Jordan Motorsports," and I traveled all over the world with him and his team. That's a lot of long flights and therefore a lot of card games. No matter where we go or for what reason, Mike always wants to gamble, so there's always a game.

In 2006, Jordan returned to the NBA when he purchased a stake in the Charlotte Bobcats. As part of his deal he became the president of basketball operations. Maybe the Wizards didn't want Jordan around, but the NBA definitely wanted its biggest star to become an owner. Charlotte made sense because North Carolina was Michael's home state and the Bobcats' first owner,

Bob Johnson, was having trouble building a winner. I actually spent one season, in 2010–11, after Michael became the team's majority owner, as an assistant coach in Charlotte, but I had back problems that forced me to leave because it bothered me to just sit on the bench.

Anyway, in 2006, Mike invited me to fly with him down to Miami to watch the Heat play the Dallas Mavericks in the NBA Finals. He took off in Charlotte and was going to land in Atlanta to pick me up. He didn't like it if you were late, and he kept telling me to be on time. That's not a problem. But that day there was a bad traffic accident in Atlanta. The highway was backed up. I was running late, and when Mike landed he called me and was threatening to leave. I told him, "Watch the news. The roads are fucked up." He said he would wait for me, but I knew he wasn't happy. I finally got to the airport, the plane took off, and we started playing the card game Tonk for money.

I was the big winner, so Mike was mad about that on top of still being mad that I was late. I stepped off the plane when we landed, and I didn't realize the bag I was carrying was open. I'd forgotten to close the zipper.

It was real windy this day, as it can get in Miami, and suddenly money was fucking flying out of my bag and all over the tarmac. It was crazy. I was running in all different directions, desperately trying to pick up $100 bills. Michael was helping, but he was also upset that he was chasing the money he'd lost to me.

I can only imagine what it must have looked like for people who saw us. They probably thought it was a drug deal gone bad, or maybe we were filming a dumb scene in a movie. It was embarrassing, but I didn't give a shit. It was my money, so I wasn't just going to leave it there.

Michael finally stopped, looked at me, and said: "We're wasting our time. Fuck it. If you need money, go to the ATM."

That's easy for him to say. Michael has a lot of money, so the last thing he wants to be doing is running around chasing bills on a tarmac in Miami. It meant more to me, but what was I going to do? He'd picked me up, flown me down to Miami, and he wanted to watch the NBA Finals. I had to play by his rules. I left a few thousand on the tarmac that day.

What made the experience even crazier was we got picked up by a limo driver who was one of those guys who do a lot of talking the minute you get into the car. Of course, he knew who Michael was, and he started giving us all his NBA conspiracies. His big one was that the NBA wanted Miami to beat Dallas because David Stern didn't like Mavericks owner Mark Cuban. He said the Mavs were done.

You hear this stuff all the time from fans and you know it's mostly just talk. But you had to think twice after what happened that night. Dwyane Wade, who grew up in Chicago idolizing Michael, got fouled with 1.9 seconds remaining in overtime and the Heat trailing 100–99. It was a tough call, especially in the last seconds of a Finals game. The Mavs were about to go up 3–2 and take the series back home to Dallas. But that foul changed everything. Wade, who scored 43 that night, made both free throws to win the game. The Mavs, as a team, were 21 of 25 from the line that night. Wade was 21 of 25 from the line on his own.

The game ended with Dirk Nowitzki kicking the ball into the seats and Cuban pointing and screaming at league officials. He held a press conference afterward and was killing the referees and the league. It was pretty funny.

But you knew commissioner David Stern wasn't going to let that slide. The league fined Cuban $250,000 for what they said were "several acts of misconduct." Stern had history with Cuban. Not like my history with Charles Barkley. They didn't fight with fists. Stern went after Cuban's wallet.

"If we are going to hold coaches, players, and fans accountable, then we have to hold owners accountable, too," Stern told the reporters. Cuban took his $250,000 punishment like a man. And I thought I lost a lot of money on the tarmac in Miami. He called it "just a business expense." But I was a player. Cuban was an owner. Michael was one of the few to do both.

Miami won Game 6 in Dallas and finished the series. Pat Riley got his title with Wade and Shaquille O'Neal. When Pat coached us in New York, we never beat the Bulls when Michael played. We took them out in 1994, but that was the year Michael retired and was playing baseball. Pat has so much respect for Michael that in the Heat home arena, the club retired the jerseys of two players who didn't even play for them; one was the Miami Dolphins quarterback Dan Marino. The other was Michael, who had come into the NBA twenty-two years earlier and changed the direction of the Chicago Bulls and the league forever.

For a long time, I've also had a relationship with the other player who has done the most to change the league: LeBron James. I first met him in Cleveland when he was fourteen or fifteen years old. People were already telling me, "This kid is going to be the next superstar." My nephews and cousins in Ohio had been paying attention to him for years. He was going to be the dip to the potato chip.

After we met, I became like a big brother to him. He looked up to Michael and knew I could help him get to know Mike. When LeBron was a junior in high school, Michael and I invited him to come to Chicago to watch us play pickup. The run was at Attack Athletics, a place owned by Michael's personal trainer, Tim Grover. Tim was the guy in *The Last Dance* who said Mike got food poisoning because he ate bad pizza before an NBA Finals game against the Jazz in Salt Lake City.

You could tell how excited LeBron was to see Mike play. LeBron's mom, Gloria, who raised him by herself, and his best friend, Maverick Carter, who eventually became LeBron's business partner, also made the trip. Chicago always had good pickup games, and on this day there were a lot of NBA players running around. The look in LeBron's eyes said it all: he was in awe of Michael. What high school kid wouldn't be?

LeBron brought his stuff and wanted to play, but Michael wouldn't let him. It would have been fun to see LeBron as a junior in high school going up against a legend like Jordan, but Mike didn't want to risk LeBron getting hurt playing against NBA players. It wasn't that Michael didn't think LeBron could handle the competition. He just didn't want to be responsible in case something went wrong. That was smart of him.

Only two years later, the Cleveland Cavaliers selected LeBron with the first overall pick. That was a great day for the city. LeBron was the hometown kid. Financially, for the Cavs, it was huge to get such a compelling, budding superstar. More important, he immediately lived up to the hype.

LeBron was only twenty-two years old in 2007 when he led the Cavs to the NBA Finals. To get there, Cleveland beat Detroit in the Eastern Conference Finals, which was the first of what would soon become many classic playoff performances from LeBron. He finished with 48 points while scoring 29 of Cleveland's last 30 points. Steve Kerr, who at the time was working for TNT, called it "Jordan-esque."

LeBron didn't have much of a chance in the 2007 NBA Finals. The Cavs' starting five were Larry Hughes, Sasha Pavlovic, Drew Gooden, Zydrunas Ilgauskas, and him. They were no match for Tim Duncan, Manu Ginobili, and Tony Parker. And this is what became the persistent problem in Cleveland. LeBron couldn't get the help he needed to get the team over the edge and win rings. Over the next three seasons, LeBron and the Cavs twice lost to Boston in the conference semifinals, and also lost to Dwight Howard and the Orlando Magic in the Eastern Conference Finals.

When the Celtics beat the Cavs in Game 6 in 2010, LeBron walked off the court and famously ripped off his jersey. I had known for months at this point that he was gone. It was over for the Cavs. They gave it their best shot, but it just wasn't going to happen.

Nine months before LeBron James announced to the world on July 8, 2010, "I'm going to take my talents to South Beach and join the Miami Heat," he made it pretty clear to me that he was planning to make the biggest move of his career.

Our conversation was on November 10, 2009, when the Cleveland Cavaliers were in Florida. The Cavs were starting a road trip in Orlando, and the night before their game against the Magic, LeBron invited everyone on the Cavs out to dinner. That tells you a little something about LeBron—it means a lot when the superstar invites everybody out and pays for the meal.

I happened to be in Orlando and was hanging out with LeBron that night. We were talking about the season, and during our conversation, LeBron mentioned that his goal was to play for the Miami Heat once his contract with the Cavs expired in July.

It made sense; LeBron was about to become a free agent, and he'd earned the right to decide his future. Seven seasons into his career, Cleveland was still having trouble recruiting stars to complement LeBron's game, so LeBron figured he could build his own team in another city.

There were a lot of perks to Miami in particular. The Heat were a solid organization who were looking to win, and LeBron would get the chance to play with two good friends and great players in Dwyane Wade and ultimately Chris Bosh. It didn't hurt that there were no state income taxes in Florida. If LeBron was going to leave Cleveland for any team and city, Miami sounded like the best option.

Two nights after I spoke with LeBron in Orlando, the Cavs had continued their Florida road trip south to Miami and were playing the Heat. I called Pat Riley, my old coach, looking for two tickets to the game.

Riley had been the president and head coach of the Heat until the previous season, when he retired as coach and handed those reins to Erik Spoelstra. But in his role as the team president, Riley was still as driven and as committed as ever to winning championships.

That's a key ingredient that sometimes gets overlooked or isn't appreciated. Not every organization is as committed to winning as you think. I would say there are about ten out of the thirty NBA franchises that have that deep commitment to winning. Even fewer know how to go about it. Some teams and owners are just in it to make money.

The Heat are one of those organizations that are in it to win it. Some of that "Heat Culture" they talk about in Miami is bullshit— the Heat didn't invent the culture, and it was the same culture in Miami as it was when Riley was with the Lakers and the Knicks. Pat Riley expects you to be professional, be on time, be in shape, play hard, and be all about the team. But some of it is legitimate, too, and it was good enough to attract LeBron—the best player in the game.

I met up with Pat before tip-off and I told him straight out, "I know of a superstar that wants to come play for you next year."

That got Pat's attention. "Who?" he asked.

"You're playing his team tonight" was all I said.

I respected Pat and he respected me. For a second, Pat had a look on his face that said "Really?" But as Pat does, he played everything cool. He knew I had a relationship with LeBron, and I got the sense he took it seriously.

It wasn't like I was trying to be LeBron's agent, and I wasn't working for any team, so it wasn't tampering. LeBron didn't mind. I was just saying what I knew to be true.

I was letting Pat Riley know that things were about to get a lot better in Miami.

The truth is, most of the NBA was already preparing for LeBron to leave. He was about to become a free agent on July 1, 2010, and a lot of the big teams, the Heat included, were going to make a run at him. The Knicks were going to give it their best shot, but they didn't stand a chance. In June 2010, my former teammate Allan Houston, who was working for Knicks owner James Dolan, set up a meeting with me to discuss LeBron's free agency. He thought I might know something, given our close relationship. The meeting was at Cafe 31 in Manhattan, right next to the Garden on 31st Street. As players we'd go there to eat after games all the time. The owners of the restaurant were great guys. The food was good and it was a casual atmosphere. A lot of business got done at Cafe 31. When I got traded in 1998, I held my press conference there. I paid for anything the media wanted to eat or drink. That's the key to having a good relationship with the press: good quotes and free food.

During that lunch with Allan Houston, he didn't come right out and ask me if I would help recruit LeBron, but it was pretty obvious that Allan was trying to get as much information out of me about LeBron as he could. I don't blame him for trying, but I knew right away the Knicks were a long shot. LeBron's heart was set on Miami, and the Knicks just weren't good enough for him to take a chance on them.

What surprised me was the Knicks strategy to get LeBron. Part of their plan, according to Allan, was to have Isiah Thomas fly to Cleveland to meet with LeBron. Why the fuck would the Knicks do that? Isiah and LeBron didn't have anything in common. It wasn't my place to tell the Knicks that LeBron had basically made up his mind, but I was certain that unless something crazy happened between June and July 1, LeBron was going to Miami.

Pat Riley had already won a championship in Miami. He'd won in L.A. He was the kind of guy who makes things happen. It's true that he's controlling, and for many players, after a while that becomes tiresome. But a lot of those players get their championships first. They were willing to go along with the control because it produced the results they were after. Riley knew what he was doing.

You couldn't say the same about the Knicks. I found it kind of funny that after years of the Knicks really not wanting much to do with me, they were now asking me, if not in so many words, to help them with LeBron. Allan was close to Dolan. Allan had been working for the team since he retired. The Knicks also gave my former teammates Larry Johnson and John Starks jobs. They had once talked about offering me a contract to make fifteen paid appearances a year at games, meeting with sponsors and season ticket holders before tip-off, which is what Johnson and Starks are paid to do. But they never followed through. I didn't hear anything back from them. My guess is they offered the job to silence me, but I kept talking about the team, so they backed off. Me, Anthony Mason, and Patrick Ewing were always on the outside—they never offered us anything worth taking. I don't know, maybe we didn't kiss ass like some other guys did. A lot of guys who I fought for with the Knicks turned their back on me. While they were eating all the cake, I was getting crumbs.

I figured the Knicks must be pretty desperate to be asking for my help with LeBron. At that lunch, Allan kept telling me, "Mr. Dolan isn't that bad," and "You should work for the team." Over the next few weeks, they started talking to me about airing my cooking show on the MSG Network. They had me talk to someone from the network. But when LeBron decided not to join the

Knicks, they told me they had decided to pass on my show. What does that tell you?

When free agency officially began on July 1, LeBron met with six teams in Cleveland: the Heat, the Knicks, the Nets, the Clippers, the Bulls, and of course, the Cavs. He wasn't going to leave without at least hearing out the Cavs' offer. All these teams came to LeBron's home state to give it their best sales pitch. The truth is, only one had a realistic shot.

LeBron made his move to Miami official with his now famous television event, "The Decision."

And Riley hit it big. He got LeBron, Bosh, and re-signed Wade. Miami had its Big 3. And just like that, the Miami Heat instantly changed the NBA landscape. It was the start of what the media likes the call "player empowerment" era. Michael Jordan had a lot of power when he played, but LeBron was taking it to another level.

Superstar players now had the ability to form super-teams. There were precursors to this: in the 1980s you had the Lakers with Magic Johnson, Kareem Abdul-Jabbar, and James Worthy, and the Celtics with Larry Bird, Kevin McHale, and Robert Parish. In the eighties it was Michael Jordan and Scottie Pippen leading the Chicago Bulls to six NBA titles. In the early 2000s, it was the Lakers with Shaquille O'Neal and Kobe Bryant. In 2008, the Boston Celtics won a title with Paul Pierce, Kevin Garnett, and Ray Allen.

But what happened in Miami was different. LeBron, Wade, and Bosh were all free agents at the same time. They were teammates for the United States national team at the 2008 Olympics who became friends and talked about joining forces in the NBA. It's not easy to pull off. But they did it.

And look at what LeBron accomplished in four seasons with the Heat: four NBA Finals appearances and two championships. He made the move and got his first two rings. He's a smart player and businessman. If your company ain't working and somebody else has a company that's stable but needs a little help, you can merge with them. That's what LeBron did. In those four years he found out what it takes to win. In Miami they had good management, good role players, and three All-Star–caliber players. LeBron was the leader. He never had a good B player until he got to Miami. And Wade is better than a B player. He's more like an A-minus.

That's why I don't understand why anyone would get on LeBron for leaving as a free agent. He never asked to be traded. He played out his contracts. He didn't do what Anthony Davis did in New Orleans in 2019. Look what James Harden did in 2020 to get from Houston to Brooklyn. He bailed on the team. LeBron didn't do that. Heck, even Tom Brady left the New England Patriots as a free agent, and now you're hearing all these quarterbacks crying about their situation. My stance is straightforward: You're under contract. Stop crying.

Brady and LeBron didn't force their way out. LeBron waited until he was a free agent and did it the right way. This was his call. The media in Miami wanted to give Pat all the credit for engineering the deal. Fuck that. I like Pat Riley, and I'm not knocking him, but he's egotistical. His horse in the race could only go so far. He didn't do anything on the court, either; LeBron played the game and in some ways was the coach and the general manager, too. He got Pat two more rings.

I was a little surprised that LeBron took so much shit for leaving, especially from his own team. Dan Gilbert, the Cavs owner, went after LeBron. It was crazy. Gilbert posted a letter on the Cavaliers' team website that was nasty and uncalled for.

Gilbert wrote:

Dear Cleveland, All Of Northeast Ohio and Cleveland Cavaliers Supporters Wherever You May Be Tonight:

As you now know, our former hero, who grew up in the very region that he deserted this evening, is no longer a Cleveland Cavalier.

This was announced with a several day, narcissistic, self-promotional build-up culminating with a national TV special of his "decision" unlike anything ever "witnessed" in the history of sports and probably the history of entertainment.

Clearly, this is bitterly disappointing to all of us.

The good news is that the ownership team and the rest of the hard-working, loyal, and driven staff over here at your hometown Cavaliers have not betrayed you nor NEVER will betray you.

There is so much more to tell you about the events of the recent past and our more than exciting future. Over the next several days and weeks, we will be communicating much of that to you.

You simply don't deserve this kind of cowardly betrayal.

You have given so much and deserve so much more.

In the meantime, I want to make one statement to you tonight:

"I PERSONALLY GUARANTEE THAT THE CLEVELAND CAVALIERS WILL WIN AN NBA CHAMPIONSHIP BEFORE THE SELF-TITLED FORMER 'KING' WINS ONE"

You can take it to the bank.

If you thought we were motivated before tonight to bring the hardware to Cleveland, I can tell you that this shameful display of selfishness and betrayal by one of our very own has shifted our "motivation" to previously unknown and previously never experienced levels.

Some people think they should go to heaven but NOT have to die to get there.

Sorry, but that's simply not how it works.

This shocking act of disloyalty from our home grown "chosen one" sends the exact opposite lesson of what we would want our children to learn. And "who" we would want them to grow-up to become.

But the good news is that this heartless and callous action can only serve as the antidote to the so-called "curse" on Cleveland, Ohio.

The self-declared former "King" will be taking the "curse" with him down south. And until he does "right" by Cleveland and Ohio, James (and the town where he plays) will unfortunately own this dreaded spell and bad karma.

Just watch.

Sleep well, Cleveland.

Tomorrow is a new and much brighter day. . . .

PROMISE you that our energy, focus, capital, knowledge and experience will be directed at one thing and one thing only:

DELIVERING YOU the championship you have long deserved and is long overdue. . . .

Dan Gilbert
Majority Owner
Cleveland Cavaliers

What the fuck? The man called it a "shameful display of selfishness and betrayal." And here's the crazy thing: LeBron still came back to the Cavs! After all that was said about him, LeBron came back to work for Gilbert in 2014 and make the guy a lot of money. That will tell you what kind of guy LeBron is. He wanted to return to Cleveland for one reason: to win a championship for that city. LeBron won two championships in four years in Miami, but what he really wanted was a championship for Cleveland.

If Dan Gilbert owned any other NBA team besides the Cavs,

there's no way LeBron would have signed with him. But this was the Cavs. This was Cleveland. It's what LeBron wanted. It meant a lot to the city for him to come back after what the owner said. How hateful can you be to write that letter? Dan Gilbert is lucky LeBron was willing to put that shit aside.

Some of these NBA owners don't get it.

Dan Gilbert has his bad moments, but the worst of them all is that guy who owns the Knicks, James Dolan. After LeBron's four seasons in Miami, before he officially announced his return to the Cavaliers, NBA teams thought they had another shot at signing LeBron. But that man Dolan doesn't even know that his own actions ruled out the Knicks from ever being a serious contender to be the new home of King James. And it was all because of something he did to me.

It happened back in 2014 during All-Star Weekend in New Orleans. Dolan had run the Knicks since 1999, but it was the first time I was ever introduced to him. That tells you a lot already, doesn't it? William Wesley, aka "World Wide Wes," tried to set up the meeting. Me, LeBron, Maverick Carter, and Rich Paul, LeBron's friend and agent, were hanging out at Harrah's Casino on Canal Street in New Orleans, just a block from the Mississippi River, when Wes approached us.

I had known Wes for years, going back to my days with the Chicago Bulls. He got in with Michael Jordan. Then again, Wes got in with everybody. He was a guy from the South Jersey/Philadelphia area who at one point became close to LeBron, then Derrick Rose, and then Carmelo Anthony. He worked closely with the agent Leon Rose, who during the summer of 2010 represented LeBron and Carmelo. Leon and Wes got close to Dolan. So close that Dolan hired Leon in February 2020 to become Knicks president.

That summer Wes was hired as an advisor. Like I told you, Wes gets around.

Before Wes landed a job in the Knicks front office, when he was basically an agent without an official title, he'd had a falling out with LeBron over something shady that happened with Rich Paul. I don't know the details, but I think Rich felt Wes had tried to fuck him over. When Wes approached us at the casino in New Orleans, Rich didn't want to talk to him. He wouldn't even shake his hand.

So Wes turned to me instead and asked me if I wanted to come to this back room.

"I'm with the Knicks owner," Wes said.

I played dumb and said, "Who?"

"Jim Dolan," Wes said.

I figured, why not? After all these years not knowing the guy personally, I might as well meet him. Over the years, reporters had interviewed me about the Knicks, and I'd always given them honest answers. Their players are soft, I said. They don't defend. The organization is a mess. All of it was true. I didn't know him, but I had gotten the sense that Dolan didn't like to hear it, and it seemed to be preventing me from getting a job with the organization. So I figured we'd have a conversation and straighten things out man to man.

I walked with Wes to the back room at Harrah's. When we got there, Wes said: "Mr. Dolan, Charles Oakley wants to meet you." Fine by me, it was true.

I stuck out my hand to shake Dolan's, and he didn't move. I kid you not, he never even turned around to look at me. You would have thought I did something to his wife. Shit, Latrell Sprewell, who played five seasons with the Knicks, cursed at Dolan in front of Dolan's wife when he returned to face the Knicks back in 2003, and they still became friends.

I didn't do anything to this man. What did I ever say that was so bad that he would ignore me like that? I wondered. Man, I wanted to hit him in the head. I walked back to LeBron and said, "This motherfucker wouldn't shake my hand."

All LeBron said was: "This is why I'm never going to New York."

At least the Knicks didn't waste their time trying to set up a meeting with LeBron when he left Miami in 2014. They were out before they were ever in. Instead, LeBron went back home to Cleveland after spending the last four years winning two titles and reaching the NBA Finals all four seasons with the Heat. By the time LeBron returned, Cleveland's roster had changed. They had drafted Kyrie Irving and Tristan Thompson first and fourth overall, respectively, in the 2011 draft. They also traded the first overall pick of the 2014 draft, Andrew Wiggins, to Minnesota to acquire Kevin Love.

See what I mean? LeBron learned a lot from his time with the Heat and Riley. The Cavs had won a total of ninety-seven games the four years LeBron spent in Miami. He wasn't coming back to Cleveland to lose. And he didn't. He took the Cavs to four straight NBA Finals and finally got the city a championship in 2016.

The Golden State Warriors beat Cleveland three times before that—they were just too good. But in 2016, LeBron was unstoppable. The Warriors took a 3–1 series lead before LeBron scored 41 in both Games 5 and 6, and then had a triple-double and that famous chase-down block of Andre Iguodala in the fourth quarter.

The city of Cleveland had not won a championship since the Cleveland Browns won the NFL Championship in 1964, the year after I was born. I wasn't going to miss Game 7 in Oakland, so I bought two tickets for $4,500 apiece. I needed to be there.

When the game ended, I was on the court and started walking back to the locker room. Ty Lue, the Cavs coach, invited me in, but security in Oakland was salty. Their team lost so the security guys started grabbing me. I said, "Please don't grab me." Eight months earlier I'd had four security guards come after me at a hotel in Las Vegas. I didn't need that again. Thankfully, we got the situation worked out peacefully, and I had a good time with the team. They eventually went to Las Vegas, and I went back to my hotel room to sleep.

You have to take your hat off to LeBron. He wanted to see people in his hometown happy, and he did everything he could to make it happen. He built a school in Ohio. He does charitable work in the inner city. What he's done for Cleveland, in sports and beyond, will outlive all of us.

When he decided to go to the Los Angeles Lakers in 2018, the reaction in Cleveland was nothing like the one he got in that ridiculous letter from Dan Gilbert. I think more people were okay with it because of everything he had done on and off the court in Ohio. I know that I was okay with him leaving. He doesn't owe anyone anything. He brought revenue to the city. He gave people in the community opportunities. He wasn't doing it for the owners. He was doing it for the city.

Our city.

18 | THE OWNER

All the Knicks have done with James Dolan as their owner is lose basketball games.

After me and the Raptors surprised everyone by beating the Knicks in the first round of 2001 NBA Playoffs, Dolan fired Dave Checketts, the longtime Garden president. Considering what has happened to the Knicks since that moment—one playoff series win over a twenty-year stretch—you could say we really ended the Knicks.

Dolan makes money and he spends money, but there is no plan. They're always changing coaches and front office executives. Look at Miami, where Pat Riley has been in charge since 1995. He knows what he's doing. The Knicks don't.

For a long time, Dolan had a media relations person named Jonathan Supranowitz. Right before my former Knicks teammate Larry Johnson got his job with the organization as something of an ambassador, Jonathan said they would hire me. But then I never got called back. When I finally got ahold of him, I asked what happened and he said, "We decided to go in a different direction." I know that decision ultimately lands with Dolan. And I know it's because I've been critical of the Knicks front office.

Some owners would be able to take what is fair criticism and brush it off. Dolan isn't that guy.

And Jonathan Supranowitz is a straight bitch. For years, he continued to tell me that I should come back and work for the Knicks, but in order to do that, I'd have to stop killing the team in the press. I never trusted Jonathan, and kept being honest. The reporters asked me questions, and I'd give them my answers. Jonathan would then call me every time a story came out in which I'd criticized the Knicks.

"Walt and Earl would never talk about the team like that," he would tell me, referring to the former Knicks Walt Frazier and Earl Monroe. Well, Walt works for the team, and Earl still comes to games. Plus, I don't give a fuck what Walt or Earl says about the team.

James Dolan hires people under the requirement that you just work for the owner. You're not supposed to be your own person. You can't say anything.

By 2011, the Knicks had stopped giving me tickets to games, which was fine. When Donnie Walsh was there—a great guy and president of basketball operations for the Knicks from 2008 to 2011—he'd have me at games. But after that, I'd buy my own tickets or someone would bring me anyway. The fans were always great to me. The ushers and the security guards all talked to me. But people in the organization were keeping their distance. There was one exception: my old teammate Herb Williams, who worked as a Knicks assistant coach for a long time, always came over to say hello when I was at the Garden. Herb is a stand-up guy. Otherwise, everyone was cold to me.

Over time, my experience at Madison Square Garden continued to get worse. When they renovated MSG, they built suites on the same floor as the court and the locker rooms. I bought tickets for a few games every season that gave me access to hang around those areas before the game. But it was like they'd ordered me to be followed: there was always someone popping up and asking to inspect my ticket. Finally, I said, "How the fuck did you think I got here? Of course I have a ticket." I was getting harassed just for being at a game with a ticket that I bought.

Still, I didn't really understand how bad my standing was with the Knicks until the 2014 All-Star Game in New Orleans when Dolan gave me the cold shoulder. It was a genuine attempt to settle our differences, but he wanted nothing to do with me. It spoke clearly to his character. If he had a problem with me, he should have talked to me face-to-face like a man. I would have liked to understand why he had an issue with me. When Phil Jackson was hired to run the Knicks in 2015, he was interested in bringing me in to work with the big men. I was interested, too, but nothing came of it. I think we know why.

Even after that, I made multiple attempts to reach out to Dolan and set up a meeting. "I had at least 15 people try to set up a meeting," I told the *New York Times*. "He won't meet." I told them I wouldn't mind cooking him dinner and sitting down over it, though I also joked that I might "put something" in the meal. I said as well that if they put us in a room they should lock the door, but make sure the police were on the other side. I was trying to make light of the situation because the whole thing was stupid. Why was this man so angry with me? But the Knicks didn't find it funny.

That was pretty much the worst of it though, until February 2017, when the incident happened that changed everything.

On February 7, I went to the Thurman Munson Dinner in Manhattan. It's a charity event named for the Yankees catcher who died in a small plane crash in Ohio on August 2, 1979. I never met Munson, but he was from Ohio, and I felt a connection to him. In fact, he was born in Akron, just like LeBron and Steph Curry. Plus, I liked doing charity work.

The dinner was held the night before the Knicks home game against the Los Angeles Clippers, who at the time were coached by Doc Rivers, my former teammate. I spoke to a guy at the dinner who invited me to the game. I was going to be in town for a few days, so I agreed to go.

The game was starting at 8 p.m. because it was on ESPN, so we met at 7:30 and then headed over to MSG. There were four people in our group, and I had no idea our seats were right behind Dolan's. We walked down to our seats and the game had already started. A waitress asked me if I wanted something to drink, so I ordered a Pepsi and some popcorn. We were sitting close to the Knicks bench, so I looked over at Mike Martinez, the Knicks equipment manager, and he nodded at me.

It was about midway through the first quarter when I noticed there were cops and security guards looking at me. Then there was a time-out, and I said hello to John McEnroe, the tennis player who is a big Knicks fans and was sitting nearby. He always came to our games.

"What's up, John?"

"Hey Oak, what's up?" he said.

We were talking, and then some fans approached, I took some pictures with them, and all of a sudden, there were eight security guys around me.

"Why are there so many of you?" I asked. "Is Obama here?"

I was told that I had to leave the building. I asked why, and they said they had been ordered to make me leave.

More and more guards and cops kept coming at me. I was standing my ground. I asked again, "Why do I have to leave?" They repeated, I had to leave.

It wasn't the first time I'd had the experience of being surrounded by a lot of security guards. In 2010, I had five security guards at the Aria hotel in Las Vegas beat me up when I tried to reenter the VIP pool area at closing time. I got a back injury from that fight, so I'm not comfortable being surrounded by that many guys. No one would be. If more than two or three people walk up to you, no matter how tough you are, you'd be right to feel threatened. And this was a lot more than two or three.

Unfortunately, I ended up having a similar experience at MSG to that time at the Aria hotel. Security started grabbing at me and it made me uncomfortable. I didn't know what was going to happen. I am not a violent person, but there were so many guys in front of me and on both sides and I needed to defend myself so something really bad didn't happen to me. Total disrespect. And by then the crowd, including the players from both the Knicks and the Clippers, were watching it go down. They handcuffed me and took me away from the court, near the loading dock.

Phil Jackson was still president of the Knicks, and he came over and said, "Oak, what happened?"

"Ask your fucking boss what happened," I told him.

World Wide Wes and Spike Lee were there, too, and they came down the ramp to check on me. Then Wes called Michael Jordan. I didn't get a chance to say much to Michael before I was taken to the Midtown South Precinct, which is on 35th Street, just a block away from the Garden. The cops were actually great to me. I told them I didn't have a beef with the cops. My problem was with Dolan. I read the next day that one of the cops outside the station house was chanting "Free Charles Oakley!" That's pretty cool. I was released just a few minutes before midnight, but I knew things had only begun, and were going to get worse.

At 8:35 p.m., only minutes after I had been kicked out, the Knicks released a hasty statement on Twitter that pissed me off.

They were trying to get ahead of the story, and they were doing it by lying. It read: "Charles Oakley came to the game tonight and behaved in a highly inappropriate and completely abusive manner. He has been ejected and is currently being arrested by the New York City Police Department. He was a great Knick and we hope he gets some help soon."

Gets some help soon? What the fuck does that mean? I wondered. I went to the game, ordered a soda and popcorn, talked to some friends and some fans, and then I got kicked out. Based on everything that happened I believe Dolan ordered me to be ejected, which is crazy. I never said one thing to him. But the Knicks' front office was saying plenty about me. The morning after the incident I defended myself in a few interviews. That's when the Knicks posted a second statement on Twitter.

"There are dozens of security staff, employees and the NYPD that witnessed Oakley's abusive behavior. It started when he entered the building and continued until he was arrested and left the building. Every single statement we have received is consistent in describing his actions. Everything he said since the incident is pure fiction."

My childhood friend Eric Nolan Grant from the O'Jays was one of the first people I talked to after I was kicked out. Eric likes to describe me as "arrogantly honest." I think that's fair. What he means is, he knew I was telling the truth that I didn't say anything to Dolan, didn't taunt him—I would never lie about something like that. If I did something like that, I'd tell the truth about it.

It was now me vs. Madison Square Garden, which meant me versus an army of employees working for the powerful Dolan. Dolan was getting killed by the media and the fans for what happened, though. The whole thing looked terrible for him. So instead of releasing another statement, Dolan decided to do an interview on 98.7 ESPN radio in New York, the same station that broadcasts Knicks games. Dolan went on *The Michael Kay Show* in the afternoon. This was a big deal—Dolan doesn't do a lot of interviews. It was clear he wanted to give his side of the story, or at least his spin. But the host, Kay, asked good questions. I didn't think he was taking Dolan's side.

Before the interview began, Kay had reported that I was banned from MSG for life. Dolan, however, backed off that just a little.

"It's not necessarily a lifetime ban," Dolan said. "But I think the most important thing with that is we need to keep the Garden safe for anybody who goes there. . . . So anybody drinking too much alcohol, looking for a fight, they're going to be ejected and they're going to be banned. Everybody has a right to go to the games and enjoy them, and no one has a right to take that from them. So in this case we are going to put the ban in place. . . . Whether it's Charles Oakley or Charles Lindbergh or Charles Dolan, you come and you behave that way, and you will be banned."

Drinking too much? I'd had a Pepsi. And I wasn't looking for a fight. I was there to watch a game. I didn't do anything to deserve being surrounded by security guards. But Dolan was sticking to his script. Kay asked Dolan what "in your mind" happened, which is a good way of putting it. Dolan's mind and the truth aren't the same thing.

"It's very clear to us that Charles Oakley came into the Garden with an agenda. From the moment he stepped into the Garden, he began with this behavior. Abusive behavior, stuff you wouldn't want to say on the radio. . . .

"He did say a bunch of things along the way that looked like he was headed in my direction. I didn't hear them myself, but we heard from our employees that he was using my name a lot. But this isn't because I'm nervous. This is because you can't do what he did and stay.

"We clearly did not—we weren't perfect here, and I think Charles never should have made it to his seats. And that's on us, and we're doing things to remedy that and make sure that never happens again. . . . We know he said on TV that he was drinking beforehand. We heard statements from police that he appeared to be impaired. Our staff clearly could see that. . . .

"A, I didn't realize it was on national television, not that it would have made a difference. B, I wasn't aware that he was behind us. It wasn't until it was pointed out to me that he was behind us that I started to open my ears. The security person came to me and said, 'There's a problem behind you; it's Charles Oakley.' I said, 'Can you wait until between quarters?' He said, 'Yes.'"

There wasn't any problem behind Dolan until security guards came to my seat for no reason and told me I had to leave, not because of any "abusive behavior" from me, whatever that even means. His story doesn't make any sense.

But it got worse. Dolan then implied that I was an alcoholic, which not only pissed me off, but really upset my mother. Dolan was the one who had been to rehab. I think he's been there two times. But the recovering alcoholic is going to sit there and accuse me of that without any proof?

He slipped that accusation in when Kay asked Dolan if he is afraid of me.

"No, I don't think so. Although he's been quoted saying things like he would poison my food. I don't think he's serious about stuff like that. . . .

"To me, Charles has got a problem. We've said it before; he's his own worst problem. People have to understand that. He has a problem with anger. He's both physically and verbally abusive. He may have a problem with alcohol. But those problems with being physically and verbally abusive, those are problems.

"I do think Charles needs help. He can't want the things that have happened to him since he retired. They aren't good. He's had many altercations. He's been arrested. It all seems to come from his anger. Maybe he can't remember it, but I think he's somewhat in denial."

Denial was how this all started, that's true: Dolan was in denial about how bad his Knicks were. And when I pointed it out, he got upset. Dolan and the Knicks were building their case against me right on the radio.

"We have great relationships with all of our alumni," Dolan said. "This is an anomaly. You're not going to find ten guys out there saying the Knicks didn't treat me well. There might be one, maybe two. . . . Go ask them about how they've been treated. . . .

"All we need is for Charles to change his behavior. He was a great Knick, and we would love to have him. He should be up there at center court; he should be up there being recognized. But this behavior, it just doesn't work with that. And until he gets it under control, we won't be able to do it."

The truth is Dolan doesn't care much about the Knicks' history. The organization has this saying, "Once a Knick, Always a Knick," but it only applies to certain players. Allan Houston is still with the team after originally signing as a free agent in the summer of 1996. He's been in the front office for nearly twenty years, but I don't know what he does, and somehow he stays there even though the Knicks keep losing and changing management. I was always cool with Allan, but now I think he is a sellout.

Loyalty means everything to me. If you're my friend and my teammate, I've got your back. It was that way with MJ in Chicago, Patrick Ewing in New York, and both Vince Carter and Tracy McGrady in Toronto. If you're my coach, my general manager, or even the owner, I'll give you everything I have. But I don't always receive that loyalty in return.

The year Dolan banned me from the Garden was the same sea-son the franchise was celebrating their seventieth anniversary. In those seventy years, the Knicks won a total of two championships.

Since 1973, they'd reached the NBA Finals twice. I was the starting power forward on that 1994 team that won the Eastern Conference Championship. But the Knicks never reached out to me about being included in any celebration. Then again, Patrick is the best player in the franchise's history, and the Knicks never offered him a coaching job, even though he coached for fifteen years with the Washington Wizards, the Houston Rockets, the Orlando Magic, and the Charlotte Hornets.

Allan Houston didn't support me after I was kicked out of the Garden. A few of my former teammates did have my back. Chris Childs spoke up, but Patrick Ewing never said anything. All those years I was protection for him and he couldn't say one thing to support me? I thought that was fucked up. And I'll never forgive Patrick for that.

On February 10, two days after the arrest, the Knicks played another home game, against the Denver Nuggets. I went to a restaurant, DeNovo, in Upper Montclair, New Jersey, to watch the game, and I had so many people come over to me to wish me well. They knew what Dolan was like. He's had fans kicked out of MSG who were chanting "sell the team." It felt good to know that the fans cared. That's what I mean about loyalty and respect.

What happened on Sunday, February 12, was the exact opposite of that. Four days after the incident at Madison Square Garden the Knicks were playing an afternoon game against the San Antonio Spurs. With Dolan still being criticized for the way I was treated, he invited a group of former Knicks to sit with him. For years, Dolan had sat along the baseline, just to the right of the Knicks bench. He had Bernard King sit with him, but the wildest shit was that he even invited Latrell Sprewell to the game as his guest.

Back on December 23, 2003, just a few months after Sprewell was traded from the Knicks to the Minnesota Timberwolves—a trade that many believed was Dolan's decision, because he was upset at the fact that Sprewell had walked out of a media training session—the Timberwolves were set to play in the Garden.

Isiah Thomas had been hired the day before to replace Scott Layden as team president. The timing of it tells me that Dolan wanted to take the spotlight off Sprewell's big return. But Dolan made a mistake because he taunted Sprewell in the newspapers by saying he was looking forward to the game and seeing Sprewell. Why would he say that? Everyone knew they weren't friends. But that's Dolan. He thinks he can do or say anything and get away with it.

Sprewell, though, was ready. Every time he made a shot, he would either stare at Dolan or say something crazy. Dolan thought it was all fun and games and even stuck his tongue out at Sprewell. That was mistake number two. At one point Sprewell grabbed his crotch and cursed at Dolan. The man had his wife sitting next to him and Sprewell did that. Crazy.

At halftime, Dolan demanded that NBA security tell Sprewell to stop. It didn't work. It only got worse. Dolan was a beaten man by the end. The next day, the NBA fined and suspended Sprewell, whose relationship with the Knicks was officially over. Or at least everyone thought it was.

For a few years Sprewell, who was having financial problems, was trying to get back with the Knicks. He was hoping to get a job like John Starks had. John was employed by Dolan and mostly just made personal appearances and hung out with sponsors at games. It pays pretty well and it's really a no-pressure job. If the team wins, that's great. If they lose, like the Knicks usually did, it's not your fault. You're not a coach or an executive. You're just an ex-player hanging out with fans in a luxury suite, telling stories about the glory years.

Spree wanted one of those jobs. He needed that job. But he was told that Dolan didn't want anything to do with him. He was an outcast. When Dolan says you're done, you're done.

Everything changed after my arrest. Steve Mills, who was serving as general manager under Phil Jackson, called Sprewell and invited him to sit with Dolan at the afternoon game against the San Antonio Spurs.

At the game, Bernard sat to Dolan's left, while Sprewell and Larry Johnson sat to his right. In all the years Dolan owned the team I never saw three players, much less three Black players, sitting next to him at games. It was a bad look. Dolan having these guys sit next to him was a public relations stunt.

Larry Johnson was once my teammate, and before the Spurs game he was quoted in the *New York Daily News*, saying "It's hard to work at the Garden when Oak is not part of the family. I love the Knicks and Mr. Dolan is my guy but I feel as if I'd be disrespecting Oak if I go the Garden."

Larry's title at the time was basketball and business operations representative. His job was just like Starks's job: meeting with sponsors and season ticket holders before games. He also attended Garden charity events and outreach programs with children in the greater New York City region. That's great, but Larry went to the game. I had heard that Barry Watkins, who at the time was Dolan's right-hand man, called Larry on the morning of the game and told him it was important that he show up for work that day. So not only was Larry at the game, but he was sitting with Dolan.

He later told me, "Oak, I'm in a tough spot, it's my job."

I said, "Fuck that." Larry is still my guy, but that bothered me.

I never played with Latrell, so I didn't have much use for him anyway. But he knew what he was doing by attending that game and sitting with Dolan. A few days after the game I saw Sprewell in the airport. He went a long way to avoid running into me.

About a year later, we were together at a memorabilia event, signing stuff in a back room. Sprewell was talking to O. J. Anderson, the former New York Giants running back. When Spree said,

"What's up, Oak," I looked at O.J. and said, "Don't ever shake that man's hand again."

I could tell Sprewell was embarrassed and he asked me, "What did I do?"

"Ask your boss."

I don't work that way. You can't pretend to be my friend while you're fucking me over. When I finally saw Bernard, I was giving him shit, too. He said he was trying to get a G-League job with the Knicks and that he only went to the Spurs game because his wife wanted to go. Fuck, they've got forty-one home games, but you can only go to that one? And you're sitting next to the owner. Stevie Wonder is blind and even he can see that one.

In the days after my arrest at MSG, the fallout was continuing to cause big problems for me. I was being labeled as a troublemaker, and it hurt me financially. I had four or five sponsorship deals on the table that fell apart. The NBA and the Knicks were also getting hurt public relations–wise, which is why NBA commissioner Adam Silver called me to negotiate a truce with Dolan.

We met at Adam's office in midtown Manhattan late Monday, five days after I was kicked out of the Garden. Adam asked Michael Jordan if he would come to New York for the meeting. Michael initially agreed but couldn't make it in person, so he joined the conversation via phone.

I understand why Adam invited Michael; he was my friend and like Dolan he was an NBA owner. I actually said to Adam: let's get every owner involved and really talk about what's going on. We had two owners involved in the meeting, why not the other twenty-eight? Adam Silver banned Donald Sterling, the Clippers owner, from the NBA for life in 2014 for something he said in a private conversation on the phone to his girlfriend. Dolan publicly embarrassed the league all the time but remained in place. If I was an owner in the NBA, watching Dolan make headlines with stories that had nothing to do with winning but with causing harm to individuals, to people's lives, I'd say we shouldn't be going through this. The NBA has got to take a look at this. You can't keep closing your eyes to it. It's akin to walking the other way if you saw someone getting beat up. It just keeps happening in New York. People are not going to come to this team, and this stadium, when they see the same problem repeated over and over and over.

The sad thing is nothing came out of the meeting. The Knicks were having their annual bowling event for charity, and Dolan invited me to the party. He said it would "be nice if you walk in with me." Dolan said the Knicks wanted to retire my jersey. He said on March 14 the Knicks would play the Indiana Pacers and that he wanted me to sit courtside as a guest of the team. He just didn't get it. I didn't really care about that. This was personal. I felt that Dolan wasn't taking the problem seriously. He'd had me dragged out of the Garden. It was so disrespectful. The lies he told about me being an alcoholic were making my mother physically ill. Free tickets to a game weren't going to make things better.

I was staying in a hotel in Manhattan that week, and I was taking a nap when Silver and the NBA released a carefully worded statement saying that Dolan was hopeful I would return to the Garden "as his guest in the near future."

"It is beyond disheartening to see situations involving members of the NBA family like the one that occurred at Madison Square Garden this past week," Silver said. "In an effort to find a path forward, New York Knicks owner Jim Dolan, Charles Oakley, and I met today at the league office, along with Michael Jordan, who participated by phone.

"Both Mr. Oakley and Mr. Dolan were apologetic about the incident and subsequent comments, and their negative impact on the Knicks organization and the NBA. Mr. Dolan expressed his hope that Mr. Oakley would return to MSG as his guest in the near future.

"I appreciate the efforts of Mr. Dolan, Mr. Oakley and Mr. Jordan to work towards a resolution of this matter."

Adam wanted to end the controversy, especially with All-Star Weekend set to begin in a few days, back in New Orleans, funnily enough. Plus, the Knicks and the NBA were also feeling pressure from local politicians and civil rights groups who were threatening to stage protests outside Madison Square Garden.

The Reverend Al Sharpton and his civil rights organization, the National Action Network, had released a statement before Adam Silver's meeting, calling for Dolan to lift my MSG ban. The NAN threatened to protest outside the Garden.

"This is an issue that is not going to go away," said Brooklyn borough president Eric Adams. "Dolan must understand that the basketball court is not a place where you are going to treat people disrespectfully when they complete their careers. And it sends the wrong message to the countless number of young people, particularly in the inner city, that use basketball as a way to escape some of the difficult times that they are going through."

My mom was really not doing well with all the attention I was receiving. The stress was not good for her health. I knew I had to get back to Cleveland, and following the All-Star Game in New Orleans, I returned to Ohio.

It always feels good to be home and loved. The Cavaliers were very good to me. LeBron had ended a postgame press conference the night I was arrested by saying "Oakley for President." The next morning, he'd posted on his Instagram account, calling me a "Legend." The point guard Chris Paul, also known as CP3, said on Instagram that I always had his back and was "the realest person our league has seen." Dwyane Wade wrote on his account: "10 years!!! 10 years Oak gave everything he had for this organization and the image everyone will be left with . . . will be the [image] of him being taken down to the ground last night in the same arena he gave his all 2 as a player by the guards! This could happen to any of us!!! #StayWoke We are not above this treatment!"

Golden State Warriors great Draymond Green also came out defending me on his *Dray Day* podcast. "I'm pissed," he said. "Number one, the man is a legend—treat him as such. Why is he buying a ticket to the game? It wasn't a problem when he was speaking out then [as a player]. Why is it all of a sudden a problem now? That's a slave master mentality. That's ridiculous. It was all fine and dandy when he was laying people out, taking fines and all this stuff for your organization. But now all of a sudden when he says something that he feels, it's a problem."

He also reacted to Dolan accusing me of having alcohol and anger issues. "How as an organization can you come out and say, we hope you get help? That's pretty messed up. That's not something that you say to the world. That's not classy at all. It's not OK for you to go say to the world as a multibillion-dollar organization."

This is the kind of thing that I mean by loyalty.

Then Dan Gilbert, the Cavs owner, invited me to sit next to him at a game at Quicken Loans Arena on February 23. I hadn't liked the way he handled LeBron leaving for Miami, but I appreciated the support and the opportunity. The Cavs opponent that night? Yep, the New York Knicks. What's crazy is that Dan Gilbert has the same seat location as Dolan: on the baseline next to the home team bench. This game, just like the Clippers-Knicks game from two weeks ago, was also on TNT, so everybody saw me sitting there.

The difference was that I wasn't kicked out and arrested.

And the Cavs won 119–104.

Another loss for Dolan.

The last place you expect to be treated like a criminal is at Madison Square Garden. But this is a different Madison Square Garden from my days, a different Knicks team, and a different owner.

And it continues to this day.

Dolan got into it with Spike Lee during the 2019–20 season because he didn't want Spike using the same elevator that Spike had been using for twenty years. Spike has been a season ticket holder forever, and suddenly Dolan was giving him a hard time. Spike shouted at them: "You want to arrest me like Charles Oakley?" In the aftermath, all everyone was talking about was what happened between Spike Lee and the Garden. That's bad for the team.

This is Madison Square Garden under James Dolan. Patrick Ewing complained about being harassed by security during the 2021 Big East Tournament. Patrick should have known the Knicks front office didn't respect him. That's why the only thing they ever offered him was a G-League job. It's really bad over there. People don't want to talk about it.

19 | SAY HIS NAME

I CAN'T BREATHE.

Those three words were on the black T-shirt I wore during the protest march in Minneapolis two weeks after the May 25, 2020, murder of George Floyd.

"I can't breathe" is what Eric Garner said six years earlier as New York City cops placed him in a chokehold during an arrest that ended with Garner dying. And now here we were again. "I can't breathe" was one of the last things George Floyd struggled to say as a Minneapolis police officer, Derek Chauvin, pressed his knee on the back of George's neck. This cop choked the life out of George for more than nine minutes and twenty seconds. Think about that. Imagine having someone put all of his weight on your neck with his knee for that long.

As a Black man in the United States I, too, have experienced police brutality and harassment before, but never to this extreme. To watch the video and hear George desperately calling out to his mother for help was horrific. No one deserves to be treated like that. Within days there were protests in just about every major city in the country. Riots and looting broke out. Stores were burned. Communities were damaged. This was an awakening in the United States. The Black Lives Matter movement was going to be heard. And we're not going away. I felt the urge to exercise my First Amendment rights peacefully. Over the course of a month I participated in three marches, including two in Minneapolis. I had a good reason.

I knew George Floyd.

At the time of his murder, George was only forty-six years old, ten years younger than me. George was good friends with former NBA player Stephen Jackson, dating back to their days as kids in Houston, Texas. They looked so much alike that Stephen would call George "my twin."

Jax, as I call him, was a no-nonsense player like me. He had a long NBA career. He broke in with the New Jersey Nets in 2000 and ended with the Los Angeles Clippers in 2014. He won a championship with Tim Duncan and the San Antonio Spurs in 2003. The Spurs beat the Nets in six games with Tim Duncan recording a triple-double in the final game of the series. It was also David Robinson's last game before he decided to retire: not a bad way to go out, as a champion. Jackson started Game 6 and scored 17 points. Only Duncan and Jason Kidd scored more points in Game 6.

Although he won a ring, Stephen is probably best known for his role in the "Malice at the Palace," the infamous brawl between the Indiana Pacers and the Detroit Pistons that took place on November 19, 2004. The fight started with Indiana's Ron Artest and Detroit's Ben Wallace pushing each other under the basket. My friend Ron-Ron Artest never backs down from anything, and Ben wasn't about to walk away. Ben, who I'd known since he was about twelve and he came to the summer basketball camp I was running in Alabama, was always a hard-nosed, physical player. The referees broke up the fight and were deciding the punishment for both players. Ron was lying on the scorer's table when a Pistons fan at the Palace of Auburn Hills hit him with a drink. Without hesitation, Ron climbed into the stands and started throwing punches. Once Jackson saw his teammate fighting with fans, he jumped right in and began throwing punches, too.

In the locker room afterward it was reported that Artest asked Jackson if he thought they would get in trouble.

"Are you serious? Trouble? Ron, we'll be lucky if we have a freaking job."

It wasn't that bad. Close, but no one was fired. NBA commissioner David Stern suspended Ron for the remainder of the season, without pay. He lost $4.9 million. Stephen got suspended for thirty games, which cost him $1.7 million.

The Pacers eventually, in January 2007, traded Jackson to the Golden State Warriors, where he played for one of my former coaches, Don Nelson. That was the year the Warriors upset the top-seeded Dallas Mavericks in six games. Jackson was ejected from Game 2 and Game 5, but in the close-out game he scored 33 points and made 7 three-pointers, which was a franchise record until Steph Curry and Klay Thompson came along.

I got to know Stephen Jackson better in November 2009 when he was traded to the Charlotte Bobcats. This was after Michael had purchased the team from Bob Johnson, and I had joined the organization as an assistant coach under Larry Brown and then Paul Silas, my former assistant coach with the New York Knicks.

I first met George Floyd during that season I was an assistant coach on the Bobcats, from 2010 to 2011. He would come to games to see Stephen, and George and I would talk a little bit. I didn't know him very well, but I went out to dinner with George and Stephen once. We reconnected years later in Houston when I was coaching Stephen in the Big3, the league started by the rapper and actor Ice Cube.

I always liked Stephen Jackson because he's tough and he's a competitor. I'm the same way, which is why we get along. But it's also one of the reasons we clash. You put two guys like us in the same room—or the same team—and eventually you will see fireworks.

Back in 2017, we had a heated exchange during a Big3 game that started with Jax being upset about me subbing him out. He had been arguing with the referees, so I had no other choice but to take him out to allow him to cool down.

"He's fucking pulling on my jersey, dog!" Stephen yelled to me on the bench.

"You're not going to holler at me," I told him. "Why are you yelling so loud?"

"Because you took me out."

I told him that he had to come out because he was arguing with the refs. His response was that we couldn't win without him on the court.

"I going to check myself back in," Jax finally told me.

"You'll have to run through me then," I replied. "I wanna see this."

Eventually I put Jax back in. We won the game, and during his interview with comedian Michael Rapaport afterward, Stephen explained our relationship perfectly.

"He's probably the only coach besides Gregg Popovich and Don Nelson that I listen to. When Oak talks, I listen. He's like a big brother slash uncle. He's someone I respect. He's trying to get the best out of me."

Three years later we were back together because of George Floyd. Jax became a national spokesman on police brutality and I wanted to support him and the cause. There are certain moments when you have to act and use your platform to draw attention to an important cause. This was that moment for me and Stephen. It doesn't seem real that a traffic stop can turn into a man dying.

According to the *New York Times*, a convenience store employee called 911 and told the police that George had purchased cigarettes with a counterfeit $20 bill. The *Times* later said that "17 minutes after the first squad car arrived at the scene, Mr. Floyd was unconscious and pinned beneath three police officers, showing no signs of life." The same investigation showed that the officer Derek Chauvin "did not remove his knee even after Mr. Floyd lost consciousness and for a full minute and 20 seconds after paramedics arrived at the scene." That's why we were marching.

I went to George's funeral in Houston with Stephen. We spent the night in the Third Ward talking to people, and when we got to the church there were television crews everywhere. The Reverend Al Sharpton spoke at the service. It was a powerful day.

I've been stopped by cops many times for no reason. Even after I made the league, the cops would fuck with me. All these interactions happened while I was driving.

The first was when I was in a white BMW in Cleveland early in my career with Ron-Ron and we got pulled over for no reason. One of the cops reached into my pocket and asked, "How much money you have on you?"

It was about $20,000.

"Why so much money?"

"Because I make a lot of money," I told him.

"You're Oakley? That name is floating around town a lot."

"That's because there's a lot of Oakleys in the town."

They gave me back my money, but the experience was just crazy.

Then there was another time when I was with Ron-Ron in Cleveland, this time driving a gray Mercedes, during the off-season. We saw about five cops near the park where we would often play basketball in the summer. As I pulled away, the cops followed me. I slowed down, they slowed down. I started to go a little faster and I got pulled over. A bunch of cops had their guns pointing at me. I knew a lot of the cops in Cleveland personally, and once they recognized me they put their guns down. One guy kept pointing his gun though and said, "We're looking for a Mercedes that was involved in a drive-by shooting." Turns out the car had a Florida license plate. My car had an Ohio plate. I heard that the cop who was pointing his gun at me was actually shot one year later.

There was another night I was driving to Atlantic City with Mark Jackson, and got pulled over on the Jersey Turnpike. It was pouring rain and the cop made me get out of the car. I'm thinking to myself, Why? It's raining. What the fuck is going on?

They checked my car while I was getting drenched, of course found nothing, and handed me my license back. I thought it was disrespectful and told them that.

"I'm just doing my job" was the response I got.

Another time I was in the Bronx taking a friend home when all of a sudden a police cruiser, going the wrong way down a one-way street, stopped in front of my car. The cops jumped out with their guns drawn and yelled: "Get the fuck out of the car."

I had no idea what was going on, so I just did as I was told. That seemed like the right thing to do, until a few seconds later when I had a gun pointed at my head.

"You just did a drive-by shooting," the cop said to me. "We got a report of shots being fired from a white car."

Even though I insisted it wasn't me and that I didn't have a gun, they made me take my clothes off right down to my underwear.

That's not a great experience. You feel violated. There's nothing worse than being accused of something you didn't do, no matter how big or small. You understand how quickly things can get out of control on the streets, especially late at night in New York City. This was a life-and-death situation in the Bronx. I consider myself lucky. I can still breathe.

20 | THE BLOOD OF A LEGEND

You'll often hear me call today's NBA players soft, because they are, but one thing I really do appreciate about the players currently in the league is that they're willing to speak out on issues. I credit LeBron as the leader of this movement. LeBron is a smart businessman, but he's not just about himself. He built a school in Akron. He's there for the people. He's an independent thinker who isn't afraid to say what's on his mind. He's got his hand in a lot of different businesses. He encouraged his friends like Maverick Carter and Rich Paul to learn the business of the NBA and make a career out of it. Rich became a big-time agent. Maverick has been LeBron's business partner for years.

LeBron has had a positive influence on all sorts of players, even those no longer in the league, like Michael.

When I played, none of the big names really spoke up. Michael Jordan had the power to do that, but he elected not to. He was a younger guy and the times were different. MJ was growing his brand, and speaking out may have hurt him. In recent years, he has taken up several important causes and gotten involved in issues in ways he didn't used to. Following the death of George Floyd in May 2020, Jordan announced that his Jordan Brand would donate $100 million over the next ten years for "racial equality, social justice, and greater access to education."

He also donated $10 million to help open two medical clinics in North Carolina, one of which will be in New Hanover County, North Carolina, which is where Mike grew up. He had previously donated $7 million, which helped found two Michael Jordan Family Clinics in Charlotte.

Michael and LeBron both have the money, power, and influence to make a difference.

People always want to talk about who is the greatest NBA player of all time, and the comparison usually comes down to Michael and LeBron, as it should. I'm not into this bullshit about who has the most rings when you discuss the best player of all time. If that was the truth, you'd have to say that Bill Russell is the greatest. He averaged 15 points and 22 rebounds for his career but he's got eleven rings. There it is: Bill Russell is the greatest.

Let's get serious though. There's no doubt that since Michael left, LeBron has been the best player in the league. LeBron has the all-around game. He's a freak. He's efficient. He's not just playing for numbers. He's playing to win. I thought he should have retired after winning the championship in the bubble in 2020. Go out on top. He's got nothing left to prove.

I would say that Kobe was the second best player since Michael. All three of them—Michael, LeBron, and Kobe—share, or shared, a deep respect for the game. They didn't like sitting out. People paid to see them play and they felt a responsibility to play. They tried to follow the rules.

Mike and Kobe were close friends. That's one reason that a story the former Pistons "Bad Boy" and talk show host John Salley tells about me punching him in the stomach because he made a comment to Michael about Kobe being better than him is ridiculous.

I *did* punch Salley in the stomach, but it wasn't because he said something about Kobe beating Mike—Mike wouldn't care about that, and neither would I. Salley is a lot like Charles Barkley. He thinks he's funny but he talks too much. I punched him for something else he said. Honestly, exactly what it was, I don't remember.

It happened at Churchill Downs during the Kentucky Derby. Salley later told his version of the story on *The Dan Le Batard Show with Stugotz*. As Salley said it to Dan, he was at the Derby with Chris Tucker, Dave Chappelle, and Julius Erving, and then they ran into me, Michael, and Kobe.

Salley said: "Off to the right is Charles Oakley, who, if you don't know, is Michael's security guard forever and didn't like me. . . . I put my hand on Michael's shoulder, and I go, 'At twenty-seven years old, young boy [Kobe] would have given you the business. . . .' And out of the blue, Charles Oakley comes and punches me in the stomach. But I mean the way he wanted to hit Dolan. Not the way he was pushing the security guard. He unleashed on me, Dan. And I saw it at the last second and tightened up a little bit. He knocked all the air out of me. And Dave Chappelle said, 'This is the only time I wish I still had my show. This is a scene.' . . . Michael is like, 'No, come on, Charles. You know Sal is crazy. He's just joking. He's just joking.' . . . [Oakley's] been wanting to hit me since the eighties. But, man, he hit me with everything he could. I had a suit on, too. And I wasn't going to stand back up and fight him. I'm a karate man. I bruise on the inside."

Bullshit. I definitely hit him because he said something I didn't like, but it had nothing to do with Michael and Kobe. Whatever it was, he certainly remembers my reaction to it. That's all that matters.

While Michael and Kobe were really close, Michael and LeBron have a lot of respect for each other on both a personal and professional level, but they aren't that close when it comes to friendship. With Mike and LeBron, it is what it is. It's not like LeBron is missing anything in his life. LeBron and Michael are just different. LeBron is into Hollywood and movies. Mike is more laid back. He's playing golf, smoking a cigar, and running his brand. LeBron is more outgoing, and in this era he gets more criticism. I don't understand that. He makes all his teammates better, just like Mike did. He goes to the NBA Finals all the time. When I hear someone say it's hard to play with LeBron, I'm like, "Motherfucker, you're averaging three points. It's hard to play with you!" Michael and LeBron both know how to win. They're like Corn Flakes and Frosted Flakes—the same thing, except one has sugar on the outside.

I didn't have much of a relationship with Kobe myself. I admired and respected him as a player. And out of respect to him and his family I attended his funeral at Staples Center in L.A. in 2020. I really liked Kobe for the type of player he was. A lot of players don't hold themselves accountable. But Kobe did. I did as well. We had that in common, which I think is why we got along so well the few times we did get together.

My relationship with LeBron is different. We talk all the time. I went to his wedding a few years ago in California. I was one of the few non–Miami Heat players at the wedding. I think it was me, Carmelo Anthony, Chris Paul, and Jay-Z (without Beyoncé). Of course, I have an obvious connection with LeBron. We're Ohio guys and we represent the city of Cleveland. People like Charles Barkley talk bad about Cleveland, but he'll never come to Cleveland and talk bad about the city. That won't go over well.

Once LeBron is gone, the league is going to be in trouble. You don't have that next player right now. There is no one coming along as special as LeBron.

At the end of the day, when people ask me: Who's the greatest of all time? Is the G.O.A.T. Michael or LeBron? I say, what's the difference? They're both the greatest. They're both in the cockpit. No one is a flight attendant on that plane. No one is putting the bags on the plane. They're both pilots on that ship.

Of course, Michael and I are still close friends. We play golf all the time. We even started playing tennis in our retirement. We'll do just about anything to stay competitive. I try to stay as active as possible. I keep myself in shape because at any moment I may have to defend myself against one of my old foes.

And can you believe that after all these years Michael Jordan still talks shit to me, on the golf course, about the Chicago Bulls beating the New York Knicks in the nineties?

He'll start in with how Anthony Mason wasn't tough and John Starks couldn't guard him. I always make sure to remind MJ that he got all the calls. He should always remember that. He had more than just his teammates out there with him—he had the refs.

He had the championships, too. Michael, Scottie Pippen, and Jerry Krause won all six together. Krause passed away on March 21, 2017, at the age of seventy-seven. A few weeks later, on Sunday April 9, there was a private memorial service in Chicago to honor him. It was at the Advocate Center, the Bulls' new practice facility that they opened in 2014, across the street from the United Center. The days of living out in the suburbs and making that long commute into downtown Chicago are a thing of the past for the Bulls players.

I went, along with a few of my former Bulls teammates, including John Paxson and Pete Myers. Dennis Rodman was there, although he was a mess—he had shades on and that same scarf he always wore, and I think he had been drinking. I could smell alcohol.

But Michael Jordan and Scottie Pippen didn't attend.

MJ sent out a statement following the news of Jerry's death, writing: "Jerry was a key figure in the Bulls' dynasty and meant so much to the Bulls, White Sox and city of Chicago. My heart goes out to his wife, Thelma, his family and friends."

Scottie posted a series of tweets, including one that read: "Jerry and I didn't always see eye to eye but I knew he just wanted to win. He surrounded MJ and me with the right pieces not once but twice."

People can do what they want, but it didn't make sense to me that they wouldn't be at the memorial in person. Jerry traded me before the Bulls won their first title, and when I returned years later, he fined me $50,000 for criticizing coach Tim Floyd. If I wasn't mad at Jerry, why did Michael and Scottie have a problem with him? The person they should have been mad at was Jerry Reinsdorf.

Jerry Krause didn't draft Michael Jordan. That was Rod Thorn. But Jerry put the right teammates around MJ, including Scottie, as Scottie acknowledges. They had a great run, but once MJ and Scottie got their rings I feel like they let Jerry down, and he became the fall guy.

Krause was one of the greatest general managers in NBA history. He was inducted into the 2017 Basketball Hall of Fame class posthumously. I think that honor should have come years earlier. I always appreciated everything Jerry did for me. Like I said, he brought me to Chicago twice. He respected me and I had a lot of respect for him.

At the memorial service for Krause, there were four speakers: Karen Stack Umlauf, who after playing basketball at Northwestern landed a job selling tickets for the Chicago Bulls, eventually rose to become director of basketball operations, and also served as an assistant coach; K. C. Johnson, the longtime beat writer who became close with Krause; Jerry Reinsdorf, the chairman of the Bulls; and Jerry Colangelo, a Chicago guy who once owned the Phoenix Suns.

Krause had a collection of writings when he died, kind of like an unpublished memoir, which he gave to K. C. Johnson to work on and maybe one day make into a book. According to Johnson, in those papers, Krause wrote: "If God gave me the ability to construct the perfect rebounder, I'd want quick feet on a tall, wide-shouldered frame, strong-legged, good hands, quick jumper and a mean streak that never shut down. In other words, I'd want Dennis Rodman, the best rebounder I've ever seen. Sure, I'd look at Paul Silas first and then Charles Oakley. But eventually I'd settle on Rodman and then put him on the floor for 45 minutes a game for a bunch of years and enjoy. I had the privilege of working with Silas for a few years in Phoenix and drafting and working with Oakley for a few years. And then, because we were desperate for another great rebounder and because we were secure enough to take chances, I had the joy of watching the best of the best be a key factor in three championships."

I agree with him about Paul Silas and myself. Not so sure about the other guy. In fact, Silas was my assistant coach once with the Knicks. We once got into a little slap after he told me he could kick my ass. We were just messing around. I don't beat up old guys—unless they cross the line.

Do I think about not having won a championship? Sure, I think everybody who plays does so to win a championship. It takes hard work, great players, and a little luck. I think we were a little unlucky at times.

We were one game away in 1994. One game, and we couldn't make the plays when it mattered. I count myself in that "we." But as I've said, I do put a lot of the blame on Patrick.

There are people who think I'm too critical of Patrick as a player, but I'm just telling you what I saw over a decade. We went through a lot together over ten seasons in New York. I don't forget that. Even today you'll hear Patrick say, "Oak had my back." That's right. I played with a broken nose, broken fingers, broken toes, back and knee pain. I did any job my coaches wanted me to do. So it does still bother me that Patrick stayed silent after my run-in with James Dolan.

Patrick could score, but you need more than that, you need to rebound and move the ball. Patrick was an All-Star, but he was missing that "it" factor. I think what hurt him is that he just didn't trust the rest of his teammates. You have to be able to get everyone else involved in the mix. That's what Michael and LeBron do. You could tell that Patrick didn't trust us. If he had, he wouldn't have shot fade-away jumpers.

Pat Riley and Jeff Van Gundy catered to him. You could even say they babied him at times. Both coaches nearly won the city a championship. But in the end Patrick didn't deliver.

None of us did.

I've got more important things to do though than spend all my time thinking about the championships I didn't win. What matters to me most, as I think I've made clear, is loyalty, friendship, and being a stand-up guy for other people.

I've become very close over the years with Jayson Williams, who has taught me a lot about all that. He's turned his life around after spending time in prison, and is trying to help others who battle addiction.

In January 2010 Jayson pleaded guilty to aggravated assault in the shooting death of limousine driver Costas "Gus" Christofi eight years earlier. Jayson had a bunch of former NBA players and college players with him at his New Jersey home following a charity basketball game.

He was giving the group a tour of the house and showed them his gun collection in his bedroom. While holding a double-barreled 12-gauge shotgun, he failed to check the safety mechanism and inspected only one of the two barrels before snapping it shut. The gun fired, striking Mr. Christofi once in the chest and killing him.

Jayson spent twenty-seven months in prison and lost nearly everything. Today, he is a recovery advocate and the founder of a recovery program called Rebound at Futures Recovery Health Care in Florida.

"Through the grace of God, I finally found something I'm really good at," he says. "I'm great at helping people beat their addiction. It's a tough business, but a rewarding business."

I'll visit Jayson in Florida from time to time and cook for people at his center—that's something I love to do. When the NBA All-Star Game was in Los Angeles, my group cooked for homeless people in the city. Jayson loves to laugh. He loves telling stories about me, but like I always say, only about 30 percent of those stories are true.

One of the few that is accurate is about a trip to Hilton Head, South Carolina, we took for a charity golf event not long after I retired in 2004. Julius Erving, Dr. J, was in our group, and he kept hitting his tee shot into the woods. Somehow he kept finding it. It was a friendly game, but I've got a competitive nature so I was getting frustrated.

Later that afternoon we went to a local gym to play basketball. Jayson was putting on a small game for a few sick kids. I still loved to play, but I didn't do it much anymore. At one point, Dr. J was cruising in for a layup and I was chasing him. At that precise moment something got into me. It was as if I was still playing for the New York Knicks and Pat Riley was screaming, "No layups!"

I fouled Dr. J. Fouled him hard.

I'm not sure me having a flashback is a legitimate excuse. I made a mistake. I fouled Julius Erving so hard that I busted his lip. I wasn't trying to do that.

I drew blood from a legend in a slow pickup game of retired players.

Maybe those hard fouls are just a part of my DNA. Today, you can't foul like that in the NBA. You'll get suspended. The league doesn't like physical play. Now it's just guys shooting three-pointers and not playing any defense. It's soft. That's what the league wanted, and that's what it got.

I do like the fact that players today aren't afraid to speak up. It's a good thing that they're willing to address issues in the league as well as in our society, including social injustice. But they shouldn't forget that it's also their job to respect the game. That means more than just putting up points.

Michael, Kobe, and LeBron showed respect to the game by putting it all on the line. I was never in the same category as those guys when it came to skill or being a superstar, but I do think I shared something with them: I played every night like it was my last game.

I was all about my teammates and trying to win. I stood up for the guys around me, as well as for myself. If that meant giving a hard foul, I did it. If I had to sacrifice shots, I did that. I rebounded, played defense, set screens, and fought for everything I had.

The way I played was about more than just a willingness to get physical and not take shit from anybody. It ran deeper than that. It was connected to the things that make up who I am and matter to me most: trust, loyalty, friendship, and doing what's right. It was a code of conduct. It's the reason that I've kept life-long friends, stayed close to my family, and always looked for ways to give back to the community. It's something that's been in me for as long as I can remember, dating back to my grandfather and probably generations before him, and will stay with me until the day I die.

I was an enforcer. Maybe the last.

ACKNOWLEDGMENTS

CHARLES

Thank you, God.

Thank you to my grandmother Florence Moss and grandfather Julius Moss.

To my mother, Corine Oakley: thank you for supporting me as I grew up. Being a single parent, you did a lot for all of your kids. Love you.

To my aunts and uncles, thank you for all of your love, all of my life: Ruby Moss Adams, Edna Moss Williams, Dora Moss Campbell, Mildred Moss Evans, Johnnie J. Moss, Andrew Moss, Samuel Moss.

I want to give a shout-out to the other Oakley family, my other grandmother and grandfather, aunts, uncles, and all of my cousins on both sides. Thank you for your support. Love all of y'all.

Thank you Chesterfield Elementary School, Harry Davis Junior High School, John Hay High School—everyone I went to school with in Cleveland. Mr. Morton, my principal; Mr. Newman, the athletic director; Sunny Harris, my football coach; and Mr. Olson, my basketball coach—thank you for your support. Y'all pushed me a lot.

A shout-out to everyone who grew up in my neighborhood: 123rd Superiors.

To Virginia Union University, including all of the students that went there before and after: we're a small school, but we have a big heart. Thank you for the love.

Thanks to coach Dave Robbins for recruiting me and driving that red pickup truck to Cleveland. You left before it got dark and that was the second smartest thing you ever did. The first was recruiting me. Love to Dr. Royal and family, and assistant coach Jim Battles.

Rest in peace to my sister and my brother: Curtis and Yvonne.

I want to give a shout-out to Mr. Fields, rest in peace to him and his wife; to the Hearns family, rest in peace, Lou; the Green family, rest in peace to your son Tyrone; the Lanasa family, rest in peace, Tony; the Bailey family, rest in peace, Mr. Bailey; Drew Hill, rest in peace, the band ain't never been the same since you left. Jim Gillian and family, rest in peace to your mom.

Thank you to Johnny Newman and family. Thank you to Terry Davis and family.

To Cunningham and Kevin Patterson: me and Steve are still waiting on that next game.

Shout-out to Warren Williams and family. Shout out to my roommates Steve, Trouble, Raymond, Big Bay, WV.

Thank you Walls and family.

John Warren and family: thank you for inviting me into your house.

The Pittman family: thank you for letting me stay at your house.

And my man William Dillon, rest in peace, and Vernon Moore, rest in peace.

Ardythe and Gayle Sayers: thank you for helping me out when I was stuck on I-94W with a flat tire. Rest in peace, Gayle.

To Mr. Price and family: rest in peace. Thank you for being my first barber in Chicago in 1985.

Jim Daniels: rest in peace.

I want to thank Jerry Krause and family: rest in peace, Jerry.

I want to thank the Bulls organization for drafting me and all of the people who had something to do with it.

Thank you to the city of Chicago for embracing me. I've been in and out of Chicago for thirty-seven years and never had a problem.

Shout-out to the Gibson and Tavern restaurants. And to East Bank for giving me a lifetime membership.

Lester Lampert and family: thanks for letting me do the best BBQ ever at your house with a ten-piece band and 150 people.

I want to thank John Kelly and family for flying to Alabama for my sister's funeral. You are the number one family.

Thank you to Robert Stambolic and family.

Thank you to the Fakhouri family for the support.

Thank you to Robert Alexander and family.

Thank you to Vernado Parker and family.

Thank you to Keir Foley and family.

Thank you to Kevin Edwards. Keep working on that jump shot.

Shout-out to my guys in Chicago: they know who they are. Right to left, you probably don't want your name in the book.

Thank you to my man Pete Myers and family.

Special thank you to MJ for doing the foreword and just being a friend over thirty-five years. A lot of love between us.

Love to Angela and the kids.

I also want to thank Juanita Jordan and family for the love over the last three decades.

To Scottie, you came in cocky and you still cocky.

To my friend Jayson Williams, you've been in my corner, I've been in your corner. Keep telling those stories. You make everyone laugh even though it's the same old stories.

Thank you to my guys Ahktar and Joe.

My best three Giants guys—LT, O. J. Anderson, and Michael Strahan—much love.

To George, the best limo driver in the country.

Thank you to Mike Nelson and family.

Shout-out to the NBA for giving me a chance to better my life and the lives of people around me.

I want to thank all of the players that I've ever played with.

Shout out to my man Bruce Smith and family.

Shout-out to Marv Albert for commentating over fifty-four years. Legendary.

Shout out to Clyde Frazier.

To my man Anthony Mason: rest in peace. I wish you were at the Garden with me. We would still be fighting.

Shout-out to all of the police officers in New York.

To all of the rappers I encountered during my years in New York, it was always love. There's so many of y'all, if I write one name, I would have to write a hundred.

Shout out to Mr. Ned and family

Shout out to my business partner Harvey Diamond and family.

Shout out to my man Miles at Prime 112.

Shout out to Jeff at Carbone and friends. Great Italian food.

Seeway Barbershop had the old heads.

Crow BBQ had the best ribs.

The best pool hall ever on 125th and Superior.

Positive Vibe Lounge in Cleveland.

Shout-out to the O'Jays. To Eric Grant and family, thanks for stepping in for twenty-five years with the O'Jays.

Shout-out to Bone Thugs: Legendary rap group from Cleveland.

Shout-out to all of the talent from Cleveland: Steve Harvey, Arsenio Hall, Halle Berry, Kim Whitney, John Henton, Ted Ginn, and Ted Ginn, Jr.

I just wanted to thank the Akron crew: LeBron, Maverick, Rich,

Randy. I want to thank you guys, your moms, your families, your friends, you've all been so supportive of me.

Shout-out to Steve Stoute and family.

Shout-out to Mike Tyson: You always showed Cleveland a lot of love when you lived there. You changed the city.

Shout out to my DJ Chuck Chillout.

I want to thank Larry Tanenbaum and family and the whole Raptor nation for supporting me. I want to thank everyone in Canada for embracing me during my three years there. I know basketball wasn't a thing when I first got there, but you see what can happen when you build something.

Shout-out to Drake. How you put the city on your back is what leaders do.

Harbor 60: Thanks for always having consistent food.

I want to thank Butch Carter and his family.

My best point guard in Canada was Muggsy and my best two players in Canada were Vince and Tracy.

Shout-out to Ice Cube and the Big 3.

Shout-out to Mike Perry and Money Knight: thanks for coming to me to do a camp in Virginia for ten years.

Jeff Warren, thanks for being a partner in my camp in Cleveland for over ten years.

I want to thank my sister Yvonne and my aunt Edna for bringing to my attention that the kids needed something to do during the summer in Alabama.

Thank you to my cousin Marcus Campbell for doing a camp with me in Alabama for over twenty-five years.

John Starks, it's been great working with you on your foundation. It should be my foundation since I bring in more money than you.

Over my career in New York, I've been to over a thousand restaurants. Thank you. I'm a tough customer and y'all always tried your best.

I just want to thank the New York fans for all of the love on and off the court. You've had my back since I stepped in the city in '88.

Lloyd Carrington and family: thanks for always answering the phone.

Thank you Henry "Blaq" Butler and family.

Thank you Ken Fisher and family, Daniel Kane and family, Nate Gray and family, Doug Wigdor, Bradley Dock and family.

Thank you Lloyd Banks and family, Robert Clarington and family, Chris Russell and family, the Felder Family, Jacob Brumfield and family, Walker D. Russell and family, my point guard Kenny Thompson and family, Earl Cureton and family, Dr. J. and family, Dominique Wilkins and family.

Thank you to the Anthony Mason family, Greg McPherson and family, Crobo and family, Sam Bradford and family, Fred Ward and family, William Platt and family, Herb Williams and family, Steve Masiello and family, Bob Capolongo and family. Kevin Willis and family, Eugene Banks and family.

All of the writers who covered me over my career. Thank you for being 90 percent accurate. I can live with that.

I want to thank Alex Koblenz and 7x Media. Thank y'all for the work you've done and more work to come.

Thank you to my literary agent Sarah Passick at Park & Fine Literary and Media.

Thank you Simon & Schuster/Gallery Books and Max Meltzer for giving me this opportunity.

Frank Isola, thank you for writing this book with me. I've known you over twenty-seven years and you've been the same consistent writer. You tell the truth and always stick to the facts.

FRANK

We could not have beaten the final buzzer on this book without the help and guidance from our editor Max Meltzer. He was the calm presence in the storm. Thank you to Charles's manager, Alex Koblenz, for providing much needed background information. We got an assist from two of Chicago's top basketball reporters, Sam Smith and K.C. Johnson, and two talented Knicks beat writers, Steve Popper and Stefan Bondy. Also, we appreciate the help of our small but dedicated research team: Josh Burton, Gabrielle and Liam Isola, Joe Catania, Scott Davisson, Dave Masur, and Mike Goldstein.

My wife, Tonja, played the part of editor, secretary, IT first responder, and inspiration. The absolute best.

And a special thanks to the man himself, Charles Oakley, who I had the pleasure of covering for nearly two decades. One of the toughest dudes you'll ever meet, Charles has always stayed true to himself. He is as authentic as they come.

INDEX